7-2

D0820758

NAHANNI

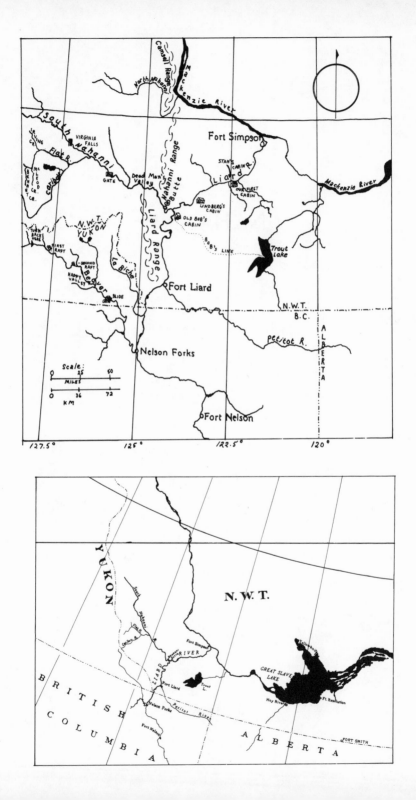

NAHANNI

by DICK TURNER

HANCOCK HOUSE

Saanichton — Seattle

Second Printing

ISBN 0-919654-46-0

Copyright © 1975   Dick Turner

Canadian Shared Cataloguing in Publication Data

Turner, Dick
    Nahanni

        1. Turner, Dick. 2. South Nahanni Valley.
3. Frontier and pioneer life - Northwest,
Canadian. I Title.
F   917.12′2
[LC: F1100.S6T87]
ISBN 0-919654-46-0

All rights reserved. No part of this publication may be reproduced,
stored in a retrieval system, or transmitted, in any form or by any
means, electronic, mechanical, photocopying, recording, or otherwise, without the prior written permission of Hancock House
Publishers.

Printed in United States of America

This book was designed and first produced in Canada by Hancock
House Publishers Limited, 3215 Island View Road, Saanichton,
British Columbia, Canada.

Published by:

HANCOCK HOUSE PUBLISHERS LTD.
3215 Island View Rd.
Saanichton, British Columbia   V0S 1M0

12008 1st Ave. S.
Seattle, Washington   98168

Table of Contents

Chapters

1

The Headless Valley

"Tell us about the headless men of the Nahanni. What truth is there to the legend of the McLeod's lost gold mine? How many men have been killed there? Do you suppose there is really an Indian curse on the valley?"

I have lived in the north for forty-five years, and have heard questions like that for forty of these years. I waited for someone else to answer.

The two Indian guides across the rough-hewn log table smiled momentarily, then went back to their food. My son Don, the outfitter, said nothing, glanced at me and lifted his coffee cup. The hunter sitting next to me then spoke. "Before I came on this hunt I was told there was a lost placer gold mine in the Nahanni, that many men had perished or had been killed in the search of the hidden valley, where the gold in the stream is guarded by headless men. I read somewhere that only one man has survived and returned after seeing this fabulous place. What is his name? Is he still alive? Did he find the gold?"

The hunters were directing their questions to the other four of us at the table, but as the native guides were obviously going to remain silent, and Don, glancing at me, said nothing, I thought I would make some observations in polite reply. But before I did, the first hunter spoke again. "Whereabouts on the Nahanni do you live, Dick? Do you stay all winter? How do you get your food and supplies into the area? Do you ever look for the lost gold yourself?"

The two hunters were from somewhere in the Eastern States and had arrived at Don's base camp that afternoon by single engine float plane. They had come on a 12 day hunt for Dall rams.

Don's Company is Nahanni Butte Outfitters and their specialty is a two week hunt for Dall rams. These majestic white sheep are found in the Mackenzie mountains and are plentiful in some parts of the Nahanni. Indeed the famous and war-like Nahanni mountain Indians who wore Dall sheepskins as clothing were called "Sheep Men" by the other northern Indian tribes.

The first hunter who had spoken was continuing, "I came on this hunt to get me a good-sized Dall ram but if I can also find that hidden valley with the gold nuggets it would be that much better."

"As to that," I replied, "there is a very good chance of you getting your ram but I would think the likelihood of finding the lost gold mine is very slim. Albert Faille, the old prospector you spoke of, has been searching in vain for it for the past 40 years. In fact he still goes back into the mountains each summer, though now he is getting very old."

"It would take a week to tell you everything I know of the Nahanni and the north, but someday I am going to write a book about it. For instance, two of the men who disappeared there were never found. But I have reason to believe that one of them did not die at all. He could be in Australia right now."

"We'll make a deal," the hunters said. "You write the book and we'll buy the first two copies."

Years later the book is written. What can I say? There were many starts and stops in attempting the task. There were many dark moments when I doubted my ability to convey to you the despair, the pain and hunger and anger and frustration that were experienced in the first years of this harsh and vast northland.

I read somewhere that "Easy writing's damned hard reading." If the reverse is true, this will be the easiest book to read you have ever seen. I hope it is both easy reading and enjoyable.

*   *   *   *   *

It has been said that most people who have escaped southern civilization to go to the northland, are just that —"escapists". Others more unkind have used such adjectives as psychotic, pathological or even paranoid.There may be some justification for these terms. For my part I was definitely escaping from an uncomfortable city environment of the Great Depression years. What I did not know was that the impact of the northern environment I escaped into would have a traumatic effect on me.

In these later years, many people from close friends to strangers passing through have encouraged me to write the following memoirs. I have chosen an autobiographical format for the book as it must from necessity be made up mostly from my own experiences. It describes most aspects of my life in the Canadian north as a trapper and pioneer. It tells of my wife Vera and me hacking out a home in the wilderness and struggling for a living at any occupation that would fetch the necessities of life. We were two of many who came north to stay and raise a family. Others came, stayed a few years, and left for one reason or another.

The Nahanni legends and mysteries are tied into my life and that of many friends and must form a large part of this chronicle, as will the man who is known to many as "Mr. Nahanni", Albert Faille.

Since 1907 when the bodies of the McLeod boys were found on the bank of the Nahanni River between the first and second canyon this rather beautiful spot has been known locally as Dead Man's Valley; and still remains so to northern residents.

If I recall correctly it was the winter of 1948 when a young newspaper man from the west coast flew into Dead Man's Valley with a ski equipped aircraft, landed briefly and flew back again to civilization. Subsequent articles appeared in some western newspapers with some pretty far out stuff on some aspects of the history of the South Nahanni River area, written by this young man. An Edmonton paper carried a drawing with the article of what was supposed to be an Indian Princess who was said to rule a tribe of mountain Indians. The whole area was dubbed "Headless Valley" and has remained that way in popular literature. The young man's name was Pierre Berton. His name today is a household word in Canada.

The name Headless Valley was chosen I suppose for the reason that the bodies of the McLeod boys found in Dead

Man's Valley in 1907 were reported to be without their heads.

The Nahanni River drains a vast land of fascinating beauty and splendor. The lure of gold has enticed many men through the canyons to this alluring land. Many have perished in its valleys and mountains; some in the search for gold. It is probable that most have died a violent and unexplained death. Conjecture has given rise to all sorts of wierd theories as to the causes of these misfortunes.

During the dog-team era of the north, the most important resource of this boundless wilderness was the pelts of fur-bearing animals. There were those who produced the wealth, the trappers; and those who exchanged goods for the pelts, the traders. The fur trade was for the most part in the hands of big trading companies. During the 1930's, these were the Hudson's Bay Company and Northern Traders Ltd. For an independent operator to break into the business, capital was needed. Those settlers who were poor had of necessity to engage in trapping. Trappers must go to the bush and live and work in the bush; they must learn the ways of all animals, large and small, predators and non-predators, ermine, rabbits, marten, beaver, wolves and moose, among others. A trapper must learn the bush lore of camping and survival, how to dress warmly and never to get wet if the weather is extremely cold. He must learn to care for, feed, handle and drive a team of dogs. He must be an expert with rifles and canoes. He must be able to stand the long tedious trips of back-packing and trail breaking and the loneliness and isolation for ten months of the year. The danger of a mishap with axe, rifle or canoe is always present, as is the chance of meeting with a moose, wolf or bear who has not read the rules of the game and in a rash moment takes it upon itself to challenge the strange two-legged animal.

As compensation for danger, hardship and isolation, a trapper has a great deal of freedom to exert his self-reliance and independence. He has no boss to please, no time-clock to punch. But some things he cannot escape. Like everyone else he has economic pressure, which is a hard taskmaster to drive him. And he is still a member of his community, albeit of one of a relatively small population. He is subject to the laws of the land even though they concern him but little.

Until the early nineteen forties, the Northwest Territories could well have been a region in another world as far as most Canadians were concerned, particularly the Federal Government in Ottawa. There was nothing here that anyone wanted, needed or thought to be of any great value. It was a cold, inhospitable land of frozen tundra, peopled by Indians and Eskimos. The Trading Companies, The Catholic and Protestant Missions, the Indian Agents and the Royal Canadian Mounted Police were left to cater to the needs of those natives, or perhaps to their own needs.

The Northwest Territories administration in 1930 consisted of a Commissioner, a deputy Commissioner and an advisory council of four appointed members, who were representatives of the Hudson's Bay Company, the Roman Catholic Church, the Royal Canadian Mounted Police and the Department of Indian Affairs. The Deputy Commissioner, Mr. R. A. Gibson, handled all the correspondence and seemed to make all the decisions. He was called 'The Dictator', as his word was final. To my knowledge he had never been in the Northwest Territories. He might possibly have had the welfare of the natives at heart, but when the Great Depression drove white trappers in from the provinces there was no encouragement given them to settle. In fact the conclusion was inescapable that there was a definite tendency for the Federal Government to discourage settlers. The Game Regulations of the N.W.T. was a powerful weapon and it was used. The N.W.T. Game Regulations of 1929 and 1930 stated quite frankly that the Northwest Territories were considered to be a Native Preserve, whatever that means. And that white trappers were not encouraged to immigrate. WE, who were Canadians from the provinces, took that to mean that officially there was a part of Canada in which Canadian citizens were not welcome. The said Game Regulations also stated that the fee for a Trapping Licence for a non resident would be seventy five dollars each year for a period of four years. Also that white trappers were prohibited from hunting, shooting, taking or killing beaver at any time of the year. The beaver population does not fluctuate as land fur does and in some years the take of beaver pelts makes up the main income of a trapper.

The excessive fee for a non-resident trapping licence, together with the restrictions on taking beaver, might have dissuaded some people from coming north; just how many we will never know. But for those of us who did come to stay, the restrictive policy constituted what amounted to harassment. The administration had the R.C.M.P. to back up the regulations, and there was very little else for them to do in those years except perhaps harass the natives for drinking "home brew". It was illegal at that time for Indians or Eskimos to buy, make, or drink any alcoholic beverages.

I believe that the prohibition of natives from the consumption of alcohol and the enforcing of the Game Regulations was a somewhat bothersome task to some members of the R.C.M.P. Why shouldn't an Indian be allowed to drink? God knows the white population did enough of it. And as to the prohibition of trapping beaver, they thought it as ridiculous as we did. But laws are laws and must be enforced, or must seem to be enforced, so it was not surprising when some humorous and pathetic situations developed.

I knew of one constable who, when on patrol with a canoe on the Liard River, would fire his rifle a mile or so before he came to a cabin or a settlement, so that his native friends could have time to hide their brew pots.

This same constable and others like him would sometimes warn their white trapper friends as to where and when to hide their beaver pelts. Illegal beaver pelts, that is. With some notable exceptions it was a rare occurrence when a member of the R.C.M.P. laid a charge on his own initiative under the Game or Indian Acts, except in some cases where a native became intoxicated and caused a disturbance.

But still and all, the situation was bothersome for this reason. Counting everyone, both native and white, there were few of us in this inconceivably vast land of the Northwest Territories, and it was inevitable that many of the R.C.M.P. became good friends with the trappers. And that left us in the position that we liked them, we respected their official capacity and wished to remain on good terms, but we had to feed and clothe our families, come what may, and if an illegal beaver or so was available, it went to sweeten the pot.

From 1929 to 1933 lynx and fox were very scarce, it being the low point in their cycle, but the white trappers hung on. We grew gardens, especially potatoes, we picked berries and made jam, ate moose meat the year 'round and ran long trap-lines.

In 1932 another law was enacted, discontinuing the issuance of trapping licences to anyone who had not held one the preceeding year. Fortunately this was in effect for only two years and was then rescinded.

After more than forty years I am still conscious of the bitterness and resentment we felt toward the absentee authorities who enacted the arbitrary and restrictive legislation in those early years. I was a young man, newly married, struggling to make a living for my family, and to say that I felt strongly about the matter is putting it honestly. I was not at all happy with having to break the Game Regulations consistently and continually for years in order to maintain a standard of living even a little above the animals. If there had been any tea to throw in the harbour or a group of rebels to join I would have been right there.

There is an interesting side-light here in regard to the relationship of natives and whites in the north at that time. The natives quite understandably resented the fact that they were classed as minors as regards liquor under the Indian Act of that time. It was not unknown for some of them to watch a white trapper carefully and to report any alleged illegal activities to the R.C.M.P.; probably in retaliation for the white man classing them as inferior citizens. In retrospect I cannot find it in my heart to blame them. To fill in this situation a little more fully I must say that I found in those early years, as I do now, that most native and white trappers got along very well together and respected each other for being simply what we all are, just people.

A trappers view of wildlife and the great outdoors generally differs in many respects from most urban residents not because he is a trapper, but for the reason that he lives his whole life in the woods and must surely have more knowledge of his environment than most others.

Some of my friends have disappeared in the Nahanni mountains, and over the years I have watched a certain segment of the popular media have a hey-day with these stories. With some cause the Nahanni has gone from fame to notoriety. It is indeed a harsh land in many ways and has no mercy on a lone man who, braving dangers, makes an error in calculation. Through mountains, on rivers or in the air, more than usual care must be taken in order to avoid a mistake. In many circumstances, if you make only one error, that is your last. Fortune, fate, or luck must also play a part, as it does so often.

2

Plans for trapping

Always since my early childhood, rivers, mountains and the bush have held a fascination for me. I would listen enthralled to stories of trapping, canoeing and hunting, anything that smacked of game trails, Indians and lonely places. As soon as we learned to read, my brothers and I devoured the stories of James Oliver Curwood, Jack London and many others. I was born on the prairies where the "Big Chief" loomed in the sky. I saw my first evergreen bough when I was five years old. I can still remember the fragrance of it. When I was eight my father took my mother and some of us younger boys with the Model-T Ford from our farm in Alberta through southern B.C., Oregon and Washington up into the Okanagan Valley. That was in 1919. There were few travellers and the roads were poor. I am sure my father had many troubles on the trip, but for me every turn of the trail among the towering evergreens, every mountain stream and every dip into a valley was interesting and exciting.

Later at our home in Rutland, school was something that had to be endured until Friday night. Then if the older boys did not have to work, my brother Stan and I with a neighbour boy would head off into the hills into what we thought was wild bush country. For a rare treat we were allowed to spend the night camping out. We found a trapline and I can still see the big leaning pine tree and the blazes marking the trail. We hoped to see wild deer and maybe a cougar. No cougar ever materialized but Stan said we could run into one anytime. Stan was thirteen and I thought he knew a lot. We did see deer several times and who could ask for more?

Eight years later in Calgary, school was no longer a bore and a drag. I was taking a three year course in Survey Drafting at Calgary's Institute of Technology and Art and enjoying every minute of it. But alas, school lasted only seven months of a year and a job had to be found for the other five months. It was 1930, the Great Depression was in full swing and a job could not be had for love nor money. Anyway who had money?

Men looking for work clung to westbound freight trains like flies to a dead horse. The trains going eastward were loaded just as heavily with men. In Calgary the Salvation Army and the City were feeding the unemployed one meal a day in soup kitchens to keep them from starving.

One day I got talking with my math instructor who was a mining engineer and went north every summer for a mining company. He told me that he had heard that the Indians at Nahanni were bad, they were reported to have killed one or several more people. He advised me to stay away from the South Nahanni. That was the first time I heard the name Nahanni. We were discussing an article that had appeared in the fall of 1929 in the National Geographic Magazine. Among others there was a photograph of Landing Lake on the Flat River. The article said that the area teemed with game; "Herds of caribou and moose could be seen at almost anytime from the aircraft, crossing the streams and lakes." This surely was a land flowing with milk and honey, or rather caribou roasts and moose steaks. It was just the place to spend a winter, garner a harvest of fur bearing animal pelts and return to civilization fat and prosperous.

My brother Stan was probably the prime instigator of the plan to go north for a year. He put up the money to buy an eighteen foot canoe, food and other necessities for the trip. He was working at the time for Calgary Power as a lineman at ten dollars per day which was really big money then. I went along with the idea wholeheartedly and we planned for months what items we would take; food, clothing, traps, guns, snowshoes, all that we would require to live in the north for a year. Then we dug out maps and planned the route. The best map of the Northwest Territories we could locate was a sheet about three feet square bounded by a wide red line going right to the North Pole. There were heavy black lines showing the main rivers, quarter inch black dots indicating Hudson's Bay Company trading posts and huge red flags denoting Royal Canadian Mounted Police detachments. That was it. Most of the paper was blank,with some tributaries of the Mackenzie River dotted in, indicating the exact position was unknown. The Liard River was marked. There was a black dot and a red flag for Fort Liard. The Nahanni River was a dotted line heading off into a large space of white paper. We spread out this hasty sketch of half a continent and studied it carefully. There was Edmonton. There was the railroad to Waterways. From there going north and west were the Athabaska River, Athabaska Lake, the Slave River, Great Slave Lake, Mackenzie River, Fort Simpson, and the Liard River. Nothing to it boys, just get on that line and follow it through.

The train ride from Edmonton to Waterways was interesting. I knew this was a recently completed rail line, but just how recent I was soon to see. After some hours the farming communities were left behind and semi-open parkland gave way to muskeg and swamp. Speed was reduced from a daring six miles per hour to a hesitant three, slightly slower than a walk. The single steam engine huffed and puffed its way along pulling its string of freight, baggage and mail cars with two passenger coaches and a caboose bringing up the tail end. The rails and roadbed sank noticeably under the weight of the engine and rose again behind it. Our coach swayed, groaned, tipping first this way then the other. The roadbed appeared to be made of moss and water. Later I realized there was no other material available unless earth and rocks were to be hauled in from miles away. The rails never did vanish entirely; they seemed to surface again after the train had passed by. Looking out of the window at the landscape, one was not aware of any noticeable progress. However, assessing the situation carefully and observing the lateral movement of the coach with the occasional gentle lurching, I felt that surely there must be some forward movement going on.

One afternoon I noticed that a number of passengers were

walking up and down and moving about somewhat more than usual. People were leaving the passenger coach. I put down my book and stood up. "By Jove," I thought, "if these people are going on ahead I may as well join them. I certainly don't want to be left behind." I stepped out of the coach door, joined the line of people marching forward and soon came upon a group of men sitting around talking. Typical northerners, I thought, never in a hurry. They are probably making a cup of coffee. Then I noticed that two men had gold braid on their caps and others were wearing blue coveralls. Employees of the railroad company obviously. My God, are they leaving too? Then who will bring the train along behind us?

The coffee did not materialize: I smelled no aroma of the Java tree and no cups were passed around. Apparently some people became weary with waiting for coffee and moved away. Then I could see that one of the baggage coaches was crosswise on the rails and the train crew and others were observing the phenomenon. Several days later the passenger coach was observed to renew the lurching from side to side and I felt it was reasonable to assume that there was also a forward movement once more. What happened to the coach that had left the rails I will never know. Perhaps a road was built around it.

When I got to Waterways I found the canoe and other equipment had all arrived safely. I erected the tent and established a camp beside the Clearwater River. Stan arrived the following day and we loaded up the canoe and pushed off. Each of us had been in a canoe about twice previously and we zigged and zagged and wobbled back and forth with some disagreement as to who was to guide the craft, the bowman (me) or the sternman (Stan). Eventually we got straightened around and pointed in a northerly direction.

Our load consisted of eight hundred pounds of food and supplies which left us with six inches of freeboard. This was fine and dandy as long as we did not encounter a wind. We soon became aware, however, that our loaded canoe would not take much of a wave as the spray and sheets of water would start coming in over the gunn'l which if allowed to continue can become uncomfortable.

As it was we did not encounter a real storm until we were on Great Slave Lake and by that time we were starting to smarten up. Also we were starting to realize that a small canoe was not the type of craft for an extended voyage on these tremendous northern rivers. The local residents used canoes for hunting on small streams and where portaging is necessary. For travel on the big rivers they used scows and wooden boats powered with an outboard motor. Going upstream a canoe can have advantages; it is easier to paddle, track or pole. But it is also easier to upset.

The size of the Athabasca River was one of the first things that impressed me. It seemed to fade into the horizon and its width was far greater than any river I had seen before. The water was a dark chocolate brown in color and contained so much silt that we advised one another to chew it well before swallowing. At all times the surface was marked by small eddies and swirls that made a constant swishing and gurgling sound. Often a large swirl twenty or thirty feet across would erupt in turbulence, then subside and disappear. The driftwood stage was over but the swirls and eddies would continue until the river level subsided to a normal stage. Sometimes an innocent looking expanse of water would suddenly surge upward in a boil ten feet across and swing the canoe violently to one side or the other.

After we had been on the river for a few minutes a welcoming party of mosquitoes came out from shore and kept us company. They swarmed around us and upon us morning, noon and night. If we paddled fast in an attempt to leave them behind they followed in a cloud even five miles out into a lake. They stuck to us like filings to a magnet. The first evening we made camp they drove us to start travelling again. The water was calm and it was light enough to see so we paddled all night. Tiredness overcame us at last and we had to stop. We put up the tent and closed all the openings as well as we could, but the little biting devils found their way in, in swarms. The more we killed the more there were to kill. Finally we slept wiping a bloody hand across our faces once in a while. At first I tried putting a blanket over my head and pulling it close around me. That kept the mosquitoes out but the heat was suffocating and I had to open up an air hole. I lay awake in pain and frustration cursing the damned insects from hell. That first night on the river I would have sold my soul to the Devil to be back in my bedroom in Calgary between cool white sheets with the breeze from the garden flowers coming in the window and where a mosquito had not been seen for a century. Until we camped on the shore of Great Slave Lake we never did have a sleep that was not broken and fitful; a sleep that was induced by sheer exhaustion.

On the two hundred miles to Lake Athabasca and Fort Chipewayan we saw several trappers' cabins and woodcutters' camps but met no one to talk to until we reached Chip. The local residents have shortened this beautiful sounding Indian name to simply Chip and rarely if ever use the complete word. I remember we crossed five miles of open lake coming in to the old fort. It was a nice evening, with no wind, which was fortunate as our little craft would not have stood much of a blow. Over the wide expanse of water the few white painted buildings of the trading post stood out for miles. First the white buildings with their red roofs could be seen far in the distance, then the Indian encampment came into view with the grey smudged tents, smoke from wood fires, brush lean-tos and some log shacks. Then about a mile away the canoes and boats drawn up on the beach could be distinguished. At Chip we left some letters for home, pushed on to the delta and camped on the bank of the Slave River.

We had embarked on the voyage with four hundred pounds of basic food supplies which we intended as a basis of a winter grubstake. We had fondly imagined that while travelling we would be able to shoot plenty of wild game and such things as ducks and geese. As the days wore into weeks we became convinced that we had been deluding ourselves and had been living in a fool's paradise. We saw no wild animals at all until we were well into the Liard River country nine hundred miles from our starting point. The water birds were extremely wild and wary and we did not succeed in killing a single one.

The trading posts in the settlements all had a good supply of food including canned goods, but the prices were getting higher as we went north and our supply of cash was extremely limited. A can of beans between the two of us and two hardtack biscuits each made up each meal. We never gave up hope entirely of getting wild meat, maybe around the next bend.

Each day now was much the same as the last. We set off very early each morning and paddled steadily all day with short breaks to roll a smoke or just to rest our aching shoulders, with a longer stop at noon to make a pot of tea and eat our beans and hardtack, then we paddled again until late evening when we would start to look for a level spot on the bank to make camp. Then to bed to fight mosquitoes all night.

After the Peace joins the Athabasca it is called the Slave River. The speed of the current was now about six miles an hour and the opposite shore-line was often half a mile away. There is sixteen miles of water below Fitzgerald that is an impassable rapids and has been named the Pelican Rapids. The trucks moved our canoe and load across the portage for less than ten dollars, if I recall correctly, and Stan and I walked the sixteen miles in four hours. Fort Smith had a few more government buildings but there was nothing otherwise to distinguish it as the capital of the Northwest Territories from most other settlements. In jig time we had the canoe loaded and were on our way again.

This was July 8, 1930, and we were quite happy with the time we were making. We had come three hundred miles so far with five hundred more to go to Fort Simpson and then two hundred more upstream to Fort Liard. Our original intention was to continue on from there to northern British Columbia or the Yukon Territory. But man proposes and God disposes, as we were to find out.

At the delta of the Slave River we missed all three of the deep channels we should have taken into the lake. We ended up on a seemingly endless flat of sandbars covered with driftwood, trees and roots with a trickle of water here and there. Standing up in the canoe we could see no end to it. Nevertheless we continued to weave our way along through the shallows and did at last reach the lake.

What an expanse of water! To a boy from the prairies it was an ocean. The lake was dead calm and glassy, and for the first time in my life I looked over an expanse of water that truly met the sky with no mark or line to tell where one left off and the other began.

A few miles to the west we rounded a point and suddenly there was Resolution. What sticks in my mind about Resolution was the myriad of Indian tents and the permeating overpowering odor of decaying fish. We took a short walk through the settlement, then hurried on.

Soon after we passed Res (again all the local people shorten the name to simply Res) the wind came from the north and we had to get to shore in a hurry and haul the canoe out of the water. We found a good camping place on a gently sloping sand beach among small birch and poplar trees. The waves came thundering onto the beach and the wind continued to blow for three days. It was three days of heaven however for the onshore wind kept the mosquitoes driven back into the bush and away from the tent. We slept in peace. The sleep of the just. Just what we didn't know.

The third evening the wind calmed, we loaded the canoe and paddled west toward Hay River. Mile after mile it was paddle, paddle, paddle until our arms were sore, and neck and shoulders were stiff with pain. We had to move on while the lake was calm and the only way to go forward was by pushing the water backward with muscle and paddle. Point after point came into sight and vanished behind. Actually they were not points at all but rather long easy bends in the shore line. They look like sharp points of land jutting out into the lake from ten miles away.

In the late afternoon a quick storm blew up and within minutes the waves were three feet high. We paddled furiously for shore, leaped into the water up to our waists and pulled the canoe to safety before it had a chance to ship much water. Looking around we found that we were in the mouth of the Hay River with the village some distance upstream. After hurriedly making camp in the small trees near the beach we headed into the settlement to get to a store before closing time; some beans and hardtack were needed for the larder. A short distance along the trail a man was cooking a bannock over an open fire. We stopped.

"How do you do?" we offered.

"Good day," he replied, "newcomers?"

"Yep. We're headed up the Liard. Might trap for the winter there."

"My name's Renny," he said, "got a line not far from here. You boys got dogs?"

"No."

"You can't run much of a line without dogs these lean years." Renny flipped the bannock in the small fry pan. Both sides were done. He set it aside and stirred up the fire. There was a wind off the lake and the air was cold.

I thought 'Here is the first real trapper we have met. We may as well learn all we can.' He was speaking again.

"I don't think anyone made a catch last winter; poor year. The only trip I got anything the wolves cleaned me out." It was not clear to me at that time what he meant by "the wolves cleaned me out" but I was too reticent to ask and kept silent.

Stan said, "How long a trapline you got?"

"Oh, about eighty miles, I guess. It's closed for beaver now, you know, so we have to depend on land fur."

We were all ears, and waited for more.

"You boys should have dogs if you are going to trap. You might be able to buy some from the Indians, they usually have lots."

We made no reply to that. We had no money to purchase a dog team, let alone the set of harness and sleigh that would be required.

The next morning we were on our way, keeping over a mile from the shore to avoid rocks and shallows. By nightfall we had worked our way the remaining thirty-five miles to Wrigley Harbour where many islands dotted the outlet of Great Slave Lake into the Mackenzie River. After the islands were passed, the river widened to more than five miles. There was but a slight current and to us in the small canoe it seemed merely an extension of the lake. On the left bank close to hand the shore was rocky, low, and covered with willows. The distant north shore was merely a thin dark line, when it could be seen at all. Near the camp that night we shot some willow grouse with the .22 rifle. It was the first game we had had to eat on the trip so far.

Forty miles farther on the river narrowed and became fast and turbulent. We saw Fort Providence ahead, a few buildings on a high bank very similar to other settlements. There was the Hudson's Bay post, the Northern Traders store, the Royal Canadian Mounted Police barracks, the Roman Catholic mission and some Indian tents.

At Mills Lake fifteen miles past Providence the river widened to a big shallow pond, then narrowed a little with a slow current for another sixty miles. Along here the banks of the river were low and covered with willows. There were weeds growing out into the river in many places.

Seventy-five miles out of Fort Simpson, at what is knows as "The head of the line", the river narrowed until it was only half a mile in width, the banks became steep and rocky, the current speeded up with swirls and eddies developing.

Next day we encountered a slight head wind with small choppy waves, but continued on with the current helping to speed us on our way. Toward evening we saw in the distance the white and red of the Hudson's Bay post and knew that we were approaching Fort Simpson. The three mile stretch of water above Fort Simpson constituted the mouth of the Liard River, and I remember thinking there should be another name for these northern waterways, they are much too big to be called simply rivers.

We pitched camp in the flats just above town and set off to find Andy Whittington's restaurant where, Mr. Renny told us, good meals were served for one dollar. It was a month since we had sat down to a table and we thought we would splurge on a decent meal.

Later two trappers, Art George and Bill Epler, came into the restaurant and sat and talked with us. Art was a heavy-set man in his forties who said he had come originally from Boise, Idaho to the Peace River country to homestead. He had been starved out and had brought his wife and son to the Liard River in 1928 to make his fortune trapping. Bill Epler and Jack Mulholland were partners and trapped in the same general area as Art George. Their home cabins were ten miles apart. Bill Epler did not say much that first night we met him, as Art was doing most of the talking. They both were quite friendly and Stan and I liked them right away. The first thing that Art said was, "You boys newcomers?"

"Yes, we're heading up the Liard into B.C."

"You can make it to Liard alright," Art replied, "although thirty miles up the river there are about eight miles of rapids that you might have a little trouble getting through without power."

"Rapids?" we said, "we hadn't heard of any so near to Simpson."

"They're there all right," said Bill Epler, "but with a track-line you shouldn't have any trouble, there's only about five miles of the worst ones."

"I don't think you'll get more than about a hundred miles above Liard," Art volunteered, "the main Liard is almost impassable once you get that far; Devil's Canyon is supposed to be one hell of a place with a six mile portage around it. The word around here is that only one person has survived a trip through Devil's Canyon, and she is a young girl named Jenny Smith who survived when her father was drowned trying to run the canyon with a raft. She is living in Fort Smith now."

"We had hoped to get up to the headwaters of the Liard" Stan said, "but it looks as if we'll have to shorten our objective a little."

I did not say anything. I was pretty damned disgusted

with the country so far and didn't care if we went north, south, east or west. There was no game and no fur, so what was the use? But willy nilly, it looked as if we were stuck in the north for a year anyway.

Bill Epler did not have much to say that evening except to describe the Liard rapids in some detail to us. The river was wide with high limestone cliffs on each side for perhaps ten miles. There were a lot of big waves in places and the current was possibly ten miles per hour. Most of the trappers, he said, used scows and outboard motors nowadays to take their supplies to their traplines, although a few still used canoes and track-lines. Bill said the first "riffle" we would come to would be the Beaver Dam; which was of course not a dam made by a beaver, but a limestone ledge on the river bottom which extends from one shore to the other and over which the water cascades, then curls back in a monstrous wave. It does indeed resemble a beaver dam except for the fact that the Liard River is much too big. To build a dam across the Liard the animals called beaver would have to be much larger, more numerous and more industrious than they are now. Bill also said that the level of the water in the Liard was about right at this time. It was in very low water that the Beaver Dam and other riffles were at their worst.

It was nine o'clock at night when we walked back to our tent and canoe, but the sun was still high. It was July 27th and it would be dusk for only two hours around midnight. We had become used to the long hours of daylight and already accepted it as quite normal.

Raymond George, Art's son, came along to visit and to sit and talk with us as the sun was going down. He was nineteen then and had been trapping with his dad for two years.

Stan and I listened to Raymond and slowly absorbed more knowledge of rivers, trapping and the bush. I found the nomenclature of northerners highly intriguing. Raymond, Art and Bill spoke of synes, kickers, toggles, cubbys, track-lines and riffles, free traders, the N.T., the Bay, Indians, breeds, missions, sheer-pins, sandbars and mukluks.

I couldn't help but notice that everyone saw that we were "newcomers" from a mile off. Now I know why. A new arrival in the north walked rather stiffly. He seemed to be either too formal or overly friendly, as if trying too hard to be accepted. He was pale of face and a bit unsure of himself. Among trappers who are tanned, relaxed and friendly an outsider shows up like a coal miner at a Ladies Aid tea.

At the time I thought if I could make a stake of any kind that first winter I would be only too glad to leave the north to the Indians and mosquitoes. However there are wise words that have been said that if you drink from the northern rivers you will never be happy away from them. Certainly for most of those who leave there is a pull that draws them back, an intangible sense of freshness, freedom and adventure that causes us all to succumb to the magic and enchantment of the big rivers.

After resting in Simpson for a day or two we launched and loaded the canoe and paddled around the long sandbar into the waters of the Liard where the current was slack for the first four miles. We soon found that paddling the heavily loaded canoe upstream was very hard work indeed, so like the voyageurs of old we ran out the line and went to tracking. Only this operation was just a little different. I blush to tell you of what our "trackline" consisted, but the truth must be told. It was two hundred feet of half inch manilla rope, strong enough to pull a battleship. When wet, which was always, it was an inch in diameter and weighed over one hundred pounds. A proper trackline, we learned later, was a hundred yards of cod-line, which was a quarter inch oiled fishnet line. It did not absorb the water and could be flipped over stones, roots and other obstructions along the beach. Using the rope we had for the job on hand was like using a bulldozer to mow a lawn. We didn't even know how to make a bridle for the canoe and had no cord suitable if we had known. But ignorance being bliss, away we plodded with our heavy duty equipment: one man pulling on the rope and the other one keeping the canoe out in the stream by means of a pole tied to the bow. In this manner we proceeded up the river, wallowing through the mud, over boulders and often walking in the water. In said moments we compared our trackline to a logging chain. Poling a canoe or boat is a very handy technique that we mastered later and it speeded our progress considerably.

The third day found us in the rapids where the shale bank was steep, wet, rough and slippery. The water was fast and turbulent with nasty little points of rock and shale jutting into the stream every few hundred feet and swift eddies below them. For three or four miles we plodded right along making good progress. With both of us out of it the canoe rode high and had shipped no water.

Rounding a bend the water increased in speed and at the head of each eddy there was a drop of a foot or more where the water changed direction from going upstream at five miles an hour to going downstream at ten miles an hour.

Naturally the inevitable happened. Stan was tracking and I was holding the bow out with a pole. The eddy took the stern of the canoe right into shore and the bow hit the oncoming water pouring over the point, at ninety degrees. Before you could say "This is a nasty kettle of fish," due to our inexperience and the perversity of inanimate objects generally, but mostly due to natural physical laws of buoyancy, the canoe filled with water and sank. Stan hung onto the rope for grim death and shouted, "Jump in you fool, and grab it." So I, the fool, jumped in. All I grabbed was a mouthful of water: it was very deep and I did not see the canoe. When I came up I scrambled for shore (minus my hat). Getting hold of the rope we pulled the canoe and its load up out of the water and onto the shore. As a precaution before we hit the rapids we had put all our stuff in canvas bags and lashed them down, so nothing was lost but oh man, was everything wet! Fortunately the beach there was large enough to spread everything out to dry, a task we completed very quickly. Blankets, a few books and papers, sacks of flour, packets of rice, raisins, prunes and rolled oats and other items including a Christmas cake in a coffee can (from home) were laid out on the rocks. The water had not penetrated the flour sacks and had done the dried fruit no harm. The bit of canned goods were all right. The rice and rolled oats, however, were soaked, and seemed to get wetter after they were laid out. To deal with this problem we simply ate them up.

Sleeping on the sharp jagged rocks must have been uncomfortable but I remember nothing of that.

During this time we were blessed with good weather and on the morning of the third day we loaded up and tried again. Splitting the load in half we made two trips to the head of the rapids and all went well. On coming to the head of each of those miserable little drops I would jump into the water and lead the canoe to safety above.

A day and a half later we were through the rapids and the limestone cliffs gave way to high clay banks with a shoreline of boulders and mud. Then the banks became still lower and the beach turned to sand and gravel bars. The heavy stands of spruce and poplar grew right to the river and in places gave way to birch, alders and willows.

Passing by one of the high mud banks, Stan provided a diversion that cheered me no end. The canoe trip so far had been a bit monotonous, a lot of darned hard work and not much else. We slept well when the mosquitoes allowed, were up bright and early to eat our skimpy meal and struggle on. No humor or joy or change from day to day. Ahh—but this day *was* different.

Up to the middle of this hot quiet afternoon there was not a sign that something new was boding. It happened suddenly, which perhaps lent to the joy of the whole occasion. By this time we had learned that one of us could sit in the canoe and guide it quite easily with a paddle while the other took his turn on the line. Stan was tracking, the bank was steep and muddy where great gobs of clay had slid into the deep slow-moving stream. The pulling was easy: Stan had the rope over his shoulder and was probably daydreaming as was his wont. He stepped around a clump of birch trees that had slid to the edge of the stream and suddenly he was gone. It is the absolute truth—I did not see him go anywhere, up down or sideways. (I suppose I could have been looking somewhere else or daydreaming as is NOT my wont). I blinked my eyes in astonishment, he was there, then he wasn't there. He had completely and absolutely vanished. I sat in the canoe taking stock of the situation, hardly daring to breathe, for I didn't want to disturb the tranquility of the scene. The suddenness of the thing was sorely perplexing. If he had given me some small warning, I could have been prepared to solve the mystery. But no, he had to act abruptly as he always does. I then took careful stock of the facts as I saw them and came to the conclusion that he was gone forever. Well, I thought, the Lord giveth and the Lord taketh away, and I will just have to carry on alone. I will gather in the rope and proceed. Then it struck me just like that. The whole thing was solved. Nothing to it. The rope lay upon the water and ended in a gentle curve at the small group of trees where Stan was last seen. He is in the water, I concluded; logically I think. He must have become overheated and wishing to cool off he had eased himself gently and swiftly into the stream, for there was not a swirl or ripple upon the surface of the water. I must, I said to myself, get a pole with a hook upon it and fish him out.

At this point in my deliberation there appeared a great eruption in the river near the spot where Stan had vanished, and lo and behold, there he was as before with the rope over his shoulder continuing his walk around the birch tree. He had come up like a cork shot from a bottle, bounced onto shore and proceeded without missing a step. You may imagine my consternation. After thinking I had lost him, there he was as good as new. He didn't even look wet, dammit. Then all at once he put his hand in his pocket and pulled out his turnip as he called it; a Pocket Ben watch. He shook the poor thing violently, as if blaming it for his mishap, put it to his ear, shook it again more violently than ever, then stuffed it back into a pocket. I thought for a while he intended to fling it in the river, but no. All this was done without either increasing or decreasing his stride through the mud: plop, squilch, glook; plop, squilch, glook, and without once turning his head. Because I was bent over, the canoe did not track properly and Stan, turning and saying some unkind words to me, saw me doubled over gurgling and gagging with tears in my eyes. Seeing the serious concerned look on his face I soon recovered from my choking spell and he resumed his stroll.

At the foot of the Long Reach, which is the local name denoting a long, wide stretch of the Liard River, we could see the mountains to the west and a five thousand foot rock where the Nahanni River joined the Liard.

"Haw humph," said Stan. "Should be game in the mountains, bound to be game in the mountains."

"Of course," I said. "Those hills look very like the ones west of Calgary, and there is plenty of game there."

"But I know we're deluding ourselves," I thought. "There is probably as much game there as there was in the last eight hundred miles, and that is, none."

Still and all, I had visions of moose steaks sizzling over a fire. We had come a long way and had seen only a few ducks and spruce hens. It would help this empty feeling inside me where there is supposed to be food. The small rations of beans and hardtack at mealtime were getting me down. True, we had some wet groceries in the canoe but we also had a long cold winter ahead. There were stories of people having seen moose in the north but I was starting to think that a moose was an imaginary creature similar to the unicorn.

At noon one day we came to a trapper's cabin and talked for a while with the trapper and his wife. He said he and his neighbor were thinking of moving to Bear Lake the following summer as the trapping had been very poor here. He said they had made a very poor catch the last winter. A poor catch, we understood by now, was a quantity of fur that was insufficient to purchase even the basic necessities of a grubstake.

We noticed that this trapper had five big sleigh dogs tied in his yard, great amounts of traps hanging under his "cache" and a twenty-two foot freight canoe with a five H.P. Johnson motor on the beach in front of the cabin. It began to dawn on us that trapping required a sizeable investment of money. But we had no intentions of spending our lives trapping and I was anxious to get back to Calgary to finish my last year at Tech.

Here in the "Long Reach", the river was slow and wide. There were good tracking beaches and often we could make good headway by paddling. We were making twenty miles a day against the current in contrast to sixty miles a day we had made downstream on the Slave and Mackenzie.

At the head of the Long Reach we passed Ole Lindberg's home. I say "home" instead of cabin, for the Lindbergs had a big clearing and a big garden. They hardly went to Simpson at all and were real settlers. They were eventually to become our very close friends. Their cabin was set back from the river a good distance, and as we saw no one we did not stop. The following spring in June when I did stop at their cabin and met them for the first time, Ole told us he was away when we went by but his wife Anna had seen us and knew that we were the Turner boys heading up to northern B.C., and that we had "swamped" in the rapids. This information had come to them by "moccasin telegraph", a truly amazing rapid and not always accurate form of communication. If I had to define the term I would say that it was bits and pieces of information passed by word of mouth that is well amplified with conjecture as the gossip moves along. Eight days later when we arrived at Fort Liard the residents there seemed to know more about us than we did ourselves. Moccasin telegraph, we learned, was as much a feature of the north as the big rivers, the dog teams, and the hospitality of the people. And when I say people, I mean everyone, Indians probably more than others.

The next day we actually saw some animals: a mother black bear ambling along the bank of the river among the big spruce with her two cubs.

Although the river was nearly half a mile wide in some places and took five minutes to paddle across we found that we could make the best time by crossing over and taking the inside of the bends of the stream and tracking along the sand

and gravel bars. Thus we kept away from the fast deep water below the cut banks. At the foot of the mountain that is called Nahanni Butte the river turned south and kept to the east of the Liard Range. We found the mosquitoes in this area the worst we had experienced on the whole trip.

About forty miles below Fort Liard we were both in the water walking the canoe through a small rapids when a cow moose ambled out from the trees and almost ran into us. We camped right there and ate moose meat far into the night. That finally was the end of our hunger strike for the summer.

Three days later at sundown we were tracking around a bend when we saw in the distance the white buildings of Fort Liard with their green and red roofs. The next morning we pulled in and tied the canoe in front of the R.C.M.P. barracks. It was August 17, 1930. Constable Burstall asked us in to dinner, which he had prepared for us. Constable McCarra, who was the senior constable, was away on patrol on the river with a three picker and canoe. An Indian special constable was with him as the police seldom travelled alone.

Burstall told us that there were eight white men in Fort Liard—two single constables, a Northern Trader's store keeper, a Hudson's Bay manager and clerk, a Catholic priest, a lay brother and a white trapper, Bill King, who trapped out of Fort Liard. These, with a few natives, made up the population of the Fort. Constable Burstall impressed us as a very decent chap. He told us that if we wanted to kill a moose we should do it before we crossed into B.C. as the Game Warden in that area was a bit sticky about things of that sort. We found later the constable in charge of the detachment was not of the same mind as Constable Burstall on this matter. As a matter of fact they differed widely in the field of character and personality. Burstall was not a man to bother about little, two-bit stuff, whereas McCarra was out for stripes.

Like all northern forts, Liard was spread out along the river bank for three quarters of a mile with the Northern Trader's Post farthest upstream, just below the mouth of the Black River. All the buildings were close to the river bank as the river was the road of communications, and all that was to be moved had to be carried up or down the river bank, including water for household use. So there was good reason why most buildings were close to the river.

We walked the canoe upstream to the N.T. post and went up the hill to the store. The manager was Gerald Hanssen who had traded at Fort Rae previously. He was busily engaged in building a new log house and store and almost immediately asked us if we would like to work for him for two weeks or so at five dollars a day and all we could eat. It did not take us long to accept as we felt we could use some money and some good meals.

Our tent was set up among the trees in the back yard and we went to work on the building. Gerald had three trappers helping him besides ourselves: Jack Stainer who had been in the Klondike in '98, and now had a trapline eight miles above Fort Liard; Bill King, a local trapper who had married a native girl and gone to seed to some extent and was not too ambitious, although he was an excellent carpenter and was good at setting in doors and windows; and last but not least, Boo Jodah, a trapper from Netla River near Nahanni, who was very good with a broad-axe.

Jack Stanier was the cook and a very fine cook he was. His home-made bread and biscuits were excellent and his sourdough hotcakes were something out of this world. His raisin pies certainly did not rot in the cupboard; as a matter of fact they hardly had time to cool. We asked about the fresh potatoes, carrots and cabbages that were often served and were told they were grown locally in Liard. In fact we found later that Liard was famous for its garden produce with the lay brother excelling all others, even ripening tomatoes against the south side of the buildings. Whenever one of us complimented Jack on the sumptuous meals he dished up I noticed that Boo Jodah was silent, although he ate as heartily as the rest. Then one day Jack made a somewhat watery stew of which he was not too proud. He set a big pot of it on the table for supper. Old Boo's eyes glistened. He got to his feet and with a wide grin ladled a generous helping onto his plate, saying as he did so, "Jack, you old bastard, I wondered when you was going to dish up some good grub." The others smiled and let Boo ramble on about his potato garden and the stews he called "booyaw" that he made.

Some evenings the conversation would get around, as it sometimes does among males, to the subject of women. And in this case, native women and native girls. There was some talk of conquests and alleged conquests. One man's wife was a native girl who spoke English very well, and we came to understand that persons other than her husband were using her for marital purposes. As a matter of fact, a year or so later when (we'll call him Joe) was getting on in years, a native trapper from up the Liard paid Joe thirty-five dollars per winter for the use of his wife. Gerald told us that not too many moons previously, when a dozen people were in the store including a constable, a young Indian widow came in and handed the constable his pipe, saying as she did so, "You left this in my tent last night." An old, old man who should know told me once, "A white man who sleeps with an Indian woman can never hope to keep it secret for the women are proud of it. They are delighted to have a blue-eyed baby."

3

Background of trapping

The first white men who came north were the fur traders, who came to exchange trade goods for the Indians' fur. Then the missionaries came to bring Christianity to a people some considered pagans and savages. The Royal Canadian Mounted Police came to bring law and order to the Indians. The Department of Indian Affairs sent representatives, ostensibly to protect the Indians' interest. Then came white trappers to harvest a crop of wild furs which until that time had been the domain of Indians alone. Indians are now, and were in the first days of the settlers, a very important part of life in the north. The changes that have taken place in their culture in a relatively short period of time are phenomenal. The mingling of native blood with white; the impact of the culture of an acquisitive society on a stone-age people and the reaction of all northerners to the effects of these happenings is of great concern to many people. Western society itself is changing more rapidly than most people can comprehend. Scientists have said recently the field of knowledge is doubling every ten years and the world population doubles every thirty years. Where does that leave the Indian and, by implication, the rest of us northerners? I have known Indians intimately for the past forty-five years and have been as close to them as most

white men get, and have observed them emerging from a
primitive culture. My observations are based on a great deal
of knowledge, a modicum of intelligence, and much human
understanding and compassion.

The barge arrived at Liard from Fort Simpson the first
week in August on the annual trip with a year's supplies for
the stores, the Mission and the R.C.M.P. We were rather
amazed to find the freight rate from Edmonton was two
hundred and sixty dollars per ton. The price of goods in the
stores was correspondingly high. Gerald told us that up to a
few years previously the general trade with Indians had been
mostly tea and tobacco (which they consumed in vast
quantities), print goods, yard goods (material for dresses for
women and children), guns, axes, knives, tents and tin stoves,
traps and canoes. Now they were starting to buy more of a
variety including some luxuries when their finances allowed or
when the traders could be talked into giving credit, or
"jawbone" as it is still called among the Indians of the bush.
Canvas tents and factory made canoes of all sizes up to
twenty-two feet in length were big selling items. Tents at
least were a necessity to most families. In the 1930's every
tent in the summer time had its hand-wound portable
gramaphone, and in the evenings the sound of jigs and reels,
western and old time tunes issued forth.

People who live within a hunting culture, as distinct from
those who domesticate animals and grow part of their own
food, must inevitably be constantly on the move. This nomadic
life of the Indians continued well into the 1940's. It was
estimated there were about two hundred and fifty Indians
within a hundred mile radius served by the trading posts at
Fort Liard. Most of them came into the Fort after the beaver
hunt was over toward the end of May. They came usually in
family groups, with pack dogs if they came overland, or canoe
and skinboat if travelling by river. They would set up their
tents among the trees near to the river. The sleigh dogs were
chained to trees nearby. Children were known to have been
killed by sleigh dogs, and long before I came north, people
realized that all dogs must be kept tied while they were in the
settlement. You just could not have two or three hundred dogs
all running loose.

While at Liard I bought my first pair of moccasins, never
dreaming it would be thirteen years before I was to wear a

pair of factory-made shoes again. The Indians of course all wore moccasins as did most of the white men. A lot of the older people wore big wide-brimmed black hats. The Bay sold a lot of post-man type caps, dark in colour. All the men wore blue serge trousers winter and summer with a variety of coats, windbreakers and moosehide jackets. Fleece-lined underwear was universal for all males. Often the men wore scarfs at their necks as cowboys do. The women wore very long voluminous skirts, often a wool plaid material. In summer they wore fleece-lined bloomers and in winter they would pull on a few extra pairs, depending on the temperature. They wore cardigan sweaters the year round, several layers when winter came, and shawls over their heads, dark colours for the older women and gaudy red and blue ones for the girls. They wore skirts that almost trailed the ground. Most women, especially the young ones, would pull their shawls over their faces when meeting a stranger on the path or trail. Shyness and gentleness were characteristics of these people.

Willie McLeod of Fort Liard, a surviving nephew of the McLeod boys of Nahanni fame, says he remembers one old man who still wore the traditional Indian clothing that was used before the first traders came. His garb consisted of tanned moose-skin leggings and jacket. The leggings were very like cowboy chaps and fastened to a belt at the waist. The moosehide coat came down to his hips, and this was about all he wore besides moccasins.

From the 1930's onward the Indian men were dressed exactly like everyone else with the exception of distinctive odd hats and beautiful beaded moccasins. Now the odd looking hats are gone, and when his wife makes a pair of beaded moccasins they usually go to the handicraft store where they bring a goodly sum. The women clung to their long skirts for years. The older women living in the bush still do not wish to expose their arms or legs with the way they dress. But that too is going by the board, as the native girls today are as nicely dressed and as snappy looking as anyone.

For a month or two Liard would be a regular hubbub of squealing children, barking dogs and the beat of drums far into the night. By the middle of August when Stan and I arrived at Fort Liard some of the hunters were already departing for the bush. It is odd that the Indians living in the bush were always termed "hunters", whereas white men living much the same life were termed "trappers". Perhaps it was because white men were trapping to make a living and the Indian was a hunter to whom trapping was incidental. Anyway some of these hunters would return late in the fall to take last minute supplies to their hunting area, and some did not come back until winter had set in, usually at New Years. That first summer and for many years after I had a chance to observe the Indians at their gambling game and tea dances which went on almost every night while they were gathered at the fort.

For various reasons this old part of the native culture started to decline soon after that and in the last years has ceased entirely. I think there is an odd case where a 'show' is put on for a visiting dignitary or when a modern native politician decides to assert his aboriginal rights, but certainly the spontaneous gatherings of the kind I describe have gone forever.

The gambling would start about nine or ten o'clock at night and take place in an open tent or under a tarpaulin. Smoke from a nearby camp-fire or smudge tended to keep the mosquitoes under control. The fire often had a tea pail hanging over it, cared for by the women and children. The gamblers were always male and usually older men. They squatted on a mat of spruce boughs in two rows of four each, facing one another. Each man had a quantity of 30-30 rifle shells at his side for wagering; I have never seen other than rifle shells used for this purpose. Close by and on the same mat of boughs sat another man with a moose-skin raw-hide drum. When the gamblers had taken their places the drummer would begin—boom-boom-boom-boom, always a consistent time of close to one hundred beats to the minute: not fast and not slow, just enough to stir the blood a bit.

In the early part of the evening there would be many onlookers, always male, youths and adults. I never noticed a woman taking part in the gambling. One of the men would have a token in his hand, usually a small piece of wood. He and the other members of his team would put their hands behind their backs and pass the token back and forth among themselves, swaying their bodies back and forth in rhythm with the drum and all joining in the cry of hey-hey-hey, in a singsong tone. Then they would stop swaying and singing and put their hands in front of them, closed, with the palms down.

A member of the opposing team would guess the one who held the token. Cartridges would pass from the losers to the winners and at a correct guess the token was passed over to the other team. With members of both teams being replaced and the drum duties being taken over by another, the gambling would continue until long after sun-up, often until 5 or 6 o'clock in the morning.

About one night a week a tea dance would take place, providing one of the traders or the Indian Agent could be persuaded to donate the tea and flour for the bannocks. Great quantities of bannock about the size of a baking powder biscuit would be cooked up by the women and black pots of strong tea brewed over an open fire. Then in the cool of the evening the men would gather round in a circle of from thirty to fifty, each one linking arms with his neighbor on either side. The drummer would start up, boom-boom-boom-boom, at the same tempo as the gambling drum. The head men would begin and the rest would follow with a chant of —Hi-hi-hi-hi-Ho-ho-ho-ho-, with a pause after the first Hi and a pause after the first Ho. At the same time everyone stepped sideways with short high steps, two to the right and one to the left, with the body bent forward. The whole circle of men would make two or three complete revolutions, the drummer would stop and all would rest. After some minutes the drummer would start, the circle would form and the chanting and movement would commence. With periodic rests for feasting and tea drinking the dance would continue until the small hours of the morning.

When I asked why the women took no part in the tea dances or the gambling, the question was politely but firmly turned aside. I assume that it would have been taboo, as at that time the Indians had very strict rules as to the different roles that males and females played in their society. Their customs were inviolable and were never questioned. Although their lives were governed by superstitions and taboos, some cruel and some ludicrous, the relations between members of their own group seemed to me more civilized than people in our so-called superior culture.

In all the years that I observed the Indians at their gambling and tea dances and other social functions such as family calls, I never once saw any quarreling or heard voices raised in anger. Alcohol has brought changes in later years, but I am speaking now of the era that ended about 1942.

Sarcasm and irony were foreign to their nature. Mild teasing between the sexes was gentle and discreet. Certainly to show anger or impatience was to lose face. The serious occasions were calm and quiet, at all other times there were smiles and laughter. In fact they would laugh at just about anything except another person. They did not laugh *at* another person. The only time I saw emotion expressed was after a death in the family. The men appeared stoical but the women felt called upon to wail and moan quite loudly in what seemed to me a ritual that lasted two or three days. Then they were back to normal and carried on as before.

If people manifest their reactions to death in different ways, the Indians then are like the rest of us. When someone died they would first hold the mourning ceremony, then if it was winter they would put the body on a platform high up in the trees. Next they would gather all belongings of the dead person and burn them. Things like guns would sometimes be left on a 'cache' near the body and no one would touch it ever again. There was a strong belief among them that a man would come back to earth in the form of a wolf or a dog, thus their reluctance to shoot wolves or dogs until later years. The Indians that I have approached with questions on these matters were reluctant to discuss the subject and appeared embarrassed.

There were certain taboos in their hunting and killing of animals that had to be observed. One was that a certain part of the animal, the bell of the moose for instance, must be hung up in a tree where the animal was killed, in order to maintain the good luck of a hunter. And if you heard moose talking in the winter time you must go home immediately and not shoot them. If not, you would not be able to kill a moose for a good long time. It is well known that moose call to one another in the mating season and it is all right to shoot one then. But if you hear them call in the winter time, that is a no—no, and you must let them be. Come to think of it, one of the last moose I ever shot was a cow moose, and she was with a group of bulls and calves that were calling to one another. It was winter! I don't care. I don't want to kill any more moose anyway.

It was a man's job to provide his family with meat, and the women were not to help in any way until the animal was shot, skinned, and delivered to the lodge or the cabin or whatever. Then came the task of cutting the meat in strips for drying and tanning the hide etc. That was for the women. A man would never lift a hand to help his wife flesh or tan a hide.

I asked an Indian friend of mine what he thought about 'sex' and he answered, "That's what women are for." As simple as that. The darned male chauvinist.

They had one taboo that was senseless and cruel, in regard to women, or rather young girls. When a girl was menstruating she could not stay with other members of her family but had to stay in a tent by herself, and if the family were travelling at this time the girl must remain separated from the others. In the winter this meant breaking a trail of her own through the snow, and struggling along behind the others as best she could. It seems too cruel to believe but the old people tell me it was done.

Strange to say, it was the women who were considered to own all the land. When a young man was courting he went to her family's camp as often as he could and was nice to her mother and respectful to her father. When they were ready to marry, he simply moved in with her, and that was that. They were married by the simple fact that he had publicly moved to her camp of his own free will. Divorce or separation was unknown. When children were born they were always treated kindly although boys were favored and made more fuss of. Girls were simply tolerated. The children of both sexes were always treated kindly and *never* punished, and I think they were better behaved than children of our more modern culture. Juvenile delinquency was unheard of. The Indians had one trait that seems similar to one that some Asiatics are supposed to have, and that is, 'face saving.' I have noticed time and time again this trait, among men at any rate. They consider it important that a man's dignity be preserved in the face of being caught out, let us say. He will come to your tent and ask you for a cup of sugar, or a roast of meat, or to borrow your dog, or your rifle. Instead of saying, "No, I won't let you have it," which would embarrass both of you, you had better say, "Sit down, Joe and fill your pipe, while I tell you of my dream." Then you go into a long involved story about seeing a bear in your dream, or a man, or a raven, it matters not. Then the raven speaks to you and says, "Joe is coming to your house tomorrow to borrow your rifle. If you loan him your rifle it will never shoot properly again, so tell him he can't have the rifle." So said the raven. Now, Joe will get the message and you will keep the gun. And what is more, Joe will not go away mad.

There is one great redeeming feature to the old Indian

culture and that is their unselfishness and generosity. It was a way of life with them, as it is not with our culture. I like to think that it still exists in the north today. You were not expected to give a neighbor your canoe, or your tent or the new axe you just bought, but you were expected to take him in if he was cold, or feed him if he was hungry. A man was forgiven if he was weak, or lazy or foolish, but not if he was stingy. An old man once told me that the thing they most hated about white men was that they were greedy.

It seems inevitable that the static culture of a primitive people, regardless of what good or bad features it contains, must give way to the sweeping onrush of the new western culture. Our acquisitive society with its myriad sets of double values must seem confusing to the Indians. We are inducing him to abandon his customs and to accept ours. It has tended to leave him doubtful and confused, with consequent loss of pride and confidence. This situation has been made worse by the easy availability of alcohol, in which he drowns his sorrows or thinks to regain his confidence. The older Indians are putting up a good battle in some cases to retain their better values and to reject ours, but some of the young ones go completely to pieces, by rejecting the old values and taking up all the worst featues of ours. Coupled with the excessive use of alcohol is the aptitude for theft, lying, sexual promiscuity (no worse than the whites in this respect) and acquiring firstly in their English vocabulary the very worst words of language.

The degeneration of the life-style of the Indians has taken place since the end of the second world war, and has come to a head in the last decade. Over these years I could see some government policies taking shape that seemed to be hastening the process. The most far-reaching and presumably unforeseen consequences came about from the action of the Education Department, under the jurisdiction of the Federal Government. It started in the 1950s when Indian children of school age were gathered in from distant camps and villages and brought to hostels in the large settlements. Coercion was alleged during the first years of this operation. Right away problems mounted. Parents were unhappy at having their children dragged away to school. For the younger children especially the change was traumatic. They were home-sick and unhappy. Most could speak no English. They had the best of teachers, modern equipment and good food and nice rooms. But some had never seen a flush toilet in their lives. There were hundreds of children in each of these hostels and some from the bush picked up undesirable habits from the others. Then each summer they were all taken back to bush camps or whatever for two months.

One girl my wife and I know very well arrived home to her mother's cabin after three years at school. She was probably fourteen years old then. Her parents have a big family and their three room cabin was crowded and dirty. The inhabitants of the village were perhaps noticeably grubby and unwashed compared to the people she knew in the hostel, the teachers and supervisors and so on. When this girl stepped off the aircraft at her native village, she was clean, well dressed and pretty with a confidence and pride in her new life. When she saw her parents and her little grimy brothers and sisters she realized she had forgotten just how much they and their life differed from hers in Fort Simpson. She burst into tears and started scolding her parents in frustration. They were hurt and amazed at her behavior, but were secretly proud of their daughter who looked so strange and handsome; just like a white girl.

After some years the policy changed abruptly. The thing to do now was to build schoools in the small villages, close up the hostels and send the children home. That has not worked too well either. After up to eight years of village schooling most of those kids could only have competed with grade three children from 'outside'. Since many of the parents at schools I was familiar with resented their children learning the white man's language and ways, the close proximity of the village schools further aggravated the situation.

When the government decided to build a teacherage and a school in each of the villages, they had also to bring a number of the parents in from camps in the bush and build them houses near the school. When some parents objected and said they could not make a living if they had to leave their trap lines, they were told they would be given welfare if they moved to the settlements.

Each year now sees fewer full time trappers and less fur coming in to the towns and auction houses. We have changed from a fur to a wage economy. Now the young people are anxious to get jobs and have a regular pay cheque coming in. There is an advantage for those who can speak fluent English, are presentable and knowledgeable, with at least a modicum of formal education.

The generation gap among the Indians I would say is somewhat less than it is in the 'Outside' world. The attitude among my Indian friends to Government is generally much the same as mine; we like our form of government, but we detest red tape and bureaucracy.

During the last two years I have been working in a Government construction camp in the MacKenzie Valley. It was set up to employ native help in clearing the Mackenzie Highway. In my camp were three or four white men and fifty or sixty native men and women. I have learned a few things and some of my observations are these:

There are very few differences in the qualities or characteristics of people generally even if they are of different ancestry. We all have the same basic strengths and weaknesses. For men, sex is a basic driving force. Men must have women; if they are deprived of this their behavior is affected as is mine. There are as many naked women pin-ups in the Indian rooms as there are in the whites. I found it interesting to note that when I took over my last camp in January, there were several pin-ups of naked women in the office. As they were rather interesting, I left them there. My office girl's name was Virginia, a full blooded Indian. She was competent, neat and very pretty. Sometime soon after we got the office in operation I noticed that my pin-up girls were all gone. I was expecting this and knew darn well what had happened, but I said to Virginia, "Virginia, whatever happened to the pictures of those nice girls that were on the wall?"

"I took them down and burned them."

"Why in the world did you do that? They were nice."

"I didn't like them." And she bent her head to the desk and went on furiously typing.

There were eight girls working in our camp, in the laundry, kitchen and office, all native but one. Some were shy when they first came. I ran a very strict camp and insisted on a clean and efficient kitchen and dining room. But I also wanted a happy camp. It wasn't long before the girls were teasing me back as much as I teased them, hiding my overshoes and throwing bits of food at me. I took them for drives on a Sunday afternoon to get them out of the kitchen. No one else was allowed to take them except my General Foreman. I didn't want any incidents. I would sing a lot, driving and at camp. One of the girls was out on 'time off' when another one got a letter from her. (Everyone at camp gets time off to go home after thirty days work.)

"Listen to this, Dick," she said. "Bella wants to know how is Johnny Cash, she misses your singing."

Once when I came back to camp from my time off dressed in my city clothes, I went to the kitchen for coffee, and was greeted by the girls with howls and wolf whistles.

I think it is obvious that Indians have the same objectives in life as the rest of us: a good home, wife and kids, a car, T.V., and money to travel. They know what a dollar is and are concerned with getting value for their money. This applies when they are sober. Under the influence of alcohol they go completely haywire.

This is hard for me to say, but it is part of the picture and must be recorded. Men and women alike find it hard to stay away from drink. The men will often spend their last two hundred dollars on a chartered aircraft to bring a load of booze to their village, then drink it all in a night and fight and quarrel among themselves something scandalous. When they sober up they are the finest people in the world again. There is a certain type of white man, and I hope they are in a minority, who are always ready to supply booze to the Indian girls in order to sleep with them. I don't know where to attach the blame for this, but some time ago a hotel manager told me in a northern town that he couldn't keep the girls out of the rooms. They would even steal the keys from the desk to get into the rooms. I know there were fifteen and sixteen year old girls flashing twenty dollar bills in one hotel in the north.

Out of a hundred and fifty natives that were employed at different times at my camp, I had to fire only about twelve. They were all very young men and had their hair slicked down with goo. They had never worked and didn't want to.

There were also many other young men who were very good workers. Many accepted authority and responsibility and did a very good job.

My General Foreman was a sub-chief from a Mackenzie Valley community, and a finer man you would never meet. If he ever tangles with the white society, I will not be against him. In talking of aboriginal rights one day, he said to me, "Who in the hell wants to go back to living in a teepee and working with a stone axe and watching your kids die of disease or starvation each year?"

4

Now to action

Stan and I had not been long at Liard when we realized from talking to Gerald and Jack Stanier that the supplies we had were vastly insufficient for two men for a trapping season. After considering the situation for a time we agreed to go along with old Boo on a proposition he offered to us. Boo had a hundred miles of trapline that extended from Netla village to Trout Lake and he wanted one of us to work for him for the winter at fifty dollars a month. The other could trap out from his line cabins. The other alternative we had was to go on into B.C. and trap on our own, depending on meat to supplement our food supply. Later we were to regret that we had not fended for ourselves.

The first frosts were in the air when old Boo and I set out for Netla with his old scow, powered with a nine-twelve Universal engine, loaded with his winter's supplies. Stan was to come down later with the canoe.

Boo's home cabin was a mile up the Netla River where there was a small permanent Indian encampment. Old Boo did a bit of trading with these natives.

The first day after arriving at Netla we got out shovels and started digging Boo's potatoes. He had somewhat less than half an acre of ground planted to potatoes and it produced twenty sacks of a hundred pounds each. We stashed then away in his cellar which was deep, dry and cool. Boo took great pride in his potato crop and talked of it continually all year round, and no wonder. It was a big item of his food supply. To this day I cannot think of old Boo without coupling his name with booyaw, beans and bannock. The beans were always cooked with salt pork.

The booyaw was cooked once every three days in a big black pot on top of the B.C. heater. These heaters are flat on top and serve as cook stoves. Boo would first dump in two gallons of water, then potatoes and turnips cut in big chunks, then whatever meat was at hand, fresh, semi-fresh or sour; moose or bear and no questions asked. Sometimes I was a little afraid from the look of the concoction that a dog or cat had found its way into the pot. I was always glad to see chunks of salt pork floating in the mixture for at least I knew where that had come from.

The contents of the pot would be boiled for an hour or so and then set aside in a corner of the cabin. A fry pan of it would be warmed up at every meal until it was finished. Toward the end it became so sour that it just about blew the top of your head off when the lid was lifted. It was a miracle we weren't all poisoned from the rusty old pot. Boo was always bothered with stomach trouble; he said he had four or five bowel movements a day. His verbiage was picturesque and crude. In fact those words describe Boo to a nicety. He was indeed picturesque and crude. It was not surprising that his stomach was half eaten away considering the vast quantities of sour mash he consumed along with the beans and baking powder. He had been raised on this diet in northern Ontario and didn't know there was anything else to eat in the world.

Of course there weren't great varieties of foods available. There was no fresh fruit except for wild berries in the summer months. The butter all came in cans and there were no eggs or cheese. Refrigerators were unknown in the north at that time. We heard of a few isolated cases of scurvy, and it was a marvel that more of us did not develop that nutritional disease.

Boo's cabin was built of hewn logs with a plank floor, a single room with about five hundred square feet of floor space. The large table was covered with oil cloth. The chairs were made of boxes and the bunks had straw mattresses.

On September 4th old Boo went across the Netla to hunt moose in the hay sloughs to the south. The afternoon was hot and many mosquitoes were still out. The air was cooling and the sun was going down about supper time when I noticed a shiny black spot across the small quiet river and half a mile upstream. Even to my inexperienced eyes I recognized a black bear. It was digging in the goosegrass, and had its head down and wasn't moving much. "Here's my chance to get some meat for the pot and surprise old Boo," I thought.

With infinite swiftness and caution, or so I fondly imagined, I grabbed Boo's .32 caliber Remington off the wall, slipped the canoe into the water and very quietly paddled up to where Mr. Bear was eating his succulent roots. I beached the canoe a hundred yards away and crept silently up to my quarry. I have never since been able to creep so close to a bear. I was ashamed of myself for being so close. He still had his head down in the tall grass and I was only twenty feet from him. How black and shiny he was! I leaped to my full height then found there was no shell in the barrel. Swiftly, too swiftly, I worked the action. The mechanism jammed and I stood there helpless. The bear started moving before his head came up, in the direction in which he was pointed naturally, and that was almost at me. I don't think he saw me until he went by me about six feet away and then he couldn't turn to avoid me for he was high in the air in the middle of a magnificent leap. When he hit the ground he gave a quick sharp "UMPH" and then he really started to go. By this time I had a shell in the barrel and out of pure nervousness I fired in the general direction of the bear. It was a shot in the air and nothing more. As my heart beats abated, I thought, "It's fortunate for you, Dick Turner, that Mr. Bear was not pointed about ten degrees more to his right or he would have gone right through you, and your trapping days would be over before they start."

When Boo came home that evening I told him about it, and blamed the gun for having jammed. But that excuse did not go too well.

"You got buck fever," said Boo. "You're just a greenhorn, Haw—Haw—Haw!" And he was right.

Our first trip over the trapline was in late September when we set out into the bush with pack dogs for a two week jaunt. Boo had line cabins about fifteen miles apart that needed re-roofing and he wanted to get a moose or two to cache for winter food. The dog packs were made of canvas and moose hide and were fastened to a dog's back much like the packs for horses. A moose hide thong went around the pack fore and aft, was twisted and pulled tight, then went around the pack under his belly and was tightened and tied from the top.

I was surprised to find that a good sized work dog could carry twenty-five to thirty pounds all day and follow along behind a man quite willingly. Some dogs got very adept at picking their way through tangled brush, jumping over windfalls and walking logs across a stream. Some dogs acquired a nasty habit of jumping into every pond they came to on a hot day and getting everything in their packs soaked, to the loudly expressed annoyance and exasperation of their master.

Most trap lines in this area were well-cut trails through black spruce muskeg, jackpine ridges, willow swamps and very occasionally some hard dry ground where poplar and Balm O'Gilead grew. The trail showed up as a rut in the mossy wet ground with water lying in all the low places. I was a little surprised to find the ground was wet and soggy at the end of the summer when the ground should have been dry.

Very often we had to skirt a slough or bog. It was at these times that a pack dog would show his colours as to how smart or dumb he was in picking his was through the tangle with a bulky pack that could catch on the sticks and logs in the way. A man had a problem also in worming his way through the brush and tag alders. These small thick growing alders insist on growing out instead of up, and always seem to point at one's face. We sank so deep into the muskeg at every step that, as my brother Fred once said, it was like continually walking upstairs.

The second night out on this trip it snowed about three inches and although it soon went off the trees there was some left on the ground all fall until freeze-up near the end of October.

On three of the line cabins we removed the dirt, moss and half-rotten poles from the roof. Then we added a round or two of spruce logs to the walls, put on fresh roof poles, covered them with moss and then shoveled on four inches of earth, making the cabin warm and snug for the winter.

Near line cabin number five, old Boo shot a bull moose and we built a box-like cache out of six-inch spruce logs on the ground to keep the meat until needed for dog food during the winter. Trees were piled on top to keep out to the bears, wolverines and wolves. It also kept the ravens away from the meat. They can destroy a carcass in days when they can get at it.

The nights were getting cold when we arrived back at the home cabin at Netla, about October 10th. Ice was forming on the lakes, geese and ducks had left for the south, and there was a feel of winter to the air. Stan had come down from Liard two weeks before and had a hot meal for us when we came in wet and cold. He had been shooting ducks and generally enjoying the fall weather and was keen to get started trapping.

During the next weeks the toboggan and dog harness were repaired, supplies for the trapline sorted out and general preparations gotten underway for the first winter trip by dog team to Trout Lake. This lake lay a hundred miles to the southeast at the far end of Boo's trapline. Stan was to trap out from line cabin number five and six while Boo and I went on to the lake. Here I was to stay for the winter to fish under the ice for dog food, run a couple of short lines of five or six miles each and keep the end of the main line open after any heavy snow fall.

There was half a foot of snow and the streams and lake were frozen enough to hold us when we set out on November first, the official opening of the trapping season. Boo drove the team of five dogs with an eight foot toboggan piled high with supplies. Stan and I each carried a forty pound pack with rifle and axe. Stan carried a five foot cross-cut saw in his hands too as it would not go on the toboggan. The fifteen miles to the first cabin seemed a long way with the heavy packs. The footing was very poor as there was no base to the trail as yet. In the evenings we would listen to old Boo holding forth on his self-proclaimed prowess as a hunter and trapper: how he had trapped a hundred and twenty-nine marten one winter; how he was able to kill moose when others failed, etc., etc. All this was interspersed with very corny vulgar jokes at which he laughed uproariously with a "haw-haw-haw" that I know for a fact could penetrate the bush for a mile. Thank God I was tired and could fall asleep early.

Anna Lindberg told us later that Boo had never shot a beaver in his life as he always had been a very poor shot with a rifle. He had previously trapped in the Birch Mountains in Alberta where Anna had grown up. I found out before the winter was over that it was a pure accident when Boo managed to shoot a moose. He would start running after it as soon as he saw one, shooting as he ran. He would even elaborate on it, thinking he had discovered a superior method of hunting. It would surely have been something to see.

The following March Boo had a heated argument with Art George and Jack Mulholland (Bill Epler's partner) as to how a bull moose had his antlers attached to his head, whether they were pointed forwards or backwards. You can guess the position old Boo took. Art and Jack produced pictures of moose showing the position of the antlers thinking they clinched the argument. Boo just laughed with his big "haw-haw-haw." "Don't mean a thing," he said. "That's just a magazine." His contempt for printed matter and photographs was astounding. This rather took the wind from the sails of the magazine men, leaving them somewhat weak and exhausted with nothing to say.

Boo went over his argument again about how sure he was that the horns pointed backwards. He even offered to wager a hundred dollars on the issue. Art was too much of a gentleman to take Boo up on the hundred dollars and the settled for a wager of a box of cigars instead. Weeks later Emil Lenoir, a very articulate and intelligent Indian whom Boo respected a great deal, pointed out to Boo the error he had made. Boo was a saddened man. He walked around in circles in his front yard with his head down for half an hour, as if searching for a lost article. I was inside the cabin watching Boo and felt rather sorry for him at the time, although Boo did deserve the humiliation.

Art was told about this episode later and was too kind to ever mention the subject again, and you may be sure Boo did not. Needless to say this episode did not destroy Boo's egotism, but at least thereafter we were spared the stories of his moose hunts.

We left Stan and his supplies at camp six and went on to the lake about forty miles farther. Boo's cabin at Trout Lake was set in a clump of big spruce trees well sheltered from the wind. It was ten feet square with a dirt floor, two windows, a tin camp stove, a pole table and a large bunk that I soon made comfortable with quantities of dry grass from a hay slough close by. The first day we set a pair of hundred foot gill nets under the ice which was a foot thick by this time. I lifted these nets every second day during the winter and they provided enough lake trout and northern pike for food for myself and the dog team when it was at the lake. Boo made regular trips over the line every three weeks or so and I tended the nets and ran three short traplines.

Stan snowshoed the thirty miles from his cabin to spend Christmas with me at the lake where we visited and feasted. Christmas dinner? Fried trout that was delicious (I even had it all winter twice a day); bacon and bannock with butter saved for the occasion. For dessert Stan make a Christmas pudding from flour, raisins, milk powder and sugar. For flavouring he used marten bait (banana extract). We cleaned up the pudding so it must have been edible. To finish off the meal we had coffee and Christmas cake, cooked by our mother six months before, and brought it all the way from Calgary. We verified then that it was none the worse for its dunking in the rapids.

At this time I had an old number three trap set in a hole in the bank of the creek near the cabin, where I had seen what I thought were mink tracks going in and out of the opening. I went to check on this trap the next morning and found an animal had been caught and was away back in the hole, the length of the trap chain. I pulled a little on the toggle but nothing budged so I tore back to the cabin shouting, "Stan, Stan. You's better come and bring the .22. I caught something big in the trap." He put on his cap and came along. "I'll pull it out and you shoot it," I directed.

"O.K." And he stood back ready.

I pulled and I pulled and nothing came. "It's something big," I said excitedly. I didn't catch an animal every day of the year and the pelt meant money. Stan stood back well away from the hole with the gun at the ready.

"Well yank it out, you fool," he said. I pulled a bit more and a furry head with whiskers came into view. Stan shot it and I pulled it free and laid it on the snow.

"Looks like a beaver." Neither of us had ever seen a beaver.

"Maybe a fisher." Stan sounded authoritative, but I wasn't impressed.

"I think it's a beaver, it can't be a fisher, look at the whiskers."

"How do you know a beaver has whiskers?"

He had me there. I didn't know. I just thought it was a point in my favor, or the beaver's favor rather.

"Just you look at the tail. It's got fur on it, it must be a fisher." Here I was at a disadvantage. Stan was older than I was and had been around a bit more and had seen more pictures than I had. But I was made of stern stuff and wouldn't give in so easily.

"All that may be true," I said in an assured and confident manner. "But beavers live in holes in the bank as everyone knows, and this fur bearing animal, this fisher as you call it" (to make him seem ridiculous), "was a hole in the bank and beaver it must be. So there."

"Bah-harrumph," said Stan. "Bring the thing in and old Boo should know what it is when he makes his next trip."

So there the matter rested and when Boo arrived he identified the animal as an otter. He was quite amused at our ignorance and "haw-hawed" for ever so long. In fact days later he was still chuckling over it.

Something I remember with great amusement must be told although Stan might not think it as funny as I do, as he was the butt of the joke. I had an old canvas parka with a hood that Boo had given me. It kept the wind from the face, and Stan thought he should have one also, something with a hood, with sleeves big and long enough to go over the cuffs of his mitts to keep the snow from getting inside and melting. He had a windbreaker that was three sizes too short for him. It was big enough around his chest but the sleeves were short and it had no collar to speak of.

Stan shook the garment out, looked it over with a concerned and quizzical look, and then got out his sewing kit and a yard of canvas. For a time there was some mumbling and prayer-meeting words from his corner of the cabin and I did think for a while that the thing would get the better of him but he persisted and eventually constructed extensions well beyond his face.

Man, you should have seen that garment. To walk behind him on the trail and observe this phenomenon was worth the price of a vaudeville show. Stan had a four-foot pair of snowshoes. He had long legs and took long strides, and the newly-constructed jacket or whatever it might be called would ride up on his middle until it was just below his armpits and sort of bulged out from there in all directions. The hood, I swear, stuck out in front a foot and a half and looked for all the world like an overgrown edition of a milkmaid's bonnet. His arms, stuffed into those stove-pipe extensions, seemed as long as his legs and got larger at the ends like a seal's flippers. The word 'grotesque' comes to mind but I do not like to use it in reference to a brother. I was a little afraid he would over-balance and fall in the snow. Stan looked around once (I think he heard a horrible choking, gurgling sound) and saw tears in my eyes. "It's so cold I choked, it makes my eyes water." I did not dare tell him I was simply gasping with mirth. He might not like it. He was much bigger than I and it was too cold to have snow pushed down one's neck.

And then I would have to think of old Boo who wore great heavy woolen trousers with suspenders. These were three sizes too big for him as he liked them roomy, which indeed they were. The trousers being hitched up firmly came just flush with his armpits, because Boo was not very tall. I did not have the courage to tell Stan this, but I thought if one man wore both units of clothing what a strange apparition he would be. And thinking of Boo, I thought of the boat that he built. He started at the river bank working toward the house, with the boat getting wider as it came. Then he ran into the side of the house, had no more room to work and had to bring the nose up abruptly. So the contrivance had a very wide, short and stubby bow. That man in that boat would have been very reminiscent of a creature from the imagination of Edgar Allen Poe.

Winters come and winters go. This one came to an end with Stan's and my fur catch totalling fifteen pelts. They sold for a hundred and fifty dollars, enough to pay for our two trapping licences. Boo could not pay me anything for he had made a poor catch himself.

Going outside and back to school was out of the question as we were what you might term broke. Stan did consider going out that summer as he could most likely have had his old job back with Calgary Power, but by fall he had decided to stay for another year.

5

Adventures

Toward the end of May I got hold of an old tub of a leaky boat and paddled down to Fort Simpson, about one hundred and fifteen miles. Twenty-five miles below the Nahanni was the Lindbergs' cabin and I pulled in and visited with them, Ole, his wife Anna, and their son Edwin who was then two years old.

Ole had been in the North since 1920 and was a well-established trapper. He said he had made a poor catch, as the rest of us had, but would make out somehow since he had a good vegetable garden and had moose meat on hand most of the time. He had a deep well that was very cold and meat kept in it for at least two weeks. Ole did not say so, but I learned later that he was one of the best hunters in the North, and was as good as the old Indians at hunting moose. Boo Jodah had known Ole for years but had never so much as hinted to us that Ole was a good hunter. Ole and Anna never failed to have an excellent crop of potatoes and for several years we got our winter supply from them.

So, on to Simpson the next day in the leaky old tub. Paddling and bailing, paddling and bailing. It was rather pleasant going downstream, no mosquitoes as yet, and moving along at a good clip with the current. The rapids were high and fast, with no rocks showing, and I kept near the shore against the wall to stay out of the combers.

The roar of the rapids was very pronounced, and with the roar, the speed, the bouncing and pounding of the waves, one tended to stay awake and enjoy the situation. At last the Beaver Dam, then calm water, and after six more hours paddling, the Mackenzie River and Fort Simpson.

I considered the place, just a few buildings in the wilderness, about a dozen people with the arm of the Government administration (what there was of it), the Signal Corps, a few Indians and that was about it. What in the world was there for me? There was food in the stores, and perhaps some work available. Not likely, but maybe.

Stan came down later with the canoe from Netla. It turned out that we spent two months in Simpson, and did not find a day's work. The builders of the new R.C. Hospital in Simpson imported help from outside and employed no local help. The few men that the Indian Agency needed were already at work. There was nothing else. Indians, who were in need, got rations from the local Indian Agency: white men had Hobson's Choice.

Stan had a little money in Calgary; he had it sent in and we bought a trapping licence and a basic grubstake. In August we headed up through the rapids again with our loaded canoe. We were learning as time went on, and made it to the Long Reach in three days, keeping the load dry. When two trappers left for Bear Lake, we decided to take over their old lines. Without a dog team it would be difficult, but we could get by with backpacking for one year anyway. We had enough traps to set out thirty miles of line each, and found that was enough mileage when all traps, food, bedding, axe, gun and other gear had to be carried on the back.

With a pack on the back, no matter how cold it was (fifty below zero in January), the snow from the bush always melted on one's shoulders and down one's back, then froze as the day wore on, making one a bit uncomfortable. The pack straps digging into one's shoulders day after day got to be wearisome. Thinking to overcome this problem, I visited an Indian camp a few miles away and traded some flour, lard and tobacco for one dog and a small birch wood toboggan. The dog I bought was not too enthusiastic about being a one-dog dogteam and I don't know if I gained anything or not. I still had to carry a pack, walk ahead of the dog to make a trail for him, and often pull him along with a bit of rope.

When walking behind I had to push with a stick. But I stuck with it, thinking to add another dog or two next year and eventually have a dogteam.

Land fur was still scarce that winter. Beaver were plentiful, but still there was a closed season on them for whites. I guess we were whites, although we felt like second class citizens, and the next spring found us in much the same financial position as the year before.

As the Yukon Territory permitted the taking of beaver by whites and the fee for a trapping licence was nil, we decided to try for a beaver hunt in the Yukon in April and early May. Although this entailed going one hundred and twenty miles to the area we selected, winter conditions permitted the use of dogteam and toboggan well on into April if the nights held cold. From Fort Liard there was a sixty mile portage trail westward into the Yukon and from there we would follow the Beaver River into what we were told was a good beaver hunting territory.

Four of us, Einar Pierson, Raymond George, Stan and I set out on April 6 from the Georges' cabin with five dogs and a sleigh loaded with supplies. We restricted our food supplies to beans, rice, flour, and tea since weight was a problem as dog food also had to be taken. This last item consisted of rice and tallow. It was cooked over an open fire in the evening for the dogs' daily meal. From all accounts of the Indians, there seemed no doubt that we would be able to kill what moose and caribou we required once we reached the mountains, where the portage trail joined the Beaver River. Alas, alas, no one told us we were foolish to depend on shooting game and we had to learn the hard way.

We had a good trail for the sixty miles across the portage and from there we travelled on the crust of the snow in the early mornings. Some nights it clouded over and did not freeze. The snow was three feet deep and soggy, so when it did not freeze we had to stay in camp and hope for a frost the next night.

Our food supply was getting low and we were well into the mountains when we saw our first moose. There were two of them, feeding on willows at the river's edge a good distance away; we guessed two hundred and fifty yards. They were standing to their bellies in snow and looked farther away than they were. Stan was a fair shot and had the best rifle, a .303

British. He lay down, took careful aim over a packsack, and fired. They took off right now and we had no chance to shoot again. Stan and Raymond went after them on the crust, while Pete and I made camp. Incidentally, this making camp in three feet of snow is no picnic, especially at the end of a long, hard day.

The snowshoes are kicked off and used as shovels to scoop away the snow in an area about twelve feet across. A supply of dry wood in six to ten foot chunks is cut down and dragged in for a fire on one side of the cleared area. Then spruce trees are felled for a bedding of boughs; packsacks and bedrolls are piled to one side, and the cooking things are dug out to prepare for the evening meal. The tea billy full of snow is set over the fire, and banged gently with a stick to keep the inside of the pot from burning until the snow is all melted. Another filling with snow and you have a pot of water ready for tea. By this time, the fire has burned down somewhat and there is a good bed of coals. Water, flour and baking powder are mixed together in a bowl and slapped into a fry pan with hot grease. With one mittened hand shading the face from the heat of the fire, coals are pulled out with a stick and the bannock cooking process begins. Just the right amount of red-hot coals is needed, and the correct amount of time to brown the bannock on one side, before several jerks of the pan and a quick high flip set the other side to cook. Plenty of lard to keep it from burning, and the bannock comes out a nice golden brown. Ahhh, eaten hot with butter or honey spread thickly on, it's delicious. Without butter or honey? It's still delicious if you are hungry enough.

Pete and I had the camp made when the boys came back. No moose. They had followed the tracks over the hill and down into the next valley, and although Stan and Raymond skipped along on the crust, the moose was still able to outdistance them easily. None of us were very happy about the situation, but told each other what we would do to the next moose we saw. In the meantime, we could see that a further reduction in the beans and bannock ration was in order. In regard to the one bannock which became increasingly small for each meal, whoever was taking his turn at cooking had to cut the bannock into four portions, pass it around and take the last piece for himself. You may be sure that each of us became very expert at dividing that poor little bannock into four equal parts, with not one particle of difference in weight or size.

We made good time in the early mornings now and two days after we saw the moose we came to the mouth of a large creek that was reported to lead to a valley of many beaver lodges. Here our outfit was divided into two portions, Stan and Raymond heading off up the creek and Pete and I going on up the river to another reportedly good beaver area. We left the sleigh at the creek and used the dogs as pack dogs since our supplies were much reduced in weight.

Two morning marches brought us to forks in the river. Still no fresh sign of beaver, but we had passed many old lodges and concluded that they had moved upstream for lack of food. We were to learn that they had been hunted out by the Indians a year or two before.

The right-hand fork in the stream was fast-flowing and rocky, and drained an area of steep, jagged mountains—not beaver country, obviously. The left branch wound through a shallow valley where there were willows, but no poplar or birch. We were getting up to a pretty high altitude by this time and even as young and inexperienced as we were, we started to realize it was not likely that there would be deciduous trees for beaver food from here on.

"Well," we said to each other, "the next twenty miles should tell the tale. Either we find beaver, or we have had the biscuit." Beaver meant food for us and the two dogs, and the pelts meant money, that rare green folding stuff which we had need of and which was the point of the whole journey.

The next morning we hiked along very fast and made almost twenty miles before the crust gave way and we had to camp. There were a few signs of fresh beaver cuttings here where the creek now wound and twisted through the shallow valley. But there were also fresh signs (axe marks and old camps) that Indian hunters had been through here recently and cleaned them out.

We climbed a good-sized hill that day and surveyed the landscape in all directions. Everywhere were endless miles of small black spruce and jackpine ridges, no poplar or willows to be seen. It was obviously marten country, and a very poor place for beaver. We had been led up the garden path. The miles of beaver lodges we had been told about were non-existent. We had not seen a moose track for many miles, and if there were any caribou in the country they must have kept to the distant bald hills where the snow had been mostly blown off. Here on the lower land there were still two feet of wet snow, with a few trickles of water in the small creeks during the heat of the day.

Back in camp we held a pow-wow, and considered the pros and cons of the situation. It was nearing the first of May. The days were getting hot and it barely froze at night; without a frost we could not travel. Our supply of food was almost non-existent and we simply had to get some game in the next few days or our bones would be lying in the bush for the ravens to pick. Whichever way we went, it had to be soon; we might have two more nights at the most before water began to run on top of the ice. There was moose country back down the river, we knew, and the valley where we had seen a lot of moose signs before we parted with Stan and Raymond seemed to be the best place to head. We took stock of our grub—half a pound of tea, four cups of flour, four cups of beans. For the dogs—a small bit of rice and one pound of beef tallow. Reluctantly we decided to use the rice and tallow for ourselves and try to get squirrels for dog food. We both knew without mentioning it that we were becoming weak and tired more easily, and of course were hungry at all times. For the last week we had seen nothing bigger than a squirrel in the way of game. No grouse or spruce hens, and no rabbits, not even a track. And if the black bears were out of their dens they were sure scarce.

Both of us knew that with the luck we were having and with our inexperience in the bush, whatever we did would probably be wrong anyway. But a decision had to be made, and by early morning we had decided on a course of action. We would hustle back downstream below the forks as far as we could before the water ran. There we would camp and build a raft of dry spruce logs and hunt anything that moved until the ice moved out when we could launch the raft and make for a point about eighty miles downriver, where there was a valley of poplar and willow flats, where the river split into many channels and where we had seen a few beaver lodges on they way up, and moose tracks.

If we could just keep going, surely, surely, some dumb moose would run into us. Here I thought to myself, "Yes, he'll probably stumble over our bones in the muskeg, and walk on as healthy as ever". But we both kept our pessimistic thoughts to ourselves and put on as cheerful a front as possible. Cheerfulness was a bit difficult to maintain with the old intestines empty and the stomach seeming non-existent.

Fortunately, it froze a little and we were off at three in the morning, trotting along on our snowshoes and eating up the miles. The two pack dogs had no trouble following us, as they were thin, weighed but little, and had light packs. We were about ten miles past the forks when we started to break through and had to stop and make camp. Here we stayed. The weather became warmer, it ceased to freeze at night, and the small streams ran water, bringing up the river and rotting the ice.

On the second day we had five thirty-foot spruce logs lashed together for a raft. Sweeps were cut, hewed, and made ready. Each day we would slog through the wet snow for a mile or two in search of game. We could have saved our breath to cool our porridge (if we had had any porridge).

There is a superstition in the north, widely held in some quarters, that if you are starving and desperately need meat, you will not see an animal of any kind. This of course is a myth, but thinking about it did not help our state of mind. We tried not to take a defeatist attitude and kept telling one another that we were bound to get game of some kind, if not tomorrow then the next day. While we were walking back to camp one day several spruce hens flew up and sat in the tops of some big spruce trees, giving their "cluck-cluck-cluck". I took careful aim with the .22 rifle and down one came, and then another until we had all four. As each one hit the ground Pete rushed over and got it, shouting, "Attaboy, Dick", as if I had done something worthy of note. We had a 'feast' that night. Wanting to eat the spruce hens ourselves we shot a squirrel for each of the dogs. They nosed them around for a long time before condescending to eat the little animals. The dogs had been getting very little to eat the last week and we assumed they would be ravenously hungry. We were surprised and a bit disgusted with them at being so discriminating at this stage of the game.

Two days later the ice started to move out, grinding and pushing its way, stopping and starting again. That morning an otter swam across the river right in front of our camp. It moved through the churning ice cakes graceful as a seal. The pelt would be worth as much as a beaver and the meat might be edible. I grabbed the .25—.35 Winchester and shot it through the neck. After skinning it out we looked it over for a long time, considering whether or not to cook it and try to eat it. It looked dark and snaky, very unappetizing and we at last threw it to the dogs. They nosed it over and left it. We felt better—if the dogs would not eat it why should we try?

Many years later when I was taking flying lessons in Vancouver, our instructor was fond of telling us that "He who is in a hurry, is in danger." Now there was no one to give us such words of wisdom, as we sat looking at the ice, grinding its way along. After running steadily for some hours it thinned out and the swirling waters sped by, seeming to whisper, "Come on boys. Get aboard the raft and you will soon be in Happy Valley, where the moose roam, the beaver 'plunk' and the rabbits scamper through the bush." And the simple-minded skinny half-starved boys slid their raft into the stream, heaved the pack sacks and the dogs aboard and were away.

It was fun for the first few miles. "Making time, eh boy?" we shouted, happy to be on our way, speeding along without having to crawl through the bush or wade the icy creeks. Then we hit a slowing current until our craft was barely moving, then ahead of us we saw ice. I shouted, "Ice jam, Pete, we've got to get ashore." We used the sweeps with all our might and just made it to the shore before running into the blocks of ice that were edging forward slowly into the ice jam. We threw the packs off and tied the raft to a tree.

"Looks like we're here for a while until the jam breaks," "Pete said. "Let's walk down and see how far it extends." We found the river jammed for half a mile. Below it there was clear water again. Walking back we heard a crunching and grinding, looked up and saw the ice moving again. Hurrying back to the raft we found it being torn loose from the shore as if it had been a straw. Another jam had broken above, swept in and taken the whole works. We stood looking at the river, a bit shaken as we watched the raft being twisted and broken like match wood among the heavy chunks of grinding ice. "Well Pete," I said, "man proposes and God disposes". The water dropped a foot or two, the ice thinned out and the river was clear once more.

"So it's walking again," said Pete, "I've had enough of rafting for a while." So had I. Considering our starved condition, the outlook seemed exceedingly grim to both of us that day and we spoke but little until camp was made that night. We put the dog's packs on, shouldered our own and started walking. We were convinced by what we had witnessed recently that rafting was out for a day or two anyway. We had to keep moving as our food was quite gone by this time and we were getting weaker day by day. We dared not wait around. We had to get to that valley as soon as possible. Luckily we were on the north side of the stream, where the snow was mostly gone from the slopes, so that the walking proved better than we anticipated. Except for some snow drifts in places, the going was good. We made about ten miles before deciding to camp, about eight or nine in the evening. We said little as we built a fire under a big spruce, made a pot of tea and shared the one bannock we had left. We referred to it as a 'bannock' although it was no bigger than a baking powder biscuit. My share of it was down in two bites and I believe it was absorbed into my system long before it reached my stomach. I said to Pete, "I do believe my intestines have dried up and shrunk away by now, and if we ever do get any food to eat, my rear end will be so astonished it will be unable to function."

"Hell," said Pete, "The last motion I had was two weeks ago, and it was about as big as a rabbit turd." We laughed a little over this but not too heartily. Then we fell silent once more.

Starting about the second week of the trip, whenever the four of us were together in the evenings we had talked always of food. It seemed that no matter what topic the conversation started on, from Andy Whittingtons's exploits with a poling boat to the prevailing price of beaver pelts, we invariably came around to food. Raymond was going to make pies for all of us as soon as we got home. Raisin pies, lots of them, one for each of us, or maybe more. He would describe in detail what he would put in them—what quantity of raisins, how much sugar, how long he would cook them, how many pies a drum oven would hold, and how brown he would make them with lard or butter or milk spread on the crust.

The other three of us would sit quietly and listen, just tasting those pies, and not wishing or daring to interrupt. When Raymond had finished his review of the pie making technique, then Stan would run over his projected hot-cake feast, with a lucid description of the taste and description of said hot-cakes. He would get a very large mixing bowl (he promised) that would hold ever so much. Into it would go all sorts of goodies, nothing spared—flour, sugar, milk powder, egg powder—the works. He would have two fry pans going and stack the hot cakes in front of us on a big platter. We would have a contest as to who could eat the most. There would be butter and syrup to go on them, as much as we wanted, we'd spread syrup over and around each hot cake. We would even have a four pound tin of warm melted honey with the hot cakes. But no, someone said, let's not get carried away. Butter and syrup would be quite sufficient. Then I would say to Stan, "When I have eaten a dozen or so, I'll flip them while you eat some."

Then we would fall silent, the four of us, staring at the fire. Just why we tortured ourselves like this, God knows. Perhaps by that time the pangs of hunger were giving way to general debility.

That evening we sat around the fire silently consuming several cups of sugarless tea, then quietly spread out the bedrolls and tried to sleep. Sugarless tea can at least be hot, and we did drink some at every meal-time. For my part I got to loathe and detest the damned stuff and to this day it gives me the willies.

One thing that worried me now was the mile-long canyon we had come through walking up on the ice ten days before. I remembered there were jagged rocks in it as big as a house, and it would be as well to build the next raft well below that canyon. How far ahead it was I could not be sure, perhaps ten miles or so. Then by the time we had the raft built surely the river would be clear of ice. Then turning to thoughts of hot cakes and honey, sugar and pies I fell asleep.

The morning breakfast was merely a ritual of building a fire and making a spot of tea, then on with our light packs and away. Our camp was on a timbered slope far above the river that was hidden in the valley. After an hour's walking we came upon an open glade where lowbush cranberries grew in profusion. The bushes were still loaded with berries from the previous fall, squashy but sweet. We dropped our packs and set upon the berries; what a surprise our stomachs got! That was our lunch; there was no use stopping now until we got below the canyon.

Sometime later we came out on a high bluff over-looking the river below. What met our eyes made us truly thankful that we were walking and not on a raft entering that place. We were right above the canyon with its black slabs of rock and foaming water. The current was clear of ice except for the banks and shores which were piled high with ice as far as we could see upstream.

Pete muttered, "Good God, it's a good thing we lost the raft, we never would have lived through that rock infested canyon."

"Yes indeed," I said, "we didn't think on the way up that it would be that bad in open water."

"I think," Pete replied, "that old Diamond Cee said they used to portage that canyon in certain stages of water."

"This sure looks like one of those stages. It's hard to believe that Andy Whittington poled a boat up through that place two years ago."

"Andy is a poling boat man from hell," Pete said, "and he isn't a b.s.er, but to look at that I would say it was impossible."

"And look at those shores piled with ice, Pete, we could never have stopped the raft when we saw the canyon ahead."

Pete looked at me and smiled. "I guess we're still alive." The packs were so light by this time that we had not taken them off as we stood talking, and we now edged our way down the slope to the river flats below. At the point where we came out onto the river, there was quiet water, a good camping spot and dry trees for a raft. Tired as we were, we set our packs under a tree and started falling trees right away. By nightfall we had five big logs cut and pulled to the water's edge.

We were quiet and apprehensive again that night, thinking of what the morrow would bring. We calculated it was about thirty miles down to the beaver ponds and could remember some sharp bends in the river, and cut walls, but no more canyons. I seemed to remember a number of big boulders in the river bed and fell asleep trying to dodge them.

In the morning we fashioned sweeps out of small trees and secured them with the dog chains. The logs we tied to cross pieces with moose-hide thongs and a bit of tarpaulin we had left.

By mid-morning we were ready to depart. There had been no more ice come down and we felt sure we would encounter no more ice jams. We skidded the raft along some poles into the water, got aboard and pushed off. The current was fast and we whizzed along, hardly having time to guide the raft clear of the boulders that showed up here and there with big combers of white water. There—there's one ahead, no time to—oops, bang, we were on. The bow swung in the air, the raft teetered and we were free again. I looked around. The dogs and the packs were in the water and Pete was flinging them back on. We were speeding on again, with no time to think or

64

consider the situation. Look ahead for boulders, and move the raft this way or that, it needed just a little but had to be done quickly. One ahead, to the right, swoosh, we scraped by that one. Another one, this time heave to the right, missed that one too. Christ, we can't miss them all, they're coming up too quick and the raft seems as heavy as a battleship to manouver. A black one right ahead, with no chance to swing aside. The bow hit and rode up and she stuck mid-section and stopped. I glanced around. Pete was standing to his waist in the water, vainly trying to turn the raft with his sweep, to get it sideways so that it would slip off. I got my sweep in the water and with a mighty tug, helped to swing my end a bit so that we slipped off and were away again.

"Heaven help us," I thought, "we can't be this lucky all the time. With the current so swift, one of these times she'll roll right over, with a pretty slim hope of us getting ashore."

Amazingly, the boulders thinned out and not another one did we hit. The shores were now clear of ice and we sped right along.

A feeling of relief or perhaps of mild elation seized us now. We had licked it so far—we might make it yet. In spite of being wet to the waist and cold we did enjoy the rest of the ride. Looking ahead now we could see the river turning to the left. On the right rose a high cliff with the water piled in a hump in huge combers against the cut wall. The raft dived from one wave into another and was half submerged at times with either one of us standing to his waist in the icy water. Then we were through and into a straight stretch and right now along side of us on the shore fifty feet away was a big bull moose. Pete was on the stern sweep with his back to the shore and did not see it.

"Pete, Pete, a moose" I said. He did not hear me. "Christ Almighty, Pete, a moose, a moose," I shouted. Now he heard me, turned, saw the moose and went for his rifle, which was tied to his packsack. Pete was a long time getting the gun as it had slipped down and was wedged between two of the main logs. By the time he pumped in a shell aimed and fired the moose was vanishing into the bush.

"Missed it," Pete said. He looked at the gun and said to me, "the lever action is awfully loose and I think the barrel is bent."

"Oh, fine," I replied, "just what we need right now." A few miles farther on another moose popped up, running along the shore having to dig to outdistance us. The same thing happened as before; while the rilfe was being dug out, the moose looked around, saw us, bent to his work and was gaining noticeably by the time Pete fired. The dirt kicked up at his feet, he wheeled and was gone into the bush. I turned around to Pete, "Give me that gun and the next time I'll throw the damned thing at him, it might trip him up and we can jump on him." Pete ignored my facetious remark, and stashed the gun away as before.

In less than an hour the current slowed and we passed through a series of snyes at the head of our valley. Here and there the ice was piled high on the gravel and willow bars. Suddenly, three moose leaped from a patch of willows behind a mound of ice. Pete fired instantly this time, the ice flew, and the three moose flew right into the bush. Well, maybe the old saying is right—when you are desperately in need you simply cannot kill an animal. Foolishly we had not been prepared for shooting a moose on the raft trip. We were occupied with the obvious dangers of the river. We thought it was best to tie the big rifle to a packsack so that it would not slip into the river, and were afraid of leaving the sweeps for a moment for fear of running broadside onto a boulder or a sweeper which might have capsized us with unpleasant consequences.

Now the current had slowed to about five miles an hour and soon we entered a quiet back channel where the beaver ponds were and we recognized the place we had camped on the way up. We saw a faint blue haze and smelled smoke. Ah-ha—a camp fire, must be Stan and Raymond, we'll soon see. The raft grounded on the shore and we shouted out, "Hey, Yoo-Hoo, who goes?" Came an answering call, "Hello-o-o," and out from the bush stepped Stan and Raymond. They were a sight for sore eyes, and they looked healthy; they must be eating. There now ensued a babble of voices. Questions, banter and laughter. The sun seemed brighter, the day warmer and the sky was even blue. Pete and I had not dared to hope that this day that had started out with such gloomy forebodings was to end with jollity. No one said so in so many words but by the jokes and kidding that passed back and forth it was obvious that we all felt pretty relieved.

"It's good to see you big apes, forgot just how ugly you are."

"We've been expecting you back, we've been here for more than a week."

"Killed any game?"

"Nothing much, just four beaver, Raymond dived in after one and got good and wet."

"Haw-haw, that's good, he's needed a wash for a good long time."

"Speak for yourself, man, I wash regularly."

"Regularly? You mean yearly. Ho-ho-haw-haw."

"We sure got our semi-annual today coming down on the raft, water to the waist half the time."

"We've just been three hours from the foot of the canyon. Christ, did we sail. And would you believe we saw five moose and missed the works? Pete's gun got jammed in the logs and bent in a circle, and the blessed moose refused to run in circles."

"Aw-hell, the gun's all right, Dick was wobbling the raft so much that I couldn't shoot straight."

"Boy, what a river, boulders 'til you wouldn't believe it. We hit two and Pete got washed off twice. You won't need a bath for another year, Pete."

"Yahh—you sure needed a wash yourself, I thought a grizzly bear was upwind of us all the time." Thus the banter flew as we walked to their camp under the big trees. A pot was boiling over the fire.. "What you got there, lads? Pete, look at this food, man food!"

"Raymond is cooking up a stew," said Stan.

"Yup," Raymond grinned, "should be just about done, some beaver meat, one muskrat, one squirrel, a handful of rice (I think he said) and a little muskeg moss to thicken it up."

"Well, said Pete, "let's dig in, what are we waiting for?" And he fished from his pack two tin plates and some spoons.

After a time I said, "Raymond, under the circumstances I will not complain about the fine stew, but I would respectfully suggest to the company herewith assembled that I would trade the whole damned thing for one good moose steak or a slice of apple pie."

"Bless me," said Stan, turning to Raymond, "did you ever hear such downright rude words? It goes to show the lack of appreciation for the culinary art as practiced by a master craftsman trapper."

"Simply shocking," replied Raymond, "that is a delicious stew. Now you take the one we had yesterday, it—."

"You can take it," broke in Stan, "and heave it. The damned thing was mostly water, thin water at that, with a few rat heads floating around in it. Now, that stew warranted a small amount of criticism."

"This er—mess, does taste and look like hell," volunteered Pete, "but there must be some food value in it I suppose. No offence to you Raymond, I think it is really well cooked."

"The three of you can go to hell," said Raymond good naturedly.

The atmosphere around the camp fire that night was different than it had been for many day, and I think we all felt now that we would make it home safely. We were determined from now on to kill anything that moved. Two men would be ready with guns at all times to make sure that no more moose got away.

In the next two days we built a large raft that would support the four of us and the dogs. During this time we subsisted on thin gruel, made with half a rabbit and three grains of rice. This was Stan's and Raymond's rice and they also had two cups of beans we were saving for a feast when we saw our way clear. The raft was built in fits and starts as we were all pretty weak and had to rest half the time; keeping our spirits up with such joshing, levity and rude remarks as we could think of from time to time.

One evening Stan described how Raymond came to take a very cold bath. When they returned to the valley a week before Pete and I, there was considerable ice remaining in the beaver ponds. When they went out to shoot beaver in the evening they designed a method to eliminate the chance of losing the beaver from its sinking after being shot. If the water is deep, the animal sometimes cannot be retrieved. The first night Raymond sat with the rifle ready to shoot. Stan took off his clothes and sat wrapped in his eiderdown. When Stan heard the report of the gun he was to dash immediately into the water and retrieve the beaver that hopefully was to be lying on the surface giving a last kick. All was quiet for some time. Then Raymond shot—there was a terrific 'bang' on the still night air and Stan leaped to his feet and plunged into the lake. On hitting the icy water he somewhat lost his bearings and was going in circles gasping, "Where is it?"

Raymond was pointing, "There, there." At last among the willows and logs Stan spied the thing, a muskrat, and brought it into shore. Shivering violently and drying himself with a towel he then climbed into his clothes. Raymond was in a hilarious mood. He was laughing and chortling with glee at

Stan's discomfiture.

"Oh, darn it" he gasped, "sorry Stan, I sure thought that was a beaver. I really thought it was a beaver. It looked like a beaver, you know. But still it's a nice rat. It sure is a nice rat, should be worth fifty cents."

A roaring fire and a cup of hot tea was now in order, and the night's hunt was abandoned.

The next night it was Raymond's turn to do the retrieving act. Stan sat in quiet readiness for the longest time waiting for a beaver to show. There was not a ripple on the water, not a rat or a duck or anything. Being of a very generous and of a considerate nature, in this case magnanimous might be the word, Stan felt he could not deny Raymond the pleasure of a cool bath. With his .303 British he fired at some distant object. Before the blast of the rifle had subsided Raymond had plunged into the pond with the water erupting around him in great turbulence as he struggled valiantly to get his breath. But he did not flinch. "Where is it?" he shouted.

"There—over there." said Stan, pointing vaguely at the far side of the pond. Raymond struck out manfully, but Stan relented and said, "Hey, Raymond I think I missed it, you better come back." By the time Raymond crawled on shore he was blue with cold, his lower jaw was going sixty to the dozen according to Stan.

"Gosh Raymond, that's too bad, I thought I saw a beaver, but maybe it was nothing." Between gasps for breath he continued, "Raymond, it is so hilarious for you to put on a show like that, hee-hee-haw-haw, for one man only, hee-hee, there should have been a crowd to watch. Haw-haw, it was so very considerate of you, hee-hee, oh, my God, I would not have missed it for anything."

Stan related that as Raymond was getting into his clothes his face was very pale and grim, his fingers were all thumbs and he couldn't seem to find the buttons on his shirt. He was continually hopping from one foot to the other and appeared to have difficulty maintaining his balance. Stan deemed it advisable to keep both rifles well out of Raymond's reach for some time and stay well out of his way. He decided also to keep his mouth shut until they got back to camp and Raymond got warmed up, his blood circulating again, and into somewhat less of a hostile mood.

It was unanimously agreed that henceforth some alternative method of retrieving would be devised.

At the end of two days the raft was completed and on the morning of the third day we set out. Two men sat at the ready with their guns on their knees and two manned the sweeps. The river was smooth and quiet. We slipped along for mile after mile without a sound. One small snarl from a dog brought instant chastisement. Gripping my sweep, I thought, "Now Mr. Moose, just you show your—."

"Hey," Stan whispered, pointing. "What's that?" Looking ahead on the left bank we saw a large grizzly bear ambling along among the big spruce trees. All was silent, two guns were aimed and as we came within range a regular fusillade opened up. A silver tip grizzly was hardly the animal a discriminating gourmet would choose for a meal, but it was at least meat, and was not going to slip through our grasp this time. The bear roared, spun around and fell over. The raft drifted past and we tied up below. Stan and Pete leaped ashore and headed after the bear. Minutes later after making sure the raft was well snubbed to a tree Raymond and I followed. Soon we met one of the dogs coming back, dragging one hind leg painfully. A close look revealed that his hind quarters were crushed, there was nothing for it but to dispose of the poor beast immediately with a bullet.

"Looks like the grizzly has some life in him yet," mused Raymond. Evidently the bear was alive and fighting so we advanced cautiously. Just then we heard four rifle shots very close together, then silence. Going on we heard Stan call and advancing, saw him and Pete standing over the bear. It was the first grizzly any of us had seen. It proved to be an old one and we marvelled at his size.

Stan was grinning. "He has two bullets from Pete's gun in his mouth; they bothered him like a bee sting. He was lying behind that big log, and Pete walked up saying to me 'Don't shoot, don't shoot'. We thought he was dead, but just then he rose to his full height standing on his hind legs. Pete hollered 'Shoot—shoot' and at the same time fired twice into the bear's mouth. The beast just shook his head but he dropped when I put two bullets in his neck. We poked him gingerly, but he was dead this time all right."

In skinning him out we dug the two .25-35 bullets from the roof of his mouth, where he had caught them like a baseball in a glove.

Meat was what we were most interested in at the moment. We took the four quarters and dragged them back to the raft, also saving what fat we could gather from the insides, perhaps ten pounds.

The raft still floated well enough even with the additional weight of meat, so we decided to go on a few miles to a place we called The Chutes before camping. Here a mountain slide of rocks had recently dammed up the river, making a quarter mile portage necessary. We carried the meat and our gear to the far end of the portage where camp was made. The raft could wait for the next day when we would drag it over the trail log by log. Right now we would eat. One of the hind quarters was laid out and we started on it. A bunch of steaks were cut and two fry pans were kept busy, each of us taking a turn at cooking while the others ate. For four hours we cooked and ate that grizzly bear, talking and laughing, remarking on how good it tasted and how much less tough it was than we thought it would be. When we hit the sack about ten o'clock that night, there was very little of that hind quarter left.

The next seventy miles to the mouth of the Beaver River was uneventful. It was around the twelfth of May and the Liard was running fast and free of ice, although the shores and sand bars were still piled high with ice in some places.

Late in the evening of the second day brought us to a cabin of Jack Staniers ten miles above Fort Liard. We had cached some grub on the way up and intended to camp and have a feed of hot cakes. The raft was out from shore a good way, and we were sweeping furiously to land on a gentle sloping gravel bar before being carried too far down stream by the current. Raymond and Stan were on the bow sweep and Pete and I manned the stern one. Our end was slightly ahead and each team was straining to outdo the other one. About midship and to port we had a camp stove on blocks with a fire going and a pot, containing the beans we had scrupulously hoarded, on the boil. The wind off the ice was cold and we all had on our heaviest clothes.

About thirty feet from shore the bow sweep broke and Raymond, with his back to the stove, went sailing into the air in a sort of half-assed backward sommersault. Amazingly, he cleared the stove, bean pot and all, by at least a foot and disappeared into the water head first making hardly a ripple. Stan's momentum took him along with Raymond right to the edge of the raft and Pete and I met him there.

All was calm and quiet with the three of us kneeling on the edge of the raft peering into the ice-cold muddy stream. A few bubbles came to the surface. There was no arguing or laughing for once. We were all pretty scared. Then up popped Raymond like a cork, right side up of all things, at least two feet out of the water, with his parka hood over his head—going "Oooooo—Ahhhhh—Oooooo—Ahhhhh."

Instantly we had him on board. Soon he was breathing in gasps and mumbling something that sounded like "Damnblast, Christcold, bloodywater." Then the three of us were congratulating him with great gusto and politeness for being so careful and considerate as not to spill the beans (no pun intended), seeing as these were our very last beans, and also considering that the said beans in this very pot had been carried by dog team, packsack, raft and whatnot for many many miles. We wished to extend to him our most heartfelt thanks for not dumping them into the damncold muddy water, where they would have been lost to us forever.

In discussing this afterward, Stan, Pete and I agreed that our tender regard for Raymond's care in this matter was more or less lost on him. He seemed to be ignoring our thanks and was instead concentrating very noisily on getting the water out of his lungs and some air into them. I remember hearing him at last sputter something like, "To hell with you bastards and your beans."

We were soon across the gravel bar and into the cabin. We got a fire blazing in the stove and Raymond changed his clothes and began to laugh as we again pointed out to him the humorous side of his sudden immersion.

Flour, baking powder and syrup were found and soon hot cakes were sizzling in the pan. Stan had mixed up the batter, and we told him that they were the finest hot cakes we had eaten for six weeks. Which was indeed the truth.

So ended the Beaver River episode. Stan and Raymond hunted for several days on Raymond's trapline, as beaver pelts were still prime. Pete went back to the Lindbergs where he had been trapping with Ole. He wanted to get some good grub under his belt and gain back some weight. I thought I would stop at Birch River and cut and peel some logs for a line cabin before going on to Simpson in search of work for the summer.

6

Man and animal survive

As you can see, we were totally dependent on animals in the North—for food, for clothing, for money. Out of necessity I have become a fair naturalist. I have noticed that nature in the north seems to be cyclical.

It is said that our northern snowshoe rabbits produce up to three litters a year, and even though many animals and birds prey on them, once the upward swing has begun the rate of increase is swift. After reaching a peak in three or four years a disease hits them and they die off suddenly, often going from plenty to scarcity in one year. They all do not succumb however and after a year or two those remaining gather strength and the pendulum is away again on another swing, reaching a peak every seven to eleven years normally.

As an army of men march on their stomachs so do all animals and the supply of lynx and fox in particular follow close behind the rabbits. Occasionally something will go awry and one type of animal or another will not conform to the pattern. The numbers of wild mink also fluctuate but seem to depend more on the supply of muskrats than of rabbits.

It was somewhat of a surprise to me to learn that mink dearly loved to kill and eat muskrats. Even though a muskrat is a fighter he is no match for a mink.

Marten also have their cycle but the marten is an omnivorous animal and does not depend entirely on rabbits for food, and its cycle, from what I know, is not fully understood. At times it coincides with the lynx and at other times conflicts with it. It seems that the supply of all fur bearing animals depends on three things: the amount of available food, the number of predators and the disease factor.

A forest fire, if large enough in extent, can influence the amount of game locally. The fire of 1942 is a case in point; when an area seven hundred miles by two hundred miles from Fort Nelson to Norman Wells was eighty percent burned off it seemed to throw the rabbit and fur cycle for a loop, and the pattern was disturbed for many years in the area. Beaver on the other hand, being a water animal, are affected in a different way. One year after a fire the deciduous trees start growing in profusion in the burned off area, even in places where there had only been spruce before. From the time they are saplings these poplar, birch and willows make the best of food for beaver. Consequently, since the fire of 1942, the beaver population has been steadily on the increase.

Moose are in a category of their own. The browsing area for a moose in this corner of the world is so vast and being continuously renewed that at no time has this area been in any danger of being overbrowsed. In fact, the available food supply could support fifty times the average moose population. There seem only two possible reasons why the moose remain in such short supply over the decades. These are disease and predators. As far as I know there has never been a disease among the moose that has affected their mortality rate. (I say this after discussion with government-employed biologists.) So that leaves one factor—predators. These are timber wolves, bears (both black and grizzly), and man. It is, of course, a debatable point as to what extent each of these predators influences the supply of moose. I refer at this time only to the sparsely settled areas of northern B.C., the Yukon and the Northwest Territories.

Let us take man as a predator first of all—he can reach out several hundred yards with this high-powered rifle to nail a moose, but he must find the moose first and get within rifle range, which is easier said than done. Come with me for a hunt in the bush some fine September morn and we'll try to shoot a moose. It is good moose country on the flats back toward the ridge—some old burns, lots of young poplar, and willow around the sloughs. We'll take a pack with a tea-billy, a lunch, dry socks, some shells for the gun, a knife and a file. We leave the cabin on the Liard River and head back toward the big burn between the cattail slough and the jack pine ridges. Our nearest neighbor is twenty miles away and the Indian village is twenty five miles farther on, so we can be sure we are the only hunters in this vast area. The mosquito season is just about over but there will be plenty of black flies and no-see-ums. We follow the trapline trail for the first few miles, then we turn left into the bush and head for the burn. There are low windfalls we step over, high ones we crawl under, thickets of small short spruce we must circle and willows and tag-alders we must push through. (They slap you in the face, and, "Oh damn, a torn shirt.") A few minutes later you hear a quiet oath and look around. Someone has tripped on one of a thousand roots and measured his length on the ground. The knees are wet and one hand is cut, but the gun seems O.K. after the bang against a tree, so you get up and away we go. Oh-oh, water ahead, not deep, just to the knees; now, which is the best way around this? We can see possibly thirty feet in any direction and it all looks the same. To the left? No. To the right? No. Oh, hell, let's go straight ahead. Someone puts a hand to his neck and it comes away smeared with blood, yes, the mosquitoes are supposed to be gone but there are always some in the wet places; they will be better when we reach high ground. There is jackpine ahead and good walking. We fling down the packs, wipe the sweat from our faces, and roll a smoke. Then we move on again. Ah-ha, moose tracks? Yup, there were two feeding in the willows there, maybe two days ago, see their tracks over there in the grass? They won't be far away. A mile more and there are some open, grassy dry sloughs. We must move quietly now. A moose can hear the snap of a twig for a quarter of a mile and can smell a man up to two miles away.

Off through some spruce we move; there are some burned trees ahead, a tangled mass. Moving to the right we follow the edge of a muskeg and go through some more windfalls. Still we are making too much noise, we will have to be more careful. We take a short rest, check the wind which is in our favor, then move ahead very slowly, toward an open spot. We are on dry ground now covered with small birch, willows and burned logs half rotten on the ground. We can see ahead now for a hundred yards or more and move carefully forward through a clump of poplar; some low willows to the edge of an old slough. You speak softly (barely audibly, for the moose may be very close, and possibly lying down, hidden by the tall grass). "There's a track there, no, there, and there's a smaller one. Maybe a cow and a calf."

SNAP! Someone steps on a dry twig, and it snaps with the sound of a pistol shot in the still air. There is the sucking sound of mud and water, the breaking of branches, and a black shape appears for an instant and is gone. BANG! Someone shot. No chance of hitting a moving target like that, just a flash of black in the bush. We may as well have a look though to be sure. Where the moose had been we searched the ground. Big tracks, likely a bull. He was feeding on the red willows when we heard the breaking stick and took off with a couple of leaps at a fast trot. There was no sign of blood or broken short hair showing the impact of a bullet. It was evidently a clean miss. Well, that is that. They will run for ten miles now, we may as well go home. We see no other fresh tracks on the way back, and late in the afternoon we hit the poplar ridge, then out to the river and follow the shoreline home. We are weary and wet, tired and scratched as we come up the hill to the cabin, a meal and a fresh pot of tea. That's a moose hunt in bush country.

Now let us get to the second mentioned predator, bears. It is a well known fact (among both Indians and white hunters) that black bears take some moose calves soon after birth, before they are able to follow their mother at a speed necessary to elude a bear. An old Indian first told me of the strategy a bear will use and I have since seen it borne out. The cow moose is a formidable opponent when her calf is in danger and a black bear has a considerable respect for her terrible slashing feet. So the bear will stay in the vicinity of the cow and calf and patiently bide his time, lying wait, down wind. The cow will of necessity leave the calf occasionally to feed, and as soon as she wanders a hundred feet or so away, the bear will dash in, kill the calf with one blow and be gone in a flash. The cow, of course, is after him instantly, but a bear is Speedy Gonzales himself for a short distance and the cow is soon drawn back to the calf. Eventually she forgets her sorrow and wanders away, and the bear returns to feed on the half rotten meat which he dearly loves.

In regard to bears and their taste for rotten meat,

trappers have good reason to pay attention to this fact. Meat cached in the bush at any time except during the cold winter months is in great danger of being found and eaten by bears. They are able to smell it for miles. During the months of September and Octoberm we would kill several moose to have them available for dog food during the winter. The meat would have to be cached in a log enclosure and weighted down heavily and carefully to keep the bears out, and even then they would sometimes get it.

I remember once, just a few miles from the home cabin, I was very happy to get a big old fat moose in a snare and spent a day's hard work in making the meat safe from scavengers. The next morning when I went back to finish up, I found that a bear had just been there and dragged away two-thirds of the meat. After some searching I managed to find most of it and carried it back, improved the cache and weighted it down with more logs. The next day I came out again to check and found that Mr. Bear had been there again during the night and dragged away most the meat again. He had less trouble carrying it, seemingly, that I did, though the hind quarters must have weighed close to a hundred pounds each. This time he dragged it even farther away and covered some with moss. About this time I was becoming a little annoyed with my competitor, but at the same time realized that he might also be feeling a bit frustrated with me interfering with what he most likely considered to be his property. It was a pleasant little game but the moose meat was getting a bit used, chewed and worn out with the constant dragging about, and besides Mr. Bear was eating some of the choice bits from time to time and I felt that somehow this competition must be brought to a conclusion.

The idea of a dead-fall occurred to me and I set about manufacturing one that would bring this bear's career to an end. This was my first attempt at a dead-fall and my bottom log was too small and too low. On coming back to inspect the situation a day later I found that the bear had been in and out of the dead-fall and had galloped off, apparently unhurt. I made another trip home for some spikes, a hammer and a file. After driving in the spikes and sharpening the upward pointing ends I looked at my handiwork and thought, "Well, if this does not fix him I guess I'm beat and will have to declare Mr. Bear the winner." Bright and early the next morning I was back. The dead fall was down and the bear was gone.

However the weight of the logs had borne him down onto the spikes and they seemed to have tickled his tummy somewhat, for his tracks showed that he had departed for points north in tremendous leaps that did not slacken. He had crashed through the bush without turning aside for any tree that was in his path, he had broken sticks and smashed down the brush in a straight groove in his haste to leave the immediate vicinity. It was the last I saw of that bear. I would not be surprised if he continued on to the Arctic Ocean where he would be free from trappers and their infernal machines.

While it is common knowledge that grizzly bears can and do kill adult moose occasionally, I did not think that black bears could do so until a few years later. Once, while prospecting near the Redstone River in the Mackenzie Mountains, I came upon a freshly killed two-year-old cow moose at the edge of a lake. The neck was broken, the guts were partly eaten out and the carcass was still warm. I thought at first that it was the work of wolves as there seemed to be too many droppings for one animal. I peered around in the bush a bit and there was a black bear partly hidden among the trees. He was a bold bear and died seconds later with a .303 Savage bullet in his lungs. He was gorged with meat and I just left him there, glad to avenge the death of the cow.

All trappers and woodsmen alike dislike wolves and bears intensely for their wanton predator activity, even though they are behaving as nature dictates. All things in nature are not necessarily good. There are beautiful things that fill you with wonder and awe, there are visual splendours that are truly breathtaking, and there are also cruel and merciless aspects to nature. When you are close to the law of fang and talon, hear the death cries and moans of animals of their final struggle in the grip of their natural predators, hear the dying gasp of terror and desparation, you are filled with disgust and loathing for the power that dictates such behaviour.

There is a commonly held and mistaken view that bears eat only grubs, ants, roots and garbage—and that timber wolves kill only the old, weak and sickly animals. Some conservationists seem to think that a half truth separated from the complete facts of the behaviour of these predators, repeated often enough, will engender sympathy for them in the eyes of the public and thus contribute to conserving the species. Certainly our energies should at all times be directed with a view to conserving most of our wildlife, both birds and mammals. But when some writers recommend the conservation of timber wolves, it seems to me that their scale of values, moral and economic, is at complete variance with mine.

Although they are a nuisance to most woodsmen, black bears are relatively innocuous compared to timber wolves. It is probably a little known fact that bears prefer meat to any other food, and will kill and eat any and all animals that can be had without danger to themselves. The larger animals that a black bear will avoid are adult moose, bull caribou in the rutting season and timber wolves. I believe that wolves and black bears will usually avoid one another. The story is told by observing the tracks of animals. Scent is left in the tracks hours after the animal has passed by. Another animal coming upon it will either ignore it, or take off in hot pursuit. If after many years of travelling in the bush on foot you observe that wolf and bear tracks will meet without either one being too concerned then I think it is logical to conclude that neither of these animals prey upon the other.

When a carnivore is desperate he will sometimes take action to procure a meal that perhaps is not normal. Rats will kill their own kind when they become too crowded. So, it is said, will human beings. So to me at least it is not surprising that wolves in rare cases will attack a human; or in other rare cases attack and kill a black bear.

In late November of 1968, when I was trapping south of the Long Reach on the Liard, I made a series of observations that led me to believe that a pack of six wolves attacked and killed a black bear. The wolves did not notify me of the time and place that the interesting episode was to take place, nor did they send me tickets for the occasion, nor ask me to referee the battle. In fact the evidence I have for my conclusions is purely circumstantial, coupled with the use of an unspecified amount of grey matter within my skull. In late November when, in the area I speak of, all self-respecting black bears are long ago bedded down and fast asleep in their dens, I observed the tracks of at least two medium sized black bears still wandering around in my trapping area. They did not follow my trail to do any damage to my traps for they seemed to avoid the scent from my fresh trail. I saw their tracks over an area of fifty square miles and for a period of two weeks. They were not together and each one was going his separate way. They were on the go for two weeks criss-crossing my toboggan trail every day or two. The snow was nearly a foot deep by this time and I found it most unusual for bears to be out so late. The weather was twenty below Fahrenheit some nights and I could only conclude they were looking for a suitable place to den up or that they had perhaps encountered family troubles that led them to leave home and seek shelter in a distant port. Then one day six wolves entered the picture. They came, as they always do, from nowhere, and made their home, again as they always do, on my trapline. Only this time they did not follow my trail relentlessly. They merely ate a lynx or two out of my traps and then left my line for sometimes as much as two miles. Then when eventually they came upon one of the bear tracks, interest in my trapline ceased and they took after this interesting scent. Then for about a week, and almost every day of the week, I noticed the wolves following one of the bear tracks. Then one fine morning it dawned on me that I had seen no fresh bear tracks for several days. My line that winter was roughly in the shape of a '9,' and the loop of the '9' (which comprised an area of about fifty square miles that was mentioned above), no bear track entered or left for the rest of the winter. The aforementioned pack of wolves soon after this also left my trapline for about a month when they returned minus two of their number. But before they left they followed my line for about half a mile. In an open space of an old slough they scratched around, and played in the snow, defecating and urinating frequently. In all the droppings were considerable quantities of hair from a black bear. All hair and fur from animals comes through the body of a carnivore in much the same condition and appearance as when it was eaten. Hide, flesh and some bones are digested but the hair or fur and feathers leaves the body intact.

These are my conclusions, with first some possibilities which I regretfully eliminated. Either one or both of the bears might have laid down and died and the wolves coming upon the bodies reluctantly consumed a fellow carnivore, or I should say omnivore. I discarded that possibility. Then there was still the chance that the bears found safe refuge in a den or other shelter (there were some rock cliffs in the area) and the wolves very soon after came upon a discarded bear hide that some trapper had discarded and consumed said hide. I was the only trapper within thirty miles and the only bear hide I had was home at Nahanni on our livingroom floor. And to get at that particular bear hide the wolves would have had to enter our cabin, kill our ferocious German Shepherd, who is devoted to Vera, my wife, then kill my wife, and then and only then would the bear hide be available to them. As Vera has had forty years experience with helping me keep the wolf from the door, she was not likely to let one in at this late date. No. Again I regretfully felt obliged to rule out this, to my mind, rather unlikely explanation.

I do think that a logical conclusion is that those six wolves among them did kill at least one of those bears. They might just have pounced upon Mr. Bear, killed him, and ate him. Knowing wolves as I do, I suspect the actual circumstances of the kill were this: I have stumbled on one bear den late in the fall. I almost fell over him; he was in a poor sort of place under the roots of an upturned spruce tree. He was half asleep, and looked at me in an unconcerned manner as I examined him from two feet away before I shot him and took him home for dog food. Twice I followed fresh bear tracks in early November and in each case a shallow and poor sort of den had been utilized. In each of these cases also the bears showed no fear or alarm as I poked around them with a stick for some time before shooting them. So I was forced to assume that the wolves after days of tracking the bears, had been able to find them in a half awake condition. Perhaps one good slash and bite was made at the bear in perfect safety and then the eventual weakening and death of the bear would be a foregone conclusion. A head-on attack I think would be avoided for the life of the wolf would be short indeed if he were not born with infinite patience which in some instances makes the killing of prey a long drawnout affair.

Black bears for the first month after leaving their dens in the spring of the year seem to be very hungry and are much bolder in attacking an animal than for the balance of the year. They seem to forget they are classed as an omnivorous animal and take to behaving as a carnivore.

All the small animals are too fast for a bear to bother with except baby rabbits which are a juicy mouthful when he runs into one. That leaves three main sources of meat; stores of dried meat, young caribou and moose calves, and beaver. These can be had without danger to himself, if he is very careful. Remember that a bear is as swift as greased lightening for a short distance but he hates to run far. He likes to make a few swift jumps to get his kill. He can slap quite effectively with his front paws but he is not a long distance runner. Elsewhere in these chapters I describe what every bush Indian knows, how a bear will stalk and kill a newborn moose calf, but you have to go to beaver trappers to find out the facts about a bear's taste for beaver meat and how he will relentlessly hunt and kill them. Fred Sibbeston, who is mentioned several times in these chronicles, is an experienced trapper and a well known guide of Fort Simpson. He told me he was tramping a creek one spring checking his beaver traps when he almost stumbled over a large black bear that was in the process of covering, with earth and moss, two large full-grown beaver it had just killed. Fred shot the bear and it was so full of beaver meat it could eat no more for the time being. Every trapper knows these things, they are facts of life; he lives with them every day. Albert Faille, who enters this book in a big way later on, told me it is harder to cache dried meat from a black bear than from a wolverine. Bears have trails along every beaver creek and around beaver ponds, as every trapper knows. They patrol these trails regularly, ready to pounce on any beaver, young or old, that ventures onto land or into shallow water. This is a fact that I have never read in articles on black bears. There seems to be a tendency to depict bears and timber wolves as harmless and innocuous creatures. True, they behave in the natural way of predators in the animal kingdom, but so do rattlesnakes and tarantulas.

When there are no humans in a wilderness area there is a balance between prey and predators. Not always a static balance to be sure, but a balance just the same. I suspect that over a very long period of time some species might disappear and others evolve. And there is some evidence to indicate that there were at one time fifty-year cycles of some species of big game. When man comes into the picture as a predator he upsets the balance. There must be a new set of rules.

Let us take for instance the case of moose and moose hunting in the Northwest Territories. There can be rules favoring the man, or there can be rules favoring the wolves. You can be certain of one thing, the moose are going to be killed in any case, by one predator or the other.

I understand that in West Germany there are no predators, and the amount of game harvested there is equal to that harvested in the province of British Columbia. I refer to a year old edition of B.C. Outdoors.

Be that as it may. Here are two pictures to see...

Do you see a large color picture of the north country? The trees, the mountains, the swamplands? Look long and intently. Do you see a rabbit, a wide-eyed stricken rabbit crying in terror as a weasel hangs to his neck and sucks his blood? Do you see the wild panic of two newly mated robins as a squirrel scampers up to their nest and kills and eats their young? Do you see a baby beaver sharpening his new teeth on a willow-tree? Do you not see the flash of a dark snake-like body that hurls it into the stream? The stark, soul chilling cries as of a human child in mortal agony? Do you not see a cow moose giving moans of agony that wrings your heart as she trails her intestines on the ground with six timber wolves close behind her? They are in no hurry, they know they have her now. When she falls with exhaustion they will tear at her guts until her moaning ceases. It is useless to shut your eyes to this. It is always there. I have lived with it for forty years and the death cries of these animals ring loudly in my ears.

Now look at the other side that is presented you as you sit in your living room far from the world of the wild things. It is a picture of Walt Disney's fantasies. There are Bambi and Perri—gentle little ethereal creatures floating in a world of fiction. Man is the only bad thing in that world. He is unbelievable cruel and malevolent. All wild things are sweet and gentle. Look at a Disney film on wolverines. A bare-faced travesty of the truth if there ever was such a thing. What drivel! What utter rot! To my mind it is almost criminal to paint such a warped picture of nature for the young people of today.

I am not going to base my philosophy of wild-life, or my arguments, on fantasy and half truths. Surely before we get emotionally carried away in advocating the protection of predators, we should tear away the Disney Curtain and look upon the naked truth of nature's ways: some are part of wild-life that few people see. Then let us come to conclusions that are honest and practical. Our final analysis will be more effective and lasting if we base our premise on facts and truth rather than wishful thinking.

Nature in the raw is not a pretty thing and personally I can see no point in those of us who know the facts of the struggle for survival in the wilds attempting to mislead the public in order to make the argument for conservation more convincing.

Storms and floods are destructive— I don't like them.

Pain is unavoidable— I don't like pain.

Envy and greed are all around us— They are both ugly.

Death is all around us—I hate death.

Some will say, "Nature's ways are there, they are right, you have to accept them."

And I say, "What I consider as cruel, I do not like, and will not accept, and will eradicate it if I can."

Later in these pages I will enlarge some more on observations I made on the habits and actions of well known predators.

Grizzly bears are like pigs and man in the matter of being omnivorous. They can get by on vegetation alone, but like the other two mentioned, they dearly love meat when it is available, witness the acres of earth and stones they will tear up to get at a single 'whistler' or marmot. Even a poor little rock rabbit is not safe from them. A grizzly after a rock rabbit is to me as ludicrous as a dinosaur chasing a mouse. The grizzly is large, swift and unbelievably strong. He can also run to beat hell for half a mile. But like a black bear he is lazy. At times he is shy and at other times he is as bold as brass. I wouldn't trust a grizzly as far as I could fling him by his left hind leg. They have killed too many people for my liking, and I know of many other cases where an intended victim was fortunate to escape. I can think of five cases in my area right now and four cases in northern B.C. in the last few years. None of these were in park areas. All were in very wild and uninhabited country. When I'm prospecting in the Mackenzie Mountains I have a large caliber rifle at my side at all times, I take it to bed, to the toilet with me, and to the creek for a pail of water. If a grizzy so much as looks at me cross-eyed he will get some lead in his gizzard before he rips my guts out. But if he avoids me and my camp and my canoe and my little aircraft on floats, tied to the beach, I won't hurt him either.

I don't know of anyone who understands the behavior of grizzlies completely. They are so unpredictable. Al Oeming claims they are gentle and playful. We have talked about it and I simply do not believe it. You could have a fat, well-fed grizzly cub around your house for several years, but how would you know that some day he would not return a little older, somewhat meaner, with a toothache or perhaps in a real grouchy mood, having been slapped around by his mate or an adversary, and come into your yard and gobble up your baby girl as he would a marmot. How would he know the difference?

Meat is meat to him.

The facts are that grizzlies have killed caribou and moose; those I know of have been cows or calves. I somehow doubt that even a grizzly would risk a head-on conflict with a bull in rutting season. The front feet of a moose in action, terrible as they are, are not enough to cope with a bear, but when he also has his antlers fresh from the velvet to wield with his tremendous neck and shoulders, I would think that a grizzly would have little hope of coming out of the conflict alive.

The closest I have come to witnessing a grizzly kill occurred near the edge of a small lake near Nahanni Butte. About one hundred yards from the lake shore, back in some fair-sized spruce, there had been a battle between a moose and a grizzly. I assumed it was a grizzly by the size of the tracks and the droppings and an Indian who was with me said he thought it was the work of a grizzly. The site was perhaps a day old. The bush had been tramped down, trees broken off, and the ground torn up. We stood in wonder for a minute, glad that the moose had put up such a good fight for his life. The tracks indicated a good-sized moose, and he must have got in a good lick or two before he died. It had ended in victory for the bear however, because we could see what was left of the moose—the hair, some hide and a few bones. Most of the meat seemed to have been carted away. The Indian who was with me was employed as a guide and was supposed to go on alone for five miles and set up camp. But when he saw the scene of this altercation, he immediately decided he had something important to do closer to the main camp.

Bears certainly account for some moose kills, especially of young moose, but I think that most of these are caught swimming in the water and die of a broken neck before they reach shore. A moose on land, if he has any warning at all, can outrun most other animals except timber wolves.

We now come to wolves, the first mentioned and most important predator as far as moose are concerned. In the bush country of the North moose provide ninety percent of the diet of timber wolves. This estimate is made after many years of observing wolf kills and wolf droppings. In fact the population of these two species of animals are closely tied together. When the wolves get plentiful the moose population thins out to almost none. The wolves consequently die off or move to better hunting grounds. In four or five years the moose start to breed up again and the wolves are right there behind them.

In all my experience , never once have the wolves allowed the moose to become plentiful and in seven years out of ten moose are scarce. In the northern Barren Lands the case is different. There the wolf cycle is tied to the caribou.

Some years on the trapline I have seen up to a dozen places where wolves have made a moose kill. And these are just a few of the kills, the ones that a man stumbles across in his work of trapping and hunting. The total amount of wolf kills must be staggering. All trappers have packs of wolves from two to forty in a pack roaming their trapping areas. Many times in hunting moose you find that wolves are following the same ones you are. Then you simply quit and look for other tracks, because wolves will often run a moose for days until they get him. A moose can trot, I estimate, at about fifteen or twenty miles per hour, through two and a half feet of snow, over windfalls, brush and muskeg and seldom slacken their pace. The wolves relentlessly keep on his track day after day, taking turns breaking trail if the snow is deep. The moose, like a horse, eventually must stop to eat and the wolves close in for the kill.

Some old hunters have told me that wolves will sometimes abandon the chase if they find their quarry is a bull with antlers. The cows, who have no antlers of course, are easier prey. Except in the case of a cow with a newborn calf and a bull in the rutting season, a moose will always run from wolves and submit to defeat sooner or later. When a cow shows fight she can usually hold off one or two wolves, but a pack will wear her down. If she can reach water she will stand in it, with the water just below her belly; the wolves have to swim and she stands a very good chance of killing them with her front feet if they venture too close. I have several times noticed that if a cow with her new calf can reach water (a shallow lake with a hard bottom is best for her) the wolves will leave her alone for a time and lie in wait in the bush for the cow to come out of the water. In these instances, sometimes the cow wins out and sometimes the wolves.

In the month of January I once observed a chase and a kill. There were four wolves after a cow caribou. She was pretty well exhausted at this stage of the game and had left the bush and taken to the shore of a large lake where the snow was blown hard and the footing was good. But, alas, the footing was good for the wolves too and it was just a matter of time until they nailed her. The wolves fanned out, two behind and one on each side of her, just loping along, not in any haste, seeming to know that their prey was within their grasp. A mile farther on she stumbled in a drift, they were upon her and that was the end.

Martin Maloney, who trapped for years on the Fort Nelson River, said he saw six wolves killing a young bull moose one September. He said it was a most terrifying experience and hoped never to witness such a thing again. One evening he stepped from his cabin to see a moose plunge into the river on the opposite side below the cabin and swim to the near shore. Six wolves were right behind the animal and all the way across the moose was giving the most heart-rending moans and cries he had ever heard. When it emerged from the water he saw that it was trailing twenty feet of its intestines. The wolves had attacked it from the rear and the guts were coming from the rectum. The chase vanished into the bush, darkness was closing in fast, the moaning continued for some time then ceased. Martin had stood paralyzed, his rifle hanging in the cabin, completely forgotten.

I have read some authors, whose works were prolific and whose ignorance of wolves astounding, who claim that wolves kill mostly sick, weak or old animals. This pleasant little myth does not stand up in the light of my own experience and that of all other trappers and woodsmen that I have talked to. Many of us have observed wolf kills in varying phases—some freshly killed, and some only partly eaten. The evidence is that wolves prefer a healthy animal in good condition with plenty of fat on his body. Invariably the first things that wolves do after making a kill is dig into the inside and start eating on the intestines and the fat around the kidneys. The back and the legs are eaten last. The meat of lean, sick and old animals will not even keep a dog team in shape. There must be fat in the meat for a dog to remain healthy and strong, if he is eating a straight diet of meat as wolves do. The sick, weak, old or crippled soon die anyway in this harsh climate and the wolverine and ravens soon clean them up.

It sometimes happens that an old and decrepit wolf is driven from the pack and is forced to make a living on his own. Occasionally there will be two or three of these together. They are usually thin and half starved, sick, hurt, or lacking in teeth. They are unable to bring down an animal of their own and roam the bush in search of hide and bones and remnants of previous kills.

Traplines are a made-to-order godsend to these malevolent creatures. They will cover an area of three or four traplines regularly and follow the trails relentlessly, going from one line to the other and eating all the fur bearing animals that have been caught in the traps and snares. Most of these wolves have been nipped many times in small traps and escaped. Consequently they become exceedingly wary of all sets and rarely does a trapper catch one and hold it. We refer to these wolves as old gummers and it is a sad day for a trapper when he discovers that several of these wretched, outcast beasts have taken over his lines and that he must share his hardwon income with them.

On the rare occasion when I have caught and held a wolf in a trap I have been somewhat amused to see that the fearsome timber wolf whose blood-curdling howl in the desolate Northland has sent shivers up and down the spines of fiction writers and their readers is in fact an out and out coward. All other animals when cornered will face you and show a bit of spunk, even a tiny squirrel will snap and bite your finger. The timber wolf is the one and only animal I have found that will keep his back to you and his head turned away. When the chips are down he has no courage at all and is the supreme coward of the animal kingdom. On the very rare occasions when I see or hear of a bold wolf, I feel sure that it is a rabid one.

One of the first years on the line Stan caught a wolf, a big black rascal, in a No. 2 trap set for lynx. Stan had no gun with him at the time, so he got the axe from the toboggan, took up a position where he felt he could deliver a blow to the animal's head, braced his feet carefully and let go with a tremendous swing. The blow missed the head and caught the wolf squarely on the shoulder, knocking him clean out of the trap. It scampered off in terror, and was not seen again.

Grizzly Bear are pretty well confined to mountain areas and are denned up for a good part of the trapping season so that they do not concern a trapper too much. It is somewhat surprising to me the number of times grizzlies are seen out of their dens in the month of January. I know of three cases where they have accosted trappers in the dead of winter. One was shot when trying to get into a cabin (Nahanni Butte, 1965). One put the run on a trapper in his cabin in northern British Columbia, and kept him in the loft of his cabin for several hours until two U.S. soldiers heard the ruckus from the Alaska Highway and came to the rescue and shot the bear, (Mile 440, 1942); and a grizzly hunted down a trapper on his line, killed him, and ate about half of him. (Near Fort St. John, about 1970.)

Black bear are almost always denned up from October until early April, and for the balance of the year are merely a nuisance. The population of black bears seems to stay fairly constant, and are always numerous. Since 1970 their pelts have been increasing in value and the few Indians who are still engaged in trapping are utilizing the pelts to some extent for sales purposes.

Timber wolves are always plentiful wherever the moose and woodland caribou are. Although a prime pelt is worth up to a hundred dollars, not many are caught and sold, for a wolf is extremely wary, as has been noted. It is perhaps noteworthy that timber wolves, in the bush area of the Northwest Territories at least, vary in color from coal black to an off-white color. You might notice in one pack, say of eight wolves, there will be one yellowish white one, two black ones and the rest will be dark grey. They are never patchy or dappled as dogs and horses are, but are the one color all over. Some will have beautiful silky fur and some will be matted and scruffy. Foxes have this similarity also, but not lynx, to such a degree. I have read somewhere that black wolves came originally from Siberia and the grey wolves are native to North America.

As some of the material of this book might be controversial, I may as well add more fuel to the fire, in regard to the behavior of wolves. It has been said, and I gather it is the popular view, that wolves will never attack a man and consequently never killed a man. I have no proof that anyone was ever killed in this way but I do know of four trappers, three yet living, who claim they were definitely attacked by wolves. In each of these four cases the men were alone and did manage to escape:

Case No. 1—Albert Faille. Location: above the falls on the Nahanni River. Time: Late September, probably late 1930's. The river ice was not yet running and Albert was camped on the bank of the river one evening while hunting moose for his winter's supply of meat. His canoe was tied on the beach and he was erecting a tarp to make a night camp. He was cooking a meal prior to going back to some sloughs to check on moose tracks. He heard a noise close behind his camp which he recognized instantly as made by wolves. It was an unusual type of noise between a growl, a bark and a howl. Then a ferocious chorus of many .together in a blood curdling crescendo. Then silence. Albert recognized this as part of the wolves' technique when they single out an animal for a kill. He felt they must be after a moose so he immediately picked up his rifle and working his way through the bush went toward the sound he had heard, hoping to intercept their prey. In a few moments he came out into an old dry snye, or back channel, that was all grown up with thick clumps of willows and alders about head high. He stopped to listen. There was total silence. No sound of the heavy thud of a large animal as it ran. No sound of sticks breaking as there would have been had a moose been in flight. Then he heard near to him a variety of sounds that he described to me as kittens mewing, a high-pitched, quick-tempo whine. It was a series of sounds coming from in front of him, he said likely within a hundred and fifty feet. He knew then that it was the wolves. He stood with his gun ready, waiting for developments. Then he saw movements through the willows, wolves dashing past him. I asked him how many and he estimated there must have been a dozen. It had not occurred to him until this moment that the wolves could possibly have designs on him. He was incredulous they would have the audacity to attack a man. The high pitched whimpering continued with the swiftly moving forms getting closer each time they passed from left to right, or from right to left. Never, so far, coming directly at him. Then he saw the one that was apparently going to deliver the coup de grace. It was a big brute coming straight at him through the willows. He raised the gun and shot. It crumpled to the ground not four feet from where he stood. Albert Faille was not a man to withold anything nor to exaggerate when telling a story and I have no reason to think that what he told me was anything but the truth. After he shot the one wolf he fired more shots at the general direction of the other wolves although he could not see them then, and he also shouted and swore loudly to hold them back and at the same time to bolster his own self-assurance. Then he grabbed a leg of the dead animal and dragged it back to his camp which was close by.

In discussing this episode at the time we both thought this was a normal way in which wolves sometimes approach their prey. We do know that they are never in a hurry to attack most animals, or rather to kill them. Theirs is a dangerous occupation and they can attain their objective just as well by taking plenty of time to bring down an intended victim. Their favorite method is to get close enough to inflict one wound, usually in the belly, hind legs or rump. Then they can hang back and follow the animal at leisure and go in for the kill when the animal is exhausted and perhaps half dead already. They will often follow a moose or a woodland caribou for many miles before making a try at wounding it.

Albert at any rate was convinced that on that day the wolves he heard were out for him and not a moose. Why wolves would do this, or if it was a mistake on their part, no one will ever know.

Case No. 2—Gus Kraus. Location: MacMillan Lake near the Flat River. Winter of 1935. A pack of about twenty wolves put Gus up a tree near the edge of the lake and kept him there for about two hours. He had no gun with him and hurried back to camp when the coast was clear. In talking with Albert Faille about this afterwords, Gus insisted that the wolves had thought he, Gus, was a caribou when they crowded around him in a menacing manner. Albert said he told Gus that if the wolves had eaten him it would not really matter what they thought he was: caribou or rabbit or moose or man.

Case No. 3—Stan Turner. Location: The Long Reach on the Liard River. May, 1942. Stan had taken a .22 rifle with him and was setting a beaver trap at a beaver lodge near a small lake. He saw the wolves coming at him when they were perhaps a little over a hundred yards away. He shouted loudly at them and they spread out a bit and kept coming. There were four wolves, all black, and they looked quite large (adult timber wolves will weigh around a hundred and twenty pounds: one was weighed out at exactly one hundred and sixty pounds, by Arthur George in 1929). Stan hastily leaped into a good sized birch tree. They were right at the bottom of the tree and he shot one of them. The others retreated a short distance into the tall grass. Stan wounded another and it crawled away. After a time the remaining two gave up and retreated into the bush. Those are the bare facts as related by Stan. His reaction to this experience rather convinced me that Stan had had the scare of his life. After he concluded the coast was clear he came down from the tree and went immediately to his tent half a mile away, where his wife Kay and his four year old son John were in a temporary camp five miles from the home cabin. He said nothing of what had just happened for fear of alarming Kay. On some pretext or other he said he needed something immediately from the home cabin, and said he would be back in a little over two hours. Back at the main cabin he got out the twelve gauge double barreled shotgun and a box of shells for it also. He returned to the tent and put the loaded shotgun in a convenient spot just outside the tent, saying as he did so, "The boy is not to touch this gun under any circumstances but it is here handy for you in case you should happen to need it." Kay was rather amazed at these unusual instructions but said that Stan would give no explanation. The .303 rifle he carried with him if he went more than three steps from the tent. And after that time Stan was never without a rifle in the bush. Knowing Stan as I do I feel positive that the wolf episode at the lake had frightened the supreme daylights right out of him. He was a believer from then on.

Case No. 4— Edwin Lindberg. Location: seven miles from the Lindberg's main cabin on the Long Reach. March 1948. Edwin was alone and was setting a beaver trap through the ice at a beaver pond in a partly open swamp. He was chopping away at the ice making a fair bit of noise when his team of dogs gave a "woof"; Edwin looked up and saw four wolves fanned out and swiftly drawing near. He shouted and screamed at them. They kept coming. He grabbed his .30-.30 carbine from the toboggan and found it was clogged with snow and ice; and while trying to work the action he kept shouting at the wolves. He said there was one black one and the rest were white. One wolf was very close when Edwin got a shell in the gun and fired it. He was excited and the shot was nowhere near the wolf, but the sound of the shot was loud and comforting. There were some spruce trees close with many dead dry branches on them, and he first thought of trying to get up a tree, but gave that up and started a fire instead. Very likely he fired a shot or two and made all the noise he could while getting the fire started. Even with the rifle shots and with a big fire blazing the wolves still did not retreat very far for a considerable time. After twenty-five years Edwin recalls that event as having a traumatic effect on him at the time, and is still convinced that without the gun and the fire he would have been a gone goose that day.

Coyotes—There are so few of these 'brush wolves' in the Northwest Territories that they are of no significance to a trapper. They were harmless and easily caught. The snow might have been too deep for them, or perhaps they could not compete with the timber wolves.

Fox— These are the colored fox of the bushland, I know nothing of Arctic fox of the Barren Lands. These swift running little animals are found in all of northern Canada as far as I know. Some years they constituted a major part of a trapper's catch..their cycle seems erratic and may depend on disease (rabies?) more than most other fur bearers. When the fox became very plentiful we termed it a fox run. It would last about three years. There have been only two fox runs since 1930. From 1934 to 1936 there was a fox run of unusual proportions. This was at the peak of the rabbit cycle and in the fall of 1935 we could see them at any time in front of our cabin. I mention elsewhere that Vera had one eating out of her hand. Some trappers who were well established got over a hundred fox pelts that winter. Out of a hundred they would be in this proportion— eighty red fox, twenty cross fox and five silver fox. A red fox has all red fur. A silver has black fur with white tips. A cross fox is anything in between. Some are almost reds with a few black hairs and some are almost black with some red hair.

Lynx are shy gentle creatures, dependent to a great extent on rabbits for their food supply. Lynx also eat partridge and spruce hens and mice when there are no rabbits. I have heard it said that lynx are good to eat but have never tried one. They are, after all, cats. The biggest lynx I ever caught weighed forty-two pounds and he was an old fat 'tom'.

Beaver are common throughout the bush country and favor lakes and slow-moving small streams where there is an abundance of poplar, birch or willow trees. They like the roots of lily-pad plants, but they need to chew on sticks to prevent their teeth from getting too long. As has been noted, many large carnivores prey on them, aside from trappers. The supply of beaver stays fairly constant in spite of having been trapped extensively until recently.

Marten are generally found in higher country of spruce and muskeg. They are a vicious little animal of about five pounds in weight. They have been very difficult to breed in captivity. They are omniverous and the stomachs contain berries, roots, mice, squirrel and rabbit. Marten, lynx and fox are what the fur industry call fine fur; these pelts are light in weight, have short underfur and long silky guard hairs. They do not wear too well. Prime marten must be one of the most beautiful pelts there is.

Mink— this little water animal is well known for having been bred so successfully in captivity. All sorts of different light colors have been produced by cross-breeding, but the wood mink is a dark brown in color, with a white mark on his chest. He is at home both on land and in the water. He eats rabbits, fish and muskrats. He is not subject to such wild fluctuations in population as other fur bearers are.

Otter are very much like a mink only bigger. A large otter might weigh twenty-five pounds. They are at home in or out of the water and appear to be playful, but they are actually cruel creatures who live on fish, muskrats and beaver. They are faster than a beaver in the water and can stay under water a longer time. Their fur is short and very tough and long wearing. They are never plentiful anywhere in the north except some parts of Ontario and Quebec. Like a beaver, they cannot be held in a trap unless it is set so that the animal is drowned.

Fisher— the Indians call this "nothee-cho" meaning big marten, and that is just what they are. They are never plentiful anywhere as far as I know. The dark silky females are worth up to a hundred dollars and the males bring perhaps ten dollars. Fisher are the only animals I know of besides wolverine that will deliberately tackle and kill a porcupine. Any fisher I have caught, and that has not been many, have numerous tiny porcupine quills in his hide on his neck and chest. Both fisher and marten can climb and jump around in trees like lightening. Why the fisher has such a name is a mystery to me. They never kill or eat fish, and never go near the water.

7

Troubling times

July found most of the trappers gathered in Simpson to get their supplies before heading back to their home cabins with boat and kicker. Most of them would not return to the settlement again for another year. This annual gathering was also a time for visiting with friends, card games that were mostly poker—stud, draw low-ball and dealer's choice. The stakes were commensurate with the current financial condition of the trappers, depending on last winter's fur catch and the price of raw fur. In those days the stakes were mostly penny-ante. Most evenings there was also a contract bridge game going somewhere in town.

The chances of getting work and thus getting a grubstake looked pretty slim for Stan and me until late June when we got a contract to cut fifty cords of green spruce wood in four foot lengths, split and piled in the bush, for the princely sum of four dollars a chord. The going price had been six dollars a chord up until this year, but the Bay, the Northern Traders and the Government Agencies were quick to take advantage of the hard times and cut the price down to four dollars a cord. By July 30 the fifty cords were cut, split and piled. We collected the two hundred dollars, paid our grocery bill which included some items such as sledge hammer and wedges, and had one hundred dollars left for a grubstake to do the two of us for the following winter.

Right here a small problem presented itself. If we spent a the hundred on a grubstake we might possibly be able to last out until Christmas when we would have some fur to sell to replenish our supplies; but if we bought a trapping licence, at a cost of seventy-five dollars, the remaining twenty-five would be hopelessly inadequate.

I had a private talk with the local Game Warden who was also the R.C.M.P. Corporal. He saw our predicament and agreed to wait until the end of December for the trapping licence fee. He said that this was not official of course, but he would cover it until we paid him in December.

So once more up through the rapids we went with our loaded canoe, with a proper track-line this time, making the seventy miles in three days. We spent the fall cutting trail, hunting moose and building line cabins. In October we paddled the twenty miles up stream to the Lindberg's place for our winter supply of potatoes and stashed them away in the cellar.

By November 1st, winter had set in again. The small creeks and lakes were frozen over, the big river was running, ice and snow lay on the ground. In the bush we were heartened to see more rabbit tracks than there had been the previous winter. This meant food for the lynx and fox which also seemed more numerous.

This was the third winter in the north for us, and after a few trips over our lines we knew that fur was definitely on the increase. As a contrast to the previous two winters, we were bringing in at least a pelt or two each trip. There were fox on the wide beach of the Liard River and some of these found their way into our traps. There were lynx tracks in the bush and on November 11th, I caught my first lynx of the year. Both Stan and I were optimistic about the prospects for the winter and felt we could have three or four hundred dollars worth of fur by Christmas with prospects for a good grub-stake coming up for next summer. Up to now our dream had been to be able to buy some warm clothes for the winter: a pair of Indian-made snowshoes each, a three star Woods eiderdown apiece, more traps and snares, and a complete grubstake to last through the winter. We even dared to speculate on the possibility of such luxuries as a case of canned sausage, and, dare I say it, maybe a case of tinned peaches! All these things had remained a dream—just that and nothing more. But now—with the rabbits coming back, lynx and fox on the increase, who knows? That lynx should be worth twenty dollars anyway. Art George sold some last year for as high as fifty.

I shall never forget that December 8th. We heard news of a tragedy that had immediate and drastic consequences for Stan and me. We had caught ourselves in a web, partly of our own making, that tightened in and could have destroyed us. It was a lovely clear day, warm by winter standards, maybe ten below. Stan was gone on his line and I was headed down the Liard where I had a line cabin fifteen miles away. It was about noon when I saw two dog teams coming on the ice away ahead. These were the first teams I had seen since the fall. As we drew closer I could see that it was the R.C.M.P. on their winter patrol from Simpson to Fort Liard. Inspector Martin was wrapped up inside the carry-all of one toboggan. I had expected to see Corporal Jim Halliday, an able and experienced woodsman, who was liked and respected by all of us and who usually made these tough trips himself. The special constable was driving one team and constable Littlewood (I believe) was driving the other team. The 'forerunner' was Constable Calcraft, and he was limping along ahead of the dog teams and looked to be about all in.

"Hi, Cal," I said, shaking hands. "How's the trip? Where is is Halliday?"

"Well, by Jove, Dick, the Corporal shot himself accidentally coming home from the fishery last October. I'm in charge now."

"My God," I said. "What a terrible thing. How did it happen?"

"He was putting away the shotgun after he was going to shoot a duck, and changed his mind. He was setting it down behind the door of the pilot house when it went off and got him in the head. He died instantly."

I could only mumble, "Good God. Good God. He was a fine man, we will all miss him."

"We've come from Birch River today and will camp at your home cabin tonight. Boy! Are my legs played out. This breaking trail is not for me."

"O.K." I said. "Stan's away but make yourself at home. By-the-way Cal, I guess you know about our licence, we will be in after Christmas and will get it paid then."

Cal looked puzzled. "No," he said. "First I've heard of it."

After I had explained the arrangements that we had made with Halliday, he said, "Well, I guess I can fix it somehow, and will see you in Simpson after Christmas then?"

"You sure will," I replied, "about December 26 or 27." We said 'so-long' and I did not see him again until we met in Simpson on December 28.

By this time Stan and I had acquired two more dogs and with three dogs we had a team of sorts to make the trip to Simpson. It was near seventy miles through the bush to Simpson, and was fifty below the night we camped on the portage trail. The following day we were in town by early afternoon. We went immediately to Andy Whittington's Hotel, had a meal and made arrangements to stay in town a day or two to rest the dogs and get supplies. Then we walked over to the barracks to see Constable Calcraft.

The first thing he said on seeing us was, "Sorry boys, I will have to lay a charge, the Inspector thinks we shouldn't let this pass."

I felt as if I had been hit with a crowbar. The possibility of Calcraft taking this attitude had never even crossed my mind. "But for Christ's sake Cal, we can have the money for the licence by tonight."

"Sorry, no go."

A hot flush overcame me and I started to tremble. My thought was, although I did not say so out loud, "You bastard, if you had given any indication you were going to take this attitude, I would not have come to town. You would have had to get me and bring me in, and that, my boy, would have taken some doing." I was so mad I was near crying. Calcraft could not look either of us in the eye.

Stan was more calm than I was. "O.K. Cal," he said, "have it your way." Stan had some thoughts of his own, and two months later I found out what they were. He asked Cal to put on civilian clothes and come outside and have it out. Cal refused. He was a big strong man, trained in hand-to-hand combat and should have been able to hold his own. He simply had no guts.

Cal seized our hard-earned fur and told us to appear in court the next day at 2 o'clock. We did, and there was Inspector Martin acting in his capacity as magistrate with his four constables grouped around him. We pled 'Not Guilty' and explained the whole thing to the court. One of the constables told us later that the old bastard was going to throw the case out but something made him change his mind at the last minute. He recessed the court for fifteen minutes and then said he had decided on a verdict of 'Guilty,' with a hundred dollars fine each or sixty days. He knew as well as we did there was no possible way of us raising the money immediately and he gave us no time to do so.

We put in January and February at the barracks cutting wood and doing chores and eating our meals in the barracks kitchen. We were given enough to eat but very plain food.

At that time in the north the Royal Canadian Signal Corp and the R.C.M.P. personnel were issued a ration for the year for each man. If he did not use it all he was free to sell the surplus at the end of the year. So each spring the 'wireless boys' and the police sold their surplus rations to the trappers. The price was fair and everyone happy. Selling rations was no crime, it was done as a matter of course.

In the barracks kitchen there was, pinned on the wall, a list of food, a daily and weekly ration for prisoners. We drew this to the attention of the cook, a civilian by the name of Charlie Hansen, who is still living in Alberta. Charlie said that Cal had told him not to feed us certain items on the list, and that we had better ask Cal about it. That evening in the living room we approached Cal and asked him point blank why we weren't getting the rations that were listed for our use. He could not give us a straight answer but said, "Oh, isn't Charlie giving you that stuff? I'll have to see him about it."

Charlie was in the kitchen and heard this. "The son of a bitch," he said, "he told me not to give you those items."

"Is he keeping them to sell, do you suppose?" I said.

"Look, Charlie," I said, "we had better let this drop, Cal could make it very uncomfortable for us, if he is pushed; rolled oats and bully beef won't hurt us for a while."

There were three other constables there at the time, Langfelt, Littlewood and Thomas. They were quite decent young men and probably didn't know what Cal was up to. And we were in no position to stir things up, but I thought, "O.K., if that's the way you want to play it, fine."

Our fur that was seized was valued at three hundred and fifty dollars, and I assume the amount went to the Northwest Territories administration, and although they might not know it, the money has been repaid many times over. I am speaking strictly for myself, of course.

At this time I have many good friends in the R.C.M.P.

Some are still in the force and some have retired. One of these, a very close friend who had been stationed at Fort Liard and Fort Simpson, one day asked me how the book was progressing. And I answered, "Not bad, but slow. I am now writing a chapter about all the discreditable things I know about the Royal Canadian Mounted Police."

He laughed. "Good gracious," he said. "that would take a whole book."

That was the clincher. I was not going to do it anyway, but his remark and our chuckling together about it really made up my mind. He is of course completely wrong, for the fine things they do and have done far outweigh any mistakes they have made. There is bound to be a little deadwood in any forest.

On March 1st, 1933, Stan returned to our trapline with a young trapper who had a current licence and had a month's successful trapping. (He still did not have a licence). I decided to work for a local contractor, cutting and hauling cordwood for the river steamer. I worked for four months and made very good wages.

100

A flashback

For just a moment let us go back to late August of 1927.
I had recently turned sixteen years of age; and after
roaming Alberta for a year I had landed a job with a farmer
near the Saskatchewan border. On driving to his farm that
first day he stopped at a neighbor's, and I sat in the Model
'T' ford while he was in the house. A girl came out on some
errand and went back in. We didn't exchange a word, but a
look passed between us and some words were written in the
book of fate at that moment. She was young, small, dark and
very pretty. For the first time in my sixteen years I thought,
"That's the one, I'll marry her some day." Her name was
Vera Halliday. Her folks farmed a mile or so from where my
employer lived. For a year I worked in that district, and for
the year our courtship was never really constant or steady.
We saw each other many times of course, and I felt there was
no hurry because at the back of my mind was the certain
knowledge that she would be my wife some day. It was not
that I felt sure of her or unsure of her, it was just that I
seemed to know that destiny had joined us together.

After a year, and when you are sixteen a year is a long
time, I said to her, "We are sweethearts, let's get engaged."

Her reply was wise and mature. "I think we had better

wait a while, we are pretty young yet." So there we left it for the time.

For the next five years we did not see each other. We wrote and exchanged pictures and I was starting to get impatient with Fate. "I had better take a hand in this," I thought, "fate can wait for eighty years, I can't."

The upshot of this was that I popped the question to her once more. She said "Yes" and I went about making arrangements for her to come north, which was a matter of sending her money for a train ticket to Waterways at the end of steel and the steamer fare from Waterways to Hay River for the paddle-wheelers that the Hudson's Bay Company ran on the Mackenzie water system. One steamer only operated on the Mackenzie River itself; the *Distributor*. It pushed one barge and made three trips each season of open water from Fort Smith to Aklavik and return.

Vera came in on the third trip of the *Distributor*, and I met her at Hay River with a tiny wooden boat and a 3 H.P. 'Kicker.'

On August 19, 1933 we were married in the little Mission church at the site of the old Hay River Post. After giving the Rev. Singleton five dollars for performing the ceremony I think I had only five or six dollars left to my name.

I have said many times before and will say again that Vera looked very beautiful that night in a blue wedding gown, and I just about fell off the deck of the steamer when she kissed me. It was midnight when the steamer pulled into the wharf with the lights blinking and flicking over the water. I went on board before the vessel was properly tied up and Vera retreated into the shadows to greet me. I was twenty-two and I didn't know what a real kiss was until that time. I wondered how it was that I was so fortunate to get a peach of this quality. She admitted later to me that she had had some other offers but felt that fate should not be denied.

The Hudson's Bay Transport gave us a wedding supper (2 o'clock in the morning by now) with a wedding cake and traditional good wishes. At daylight we steamed out of the harbor bound for Fort Providence. From there we went on to Simpson with my little boat.

The paddle-wheeler pulled out of Providence without unloading all my supplies, and we did not get them until a month later on its return trip from Aklavik. Among the things we missed were a tent, bedding and food supplies. We discovered our loss soon after the steamer had left but I knew we'd be lucky to ever see those items again. There were stores in Providence where we could have replenished the articles, but without the necessary funds that was no help.

That first night we camped on the Mackenzie River on a nice sand beach among willow, poplar and birch trees. For food there was a can of salmon and about half the wedding cake. A heavy rain storm blew up right then and with no spruce trees within miles for shelter, we huddled under a new flannelette sheet we had in the supplies. Time has dulled the memory of that night but if my spirits were low, it must have been worse for my new bride. I did not dare to think what thoughts were in her mind about that time. She did not say much but I knew that she had not expected anything quite like this. I did not wish to lose her, but if I could have done so at that time I would have transported her on a magic carpet back to her family and friends outside and forgiven her for her rash decision to come north to marry a trapper, a trapper who was down and out at that. But there was no magic carpet handy just then, and I had no alternative but to swallow my pride and hope that the future would hold better things.

The rain was soon over and a blazing fire kept us warm and dry. Mercifully there were no mosquitoes at all. The morning came with a bursting of blue in the sky that is seen only in the north. The day was warm and the air was still and the river ahead met the sky in a shimmering expanse that might have been endless. The kicker hummed along and we made far better time than Stan and I did paddling the canoe three years before. Art George and his wife Lodema welcomed us at Simpson. Lodema and Art had been prosperous in Boise, Idaho some years before. Lodema knew what the good life 'outside' was, and knew what a shock it would be for a girl from the south, who might not have imagined the' north to be as it is, to go directly to live in the bush, the wife of a trapper, and live very much as the early settlers who came west.

Lodema and Vera clung to each other in delight, and I have never ceased to be grateful to Lodema and Art, who were the dearest friends for many years.

I did small jobs and wood-cutting contracts that fall and during the winter got a sub-let contract to cut one hundred cords of jack-pine for the river steamer. I got three dollars a cord, cut and piled in the bush, so did not get overly rich at that.

In March I got a letter from Stan who was trapping on the Long Reach. His purpose in writing was to tell me that he had returned at the end of January from staking placer gold claims in the Flat River area. He thought perhaps I should go up in open water as soon as the ice moved out, and stake more claims. I was all for this, as who can resist a possible gold rush? Especially when we would be staking on McLeod Creed, where the lost placer mine was said to be. Stan suggested that we come to his cabin by dog team and as soon as the river broke-up we would continue on by boat to Nahanni.

By this time Vera and I had acquired a bit of necessary property for travelling in the bush. We had a dog team of sorts, harness and toboggan, a Woods three star eiderdown and other items.

On April 1st, 1934, Vera and I left Simpson by dog team with a load of food and supplies for Stan's cabin on the Liard, a trip of seventy miles over a bush train that somehow was always referred to as the portage trail.

Art George was planning to build a cabin at Nahanni Butte that summer and Vera was to stay with Lodema while I was away for a month on the claim staking. Poole and Mary Field were also at Nahanni during these years. Vera and I were later to become very close friends with them. Poole had been in the Klondike in the rush of '98, and had come to the Nahanni Valley originally about 1914, when he had come into the possession of a most intriguing letter from a man called Jorgensen who was later found dead at his burned cabin below the Virginia Falls, but more of this later.

The trail was high and soft most of the way over the portage and pulling was hard for the dogs. Steel runners bolted to the bottom of the toboggan helped it to run easier, but we made poor time because it refused to freeze at night. The trail, under good conditions, is a groove in the snow of from six inches to a foot deep, but in this warm weather the snow had settled and left the hard-packed trail sticking slightly above the surface of the surrounding snow. Vera had to walk most all the way and as I recall we were two and a half days making the seventy miles. When the loaded toboggan left the narrow trail it would settle with a soft whoosh in the loose wet snow beside the trail and it took three men and a boy with the dogs straining to get the thing back up to where it belonged.

The second day out we met a gentleman returning to

Simpson from a patrol somewhere up the Liard River, with a team of five dogs. He had given up trying to keep the toboggan on the trail, and was walking behind. His load was light and the sleigh was half on and half off the trail with one side of the carry-all dragging in the snow. This chap was a bit put out by the adverse conditions that he was encountering and I could hear him half a mile before we met. He was remarking on the condition of the trail, the character of his dogs for several generations back, the feeling of his feet which were wet and cold, the weather which he had to cope with the last few days, the distance he still had to go and the general inhospitality of the country. All this was in very choice language, with a variety of epithets that was an education even to a trapper. We were, of course, glad to see one another and to exchange greetings and bits of news. But when he saw Vera coming along behind me, his face turned a brilliant scarlet. She must have heard the music from a distance but I doubt if she could distinguish the individual notes. She did not say and I did not ask.

Until we entered the timber a dozen miles farther on, it was more difficult to keep the sleigh on the trail due to the fact that the trail was now sloping at a thirty degree angle, but I managed somehow, at the same time trying to copy some of the phrases I had recently heard, but without succeeding very well, and chuckling as I tried to recall the choice bits.

On the third day we pulled in to Stan's cabin perched on a high bank of the Liard, where we looked westward to the mountains in the distance.

The small creeks had been running water for four days, when on the 29th of April the river rose suddenly about 15 feet and the ice began to break up and move out. All night the river cracked and snapped as the ice went grinding by. In the morning the river was clear of ice and had started to drop.

On May 1st, the water was lapping on the sandy shores as if there never had been a winter. Late that afternoon a boat and kicker appeared far in the distance from up river. It was Bill Epler and Ole Loe, who had come to fetch us to Nahanni Butte, the jumping off place for our placer staking. The next night we camped at the Lindbergs and Vera met Anna for the first time. They took to each other right away and have been friends ever since. Next day we arrived at Nahanni Butte and were welcomed by Poole and Mary Field and Art and Lodema George.

Nature's bounty

Gold, like most other minerals, has been carried in solution by vapors and gases from deep within the earth and brought to the surface under great heat and pressure. The vapors will penetrate toward the surface of the earth's crust wherever there is a point of weakness. In cases where the surface rocks have been subjected to a sufficient stress they have broken and slipped. These are known as 'faults' and are sometimes used by the mineral bearing gas and vapors as a road toward the surface. For some reason that is not yet clearly understood even by knowledgeable geologists, minerals, including gold, will solidify only under very particular and suitable conditions. This seems to depend somewhat on the rate of cooling and the various types of rock encountered along the way. In the case of gold, it seems to solidify under a wide range of temperatures. It is sometimes found in very minute particles in the host rock, that is, the rock adjacent to the fault. In other cases it forms invisible specks and even large chunks along with a gauge mineral called quartz. Quartz has a definite crystal formation and looks somewhat similar to glass. Quartz veins are often near a fault zone and are probably there because the vapors found a weak line in the earth's crust to penetrate.

During the many different glacial ages ice of tremendous weight and pressure ground off mountains and gouged out trenches in the earth. Streams formed and tended to move the glacial rubble to a lower elevation. After many glacial movements and the forming and reforming of streams, the gold, along with the quartz from the veins that came under the action of the glaciers, was thus ground down and washed away and shifted from place to place many times. The gold that was separated from the quartz in the grinding process, being very much heavier than other rocks and minerals, settled into any pockets or grooves in the stream beds. This is 'placer' gold. Some is so fine it will float. This is called 'flour' gold. It has been flattened to tiny minute particles that can barely be seen with the naked eye, but much of it together will leave quite a visible 'streak' in the gold pan. Because gold is soft or 'maleable' it is sometimes flattened instead of being ground into a powder. When the gold in a stream bed is of the size from a small grain of sand to as big as a match head it is referred to as coarse gold. From this size up they are nuggets.

Placer gold has stirred men's minds and sent them searching to the far corners of the world to reward a very few, disappoint many and lead others to almost an obsession in an endless quest for the elusive yellow metal that must surely be just over that mountain or in that next creek.

A gold pan is made of iron and shaped much like a large fry pan without the handle, and is a necessary part of a prospectors equipment. He will pan the streams in the hope of finding colors, which is one or more pieces of gold that can be seen. He will dip a pan of sand and gravel, fill the pan with water and swish and rock the pan from side to side. With the pan tipped, the water with the uppermost of the pans contents is poured off and fresh water taken in. After a time he should have left only the heaviest residue from the pan of gravel. Gold is so much more heavy than most other rocks and minerals that if there happens to be a particle of gold among the original contents it will be with the black sand when all else has been washed away, and will tend to cling to the bottom of the pan when the black sand moves along with the water in the pan.

If the prospector gets many colors and thinks he might have struck 'pay dirt', he might stake a claim and build a sluice box. In the early days in the Northwest Territories a placer claim was smaller than other mineral claims and a man was allowed one claim only on each creek. The corners of the claim, as is the case today, must be marked with a four sided post giving your name, the date and other details. Today the size of all mineral claims is a square of fifty-one acres, and one man may stake up to thirty-six claims in one year in each of certain designated areas. All claims must be recorded at a mining recorder's office within about forty days.

In building his sluice box the real work begins. Sluice boxes can vary in their size and length, but the one I saw on McLeod Creek in 1934 was about twelve feet in length, a foot wide with six inch sides. It had been made many years previously and covered with moss and had almost rotted away.

Trees must be made into boards either with a whip-saw or by hewing with an axe. The whip-saw method is described later in this book, but whichever method is used the rough boards must be trimmed with a hand-plane until they are even sided and fit snugly together. Otherwise the gold will be lost down the cracks and your labor will have been in vain.

Once the box is built thin strips of wood are set in crosswise and a foot apart. The box is set up off the ground at a slight angle and water is directed into it. Now the presumably gold-bearing sand and gravel is shoveled into the box for say an eight hour day. Then the residue caught in the upper edge of each riffle is examined and any gold that has been shoveled in should be there. Panning of the overflow must be done at regular intervals to ascertain if any colors are passing through without being caught in the riffles.

If the prospector does get lucky and find pay dirt his next thought is "Where has this come from? If I can find the source or mother lode that will be where the real money is."

To my mind mother lode is rather an indefinite term. It could be the source of the placer gold, that is, the original quartz veins that a glacier had gouged out, or it could be simply a large accumulation of placer gold in a stream bed.

In a case where the gold is too fine to be picked up with a sluice box another method is used. The gravel and sand is shoveled into a 'grizzly' instead of a sluice box. These are similar to a sluice box in that water carries the materials along. But with the grizzly an iron grill disperses the larger rocks and pebbles and only the sand and small pieces are carried along. There are blanket cloths of different textures fastened to the bottom of the box and the fibres of these retain the flour gold. Every few hours the blankets are removed and washed in a gold pan. The black sand and the gold settles to the bottom of the pan and the water is poured off.

When there is an accumulation of black sand with its contents of gold, then mercury or quicksilver is used to separate the two.

Mercury will gather up the flour gold and hold it while rejecting the other minerals in the black sand. A chamois cloth is used to squeeze the ball of mercury. Most of the mercury will penetrate the wall of the chamois, leaving the gold and some mercury within. The mercury that is squeezed out can be used over again as it is expensive and should not be wasted. To separate the gold from the mercury in the amalgam that is left it is necessary to burn off the mercury. The fumes from this process are deadly, so great care must be taken not to inhale even the most minute quantity of the fumes. We used to do this out in the open air with the heat of a blow-torch. Great care must be taken to stay to windward. What is left from the burning process is a small bannock of almost pure gold.

The historical facts of the gold rush to the Klondike in '97 and '98 are well known to most people; rumours spread like wildfire all over the continent, of placer gold in fabulous quantities in the white gravels of the Yukon streams, of miners rich overnight and spending money recklessly. Men, bitten by the gold bug, dropped whatever they were doing and headed for the Yukon by the hundreds. They came by all possible routes. Some came down the Mackenzie River, up the Laird, then into any stream that led westward and over the divide to the Yukon and it tributaries. Some must have worked their way up the Nahanni and Flat Rivers, and perhaps over the divide to the Pelly and the Ross Rivers. It is generally believed that those same Klondikers were the first white men to find placer gold in the McLeod Creek and Gold Creek areas.

When you hear about these men, and see at first hand the evidence of their trek, and think of the trials and hardships they must have suffered and how some continued on when friends and companions died by the way, the faith they must have had in the end of the rainbow was truly amazing. These men, most of whom must have been inexperienced in the bush, pulled and worked their crude boats and canoes up against the current of the Laird until winter overtook them. Some built cabins where they froze. Others made sleighs, piled their supplies on them and, pulling them by hand, continued on.

Jack Stanier, who was trapping near Fort Laird when we came north, came this way from the south himself, and was one of those who got as far as Fort Laird when the ice started to form in the river. When he arrived in the Klondike in the spring of '99, he was too late for the rush as all the ground had long since been taken up. He wandered around the north for years and eventually settled at Fort Laird. He was one of the first to stake claims on McLeod Creek in 1933. Jack said that on the winter trip from Fort Laird through the mountains he and his group were following a trail with many other gold rushers ahead of them. There were also others coming behind. Around dusk one night his party came upon a cabin and were delighted to find a place to camp. Inside the cabin he was feeling around for the bunks, stove and table when he discovered that the three bunks contained men who had been dead for some time and were now frozen stiff. Jack said he and his companions went on a ways farther and camped in the open that night.

In talking to Jack, he said stories had gone round the Yukon of placer gold found on the Nahanni and Flat Rivers by some of the men who had come that way, but it could not be pinned down as to exactly where or how much there was. Then about 1905 Willie and Frank McLeod were reported to have found placer gold on the Nahanni near the headwaters. There was an Indian chief at Fort Simpson in the 1930's who claims to have met the McLeods on the river as they were returning to Liard. They showed him an Enos Fruit Salts bottle about half full of coarse gold and small nuggets. According to Albert Faille, this bottle was being passed from boat to boat when it was dropped in the river and never recovered. The McLeods went back into the hills again the following summer and perished in Dead Man's Valley which is only sixty miles from the mouth of the Nahanni River. They were assumed to be on their way home by boat when they met with some misfortune. They were found a year later and their heads were reported to be separated from their bodies. Albert Faille had a wild story that he sincerely believed, that a man from the Liard area put four thousand dollars in gold in a bank in Vancouver the year the McLeods died in Dead Man's Valley. If this was true, the conclusions to be drawn would be pure speculation.

Some years after this Poole Field and his wife Mary were

living in Dawson City in the Yukon. Mrs. Field came into the possession of a letter from a man she knew that had gone up the Pelly River and over the waters of the Nahanni to prospect a year or two before. This letter was from a man called Jorgensen and advised a friend of his to come on over to the Nahanni as he, Jorgensen, had found some good stuff. She never did give the exact words but Poole and she took off for the Nahanni soon after and found Jorgensen's body outside his burned cabin with his rifle either in his hands or close beside him. Poole told me that he did not know how Jorgensen met his death but felt sure that it was not at the hands of a man. This happened near the mouth of the Flat River and the cabin has long since been washed into the river.

Poole Field was so certain there was placer gold in the Nahanni area somewhere that he stayed in the area for many years hoping that he could find more clues to the mystery of the lost placer creeks.

John Norgaard, who trapped above Virginia Falls for several winters, told me that he panned very carefully on one of the Nahanni tributaries and found only one gold nugget the size of a white bean. He became enthused and panned the creek carefully for more 'showings'. Not another trace of gold did he find on that creek. He told no one about this for many years and as far as I know only three others have ever panned on that creek.

Albert Faille told me many times that before he had come to the Nahanni River in 1927 a Nahanni Indian trapper had found one nugget, or at least he had given one very large nugget about an ounce in weight, to a Bishop whom he knew. The Bishop was rumored to have had a watch fob made of it. No amount of questioning would persuade the old Indian to tell where he had found it or if he had found any more. Albert said he had verified the story and was convinced that it was true. He also felt that the Indian really did not know where he had found the nugget, for it had been many years before giving it to the Bishop that he had picked it up. To me personally this is the most intriguing story of all for I knew the old Indian in question. He was known as Big Charlie, had only one eye and was living in the Netla River area when I spent my first northern winter with old Boo Jodah. It was rumored even then that this old man had found some very rich mineral back in the mountains west of Nahanni Butte. Big Charlie died in the 1930's and I never did get to know him well enough to ask him about his reported find. The situation too was somewhat different in those days in this way; most of the natives did not like to be questioned about matters of this kind as there was some resentment against white men and they did not wish to encourage us to come swarming into their country.

That much was known of the 'Nahanni Legends' in 1933 when Jack Stanier and Billy Clark flew in to MacMillan Lake, staked a claim each and started to work the gravel on McLeod Creek. Jack Stanier was convinced at this time that the old sluice boxes that were rotting on that creek were built by the MacLeod boys about 27 years previously. I think they got two or three ounces of gold and then abandoned the project, but rumors spread by the old reliable moccasin telegraph and the slight amount of gold that Jack and Billy had set off a small rush.

A dozen or so local people, trappers and others, flew in from Fort Simpson. Only one one man, I believe, stayed in to work his claim; the others came right back out hoping to sell their claims. About twenty trappers from the Liard area went in by dog team in January of 1934. The Nahanni Indians guided them in, through the valleys, up over high passes and along creek beds. The trip one way was a hundred and twenty miles from Nahanni Butte.

Stan joined up with Bill Epler and Jack Mulholland for the dog team trip in to MacMillan Lake. They left Nahanni Butte on January 1st with a team of five dogs and a loaded toboggan with food and supplies for a month. There were some teams ahead of them so that these three had a trail of sorts most of the way. They ran short of food and at MacMillan Lake they borrowed a three pound pail of lard from Gus Kraus who had come in early in the fall and was trapping there. After getting the lard from Gus, they staked claims on MacLeod, Grizzly and other smaller creeks and then headed home. They camped one night near the top of the Toglosho Plateau and Stan shot two Dall Sheep, which was a Godsend as they were very low on grub and food for the dogs.

Each night of the trip they had to find a place to camp where there was plenty of dry wood for a fire so that they could dry their clothes, cook their food and keep warm until they rolled into their sleeping bags. Some nights it went to forty below. Like many others, their trials were for naught.

10

The Nahanni trip

Bill Epler, Old Ole and I planned on leaving for the staking grounds on May 4th in order to be ahead of the rush, if there was a 'rush'. As it turned out no rush developed but we did not know that at the time.

Old Ole had been trapping on the Mackenzie since 1929 and had come up to the Nahanni by dog team in April in order to get into the staking grounds in early May.

We had a twenty-eight foot river boat and two small kickers. We had enough gasoline, we hoped, to take us to Irvine Creek seventy-five miles up the Flat River. With the two little egg beaters humming we waved goodbye to the Fields, the Georges and Vera, as we disappeared up the snye and around the corner of the butte as it juts out into the river.

The first twelve miles was slow calm water and I lay back in the boat thinking of placer gold, Nahanni legends, McLeod Creek, Gold Creek, Grizzly Creek, the McLeod boys and the Klondikers; some of whom had come this way in 1898.

Then we entered the fast water and I sat up to look around. We were faced now with thirty miles of splits. Here the river is braided, wide, shallow and swift. The stream is filled with sweepers, which are trees that have been torn loose from the eroding banks, with the roots embedded in the river's bottom, lodged in mud or gravel, the water tugging at them until some are worn down like a naked tooth. Some are long and limber and bob up and down with the force of the current. Others have been worn down by ice and driftwood and are covered by the rising turbulent stream. These deadheads, as we call them, are a hazard to navigation and if you hit them just right they can tear the hull of the boat or rip the kicker off.

In fast water there is a characteristic turbulence down stream from them which warns you of their presence but in slow water you can run up onto one without warning.

We picked our way back and forth among the sweepers and gravel bars, avoiding the very shallow water and taking the slack parts whenever possible. Bill Epler ran the motors the first day and Ole and I knelt at the sides near the gunwales, each with a dry twelve foot pole. Whenever a riffle brought us to a standstill, Bill would edge over into two or three feet of water; Ole and I would jab the poles into the river bottom and pushing with our feet and knees we would heave the boat ahead. Our craft was a home-built Sturgeon head and with our light load it handled very well. After a fast place we had time to rest until we hit the next riffle.

I had looked forward to making a boat trip up the Nahanni since coming north four years before. We had heard many stories about this river and knew that it was fast and dangerous. I was interested to see the places I had heard so much about: the Splits, the Hot Springs, First Canyon, where the jagged limestone cliffs rise to thirty-five hundred feet above the water; Lafferty's Riffle, George's Riffle, Dead Man's Valley, the Gate, Figure Eight, Virginia Falls. We would turn up the Flat River twenty miles below the falls, and it was not until some years later that I was to see that awe-inspiring waterfall of over three hundred feet. We knew that Albert Faille was trapping somewhere on the Flat River and fully expected to see him somewhere along the way. Besides the three men at MacMillan Lake he was the only one we knew of who had wintered in the mountains that year.

Albert had first come north about six years previously and had trapped near Fort Providence for two winters before coming to the Nahanni. All I knew about him at that time was that he was an expert woodsman who lived alone in the mountains for ten months of each year, and I was looking forward to meeting him. He was forty-two years of age.

At the entrance to the First Canyon we encountered Lafferty's Riffle, where the river swept around a gradual bend, piling against the canyon wall in big rolling combers. Here the river dropped eight feet in less than a hundred yards. By hugging the gravel bar side and poling manfully, we were up and over in jig time. The canyon winds and twists for ten miles through a limestone plateau with walls sometimes sheer but more often broken and jagged that tower overhead. The current of the stream is fast and steady with riffles in every bend.

We had R.M. Patterson's map of the river, so we had some idea of what we were coming to. Every hour we had to stop to fill the gas tanks and now I steered the boat to a sandy beach of an island and shut the motors off. While Ole was tying up the boat, Bill said, "There's George's Riffle ahead." Looking up-stream a half mile we could see the water dancing and hear the muffled roar.

We filled the tanks and Bill said, "Should I take the kickers now?" Meaning did I want him to steer the boat through the riffle.

"Hell, no," I replied, "you and Ole can lift it through this one."

A mile above the riffle, the river, leaving Dead Man's Valley, starts to pick up speed at Stark's Rock, swings around a rock-bound island, curves against a cliff in big rolling waves and shoots across the river into a rock wall. The partial deflection induces side waves, choppy turbulence and some vicious swirls at the foot of the riffle. River men do not class this as a dangerous place, and in all but a flood stage it is quite navigable. Nevertheless one should stay awake and keep at least one eye open, for it is possible to get broadside to the waves and be thrown against a rock and capsize. With a large boat and plenty of power there is nothing to it. Ole and Bill were ready with the poles. We shot across the waves, edged past the wall and up to the rock bar and crept up and around the bend with the poles digging the gravel and the kickers humming. Then we were past Stark's Rock, through a riffle and on into Patterson's Lake where we could see into the Valley. We named Patterson's Lake after R.M. Patterson who had spent a winter trapping in Dead Man's Valley a few years previously. We call it a lake because it is a quiet stretch of water two hundred yards in length, narrow, very deep and slow. It is one of the few places on the river where you can shut down the motors and look around a bit without danger of being carried down stream or crashing into a rock. Here we camped for the night at the mouth of Sheep Creek, a favorite camping spot of Albert Faille.

The second canyon's walls were not as high nor jagged as the walls of the first canyon. In its extent of twenty miles it occasionally opens up into a small valley. There were moss and spruce trees on many of the slopes of the canyon walls, with small streams of sparkling water tumbling from the cliffs here and there. Enticing trails led up the slopes and creek valleys where Dall sheep grazed in small groups. We must have seen five or six such groups in the second canyon. But we must not stop to hunt or to roam the hills. Man! We were headed for the lost McLeod gold fields, and must not waste precious time.

The fourth night out we camped at the mouth of Mary's River, named for Mary Field, Poole Field's wife. They had camped here for some time in previous years when they were searching for Jorgensen's find.

That night at dark it started to rain and it poured all night. By morning the river had risen four feet and was running a lot of small driftwood and crud. Crud is foam and leaves, small roots, sticks and pine needles. We fought our way upstream that day for twelve miles to the mouth of the Flat River. We camped there early in the day as we were burning up precious gasoline and making poor time against the increased current of the flood. The Flat dropped a foot or more that night, the driftwood quit and in the morning we were able to make good progress again.

Here the mountains were low, the valley wide and green with the stream confining itself pretty well to one channel.

The mouth of Caribou River was twenty-five miles upstream from the Flat's junction with the Nahanni. Toward evening we kept looking around each bend in the river for the Caribou River and Albert Faille's cabin. We knew he had cabins at Caribou, Irvine Creek and Borden Creek and were not sure at which one he would be. At last we saw something moving on a sandbar way ahead. Someone said, "It's a moose. No. It's a caribou." But it was no moose or caribou, it was old Albert himself. (When I was twenty, people of forty were old. And somehow as the years go by people of forty seem a lot younger.)

The strange apparation had red wool pants, hair to his

116

shoulders and a long red beard. Ole turned to me and said, "That's Albert." He might as well have said, "This is a boat, and my name's Ole." I was on the kickers at the time and heard nothing of what more was said as Ole and Bill moved up to the front of the boat as we pulled in to the edge of the sandbar. But I saw Albert was talking before I shut the kickers off, and upon my word of honor he did not stop talking for two days and nights. He had seen no other human soul except Gus Kraus for a day or two in January.

Gus Kraus was the trapper from whom Stan and Bill and Jack had borrowed the pail of lard that last January at MacMillan Lake. A mile farther on at the mouth of the Caribou was Albert's cabin. It was clean, snug and well built with bunk, table, chair, door and windows. It was very neat and ship-shape as I found Albert's cabins always were. He loved the bush and took great pride in his work. His cache was a small cabin built up off the ground about twelve feet high, to keep his supplies safe from scavengers, bear and wolverine in particular. Albert said a bear had broken into the cache while he was away, cleaned up a bale of dried meat and ripped some of his fur pelts from his winter's catch.

One of the first things he told us was that he had just got back from away up at the head of the Flat River where he had swamped his moose-skin boat and lost all that was in the boat except his matches and his axe. It had taken him five days to walk and raft back to his main cabin here at Caribou. He had been home for two days now, but before that he had eaten nothing for those five days.

Albert had left his furthest upstream cabin at Borden Creek in March with his team of five dogs and his toboggan loaded with supplies for a spring beaver hunt. He travelled up the Flat for more than fifty miles, trapping beaver through the ice along the way. Where the beaver country ended and the stream became swift and rocky, he set up camp and waited for the ice to move out. The moose were plentiful here and he shot two large ones and made a skin boat. This was his first attempt at making such a craft and he wanted to try one out. The Indians have made skin boats for centuries for use in drifting down stream and they seemed very satisfactory. He made a frame of spruce poles and tied it firmly with moosehide babiche, (dried rawhide). Then he sewed the two hides together and stretched them over the frame of poles, tying it well with babiche along the gunwhales. Small peeled spruce were flattened and forced between the hide and frame to serve as ribs. When all was finished he had a somewhat crude looking craft, but one which he thought would be seaworthy, although a bit small to his liking.

He waited several days after the ice moved out to give the river time to clear properly. He was too old and experienced a hand to set out too early and run into ice. Around May 3rd he loaded his grub box, packsack, bundle of beaver pelts, gun, axe, a bale of dried meat, his four dogs, and pushed off. In places the Flat River has many large boulders in the stream bed. Some stick up above the water, while others are barely covered and the water pours past, over and around them in great swirls and combers. Albert had always guided his big canoe among them safely before and saw no reason why he could not do the same with the skin boat. He soon found that the skin boat which was much more cumbersome and hard to handle, as it was heavy, sat low in the water and was rather tubby.

He had gone only a mile or two when he ran slam bang up on a huge smooth boulder. The next thing he knew he was in the river, the skin boat sank, never to reappear and he and the dogs were swimming for shore. He saw the sack of fur and the packsack drifting along down the river. All he had in his pockets were his pocket knife and a waterproof match case. But a fire could wait. He ran along the bank, dodging among the trees and over windfalls in an effort to catch up to the packsack which contained some clothing and other valuables. Around a bend, there was the packsack caught up on some logs in a driftpile. He heaved a sigh of relief and looked around for a pole to reach the sack with. It was not quite long enough so he stepped carefully out onto the driftpile. The log he stepped on caught another one which touched the sack and tipped it into the river. It was forced under by the current and he never did see it again. What he did find was his frypan half full of moose fat, that by some miracle had floated free. I forget how he managed to save the axe, but I think he swam ashore with it, having intended to grab the rifle instead. His nearest cabin was at Borden Creek, and that was where he headed. At least he had a fire at night to keep warm by, and a few licks of moose grease. At Borden creek he made a raft, and another one at the canyon twenty-five miles down. At Irvine Creek he picked up some supplies from his cabin there, and from that point down to the Caribou cabin it was just routine, drifting along on the raft.

Albert left no doubt in our minds that that was the first and the last skin boat that he would ever use. He was verbally vehement about it, and used some flowery language to describe the lack of desirable features of all skin boats.

Albert's cabin had a dirt floor, and that evening he and Ole brought in great armloads of fragrant spruce boughs for a bed. Ole and Albert slept on these and Bill and I on the bunk. The other three played cribbage for a while after supper, and we all lay down about ten o'clock. Albert did not quit talking for a minute, and Ole or Bill would answer him at odd times. I fell asleep half an hour later to the sound of Albert's voice. Bill and Ole were asleep too, but once in a while one of them would move and murmur, "Yes", or "Oh", or "Ahhh" or "Ummm". And believe it or not, at six o'clock in the morning when I awoke, Albert was still talking, and Bill and Ole were still going, "Awww", and "Ummm".

We stayed at Caribou all the next day. Albert shaved off his beard, Bill cut his hair, and he looked a different man. I have regretted not having a picture of him as he was when we met him on the sand bar, with his whiskers, long hair, and homemade wool blanket trousers.

Faille is one of the few men I have known who has spent many years alone in the bush without it affecting his mind, or getting a wee bit 'tetched'. He retains a sense of humor, and always has a merry twinkle in his eye. In contrast to him, I can think of four others right now, whom loneliness and isolation got the better. One died of 'Shanty Rot'. He lay on the bed in his cabin for the best part of two years and gradually rotted away. The other three had obsessions that someone was out to get them. One man would lie on his bunk with his face to the wall when his neighbour came to see him. Another one would accuse his friends and neighbours (behind their backs) of stealing from him, and had three locks on his door. The third man was really far gone. Talking with him on commonplace subjects, I found him as normal as anyone. His friends said he was decent, honest, well-liked and a good citizen. But suddenly, in the middle of a conversation he would lower his voice and in a somewhat obscure manner, make reference to 'them'. He thought 'they' were out to get him, and drive him from his trapping territory, which was a mountainous country in northern B.C. He was convinced that 'they' took pot-shots at him occasionally, and spied upon him. He admitted that he had never seen 'them' or 'him' or 'it', but his camps were consistently being disturbed in some small way that he noted. He obviously had no desire to harm anyone and was only concerned with avoiding his tormentors. The strange thing about all this is that one spring he did fail to return to the Fort, and was never seen again and his body was never found. A raft with a dog chain tied to it was found in a driftpile, and he was assumed to have drowned.

Albert told us that soon after he swamped his skinboat and was walking back down the Flat River he crossed a big creek, coming from the granite range. It looked very promising for placer gold and he felt it should be prospected. "No better time than now," we said. So it was decided that we would all go up to the McLeod Creek area, stake some claims, and then go on up the Flat to Albert's Creek. We would leave the boat at Caribou and take Albert's big twenty-two foot freight canoe, which we could portage at the Flat River canyon, fifteen miles above Irvine Creek. By using just one kicker and tracking where we could, we might just have enough gasoline to reach our destination. As to coming back down, well, the current was fast and the four of us could provide plenty of paddle power. Our food supply was not sufficient for the additional time we wished to spend prospecting, but Albert thought we would have no trouble at all in shooting what moose or caribou we needed. As it turned out, we saw game almost every day.

One long day's travelling brought us to Irvine Creek. The current was steady but not really fast; the valley was wide and green, with some bare hills on either side. Moose and caribou tracks were everywhere. The bars were sand and gravel with no boulders in the creek. The mouth of Irvine Creek is one of the prettiest spots on the Flat River. The old Indian name for it is "The Joining of the Waters". Phil Powers had his cabin here and we examined the ashes of the burned cabin. It had burned up completely and there was nothing to see. But one thing that puzzled us was a piece of wood nailed to a tree with "Phil Powers—his finis", printed on it with pencil. The last word was spelled f-i-n-i-s. We never did find out for sure who put this up. Ole and I stood looking at the cache for a while. It was a 'T' cache platform, very high, perhaps twenty feet, and of course made the use of a very long ladder necessary. Right underneath the cache were several large stumps of trees that had been cut down for the construction of the cabin. Ole and I both thought Phil could have fallen from the cache and hurt himself, perhaps even fatally. But then, why did the cabin burn down?

The fifteen miles to the canyon was a full day's travel. The current increased in speed and there were many rocks and boulders in the stream. To lighten the load three of us walked the shore, cutting across the bends through the bush. There were well worn game trails most of the way and we got to the canyon just ahead of Albert, who ran the canoe up. At one spot at the top of a hill near the river we sat and watched as Albert worked his way up through a riffle. We said, "It is too fast, he will never make it. We'll rest a bit, then go down and give him a hand." With the motor humming along, the canoe was just holding its own with the current.

Albert stood up, reached for one of the poles, held the steering handle between his knees, and used the pole to push the canoe forward. At the head of the riffle the drop was a bit too much for him. He calmly laid down the pole, set the steering handle carefully and stepped out into the water. Working his way to the bow he pulled the canoe up and over the drop, into calm water. Then with the kicker still humming along he stepped back into the canoe and continued on.

Bill said, "The old rascal will slip and get his leg cut off sometime."

Ole said, "I had to see it to believe it."

"He loves the rivers and canoes," I said, "they will never kill him."

That night he told us, "Yes, the propeller did cut my leg once, but it was just a nick."

The walls of the canyon are very low, the stream narrow and deep, with a series of chutes and short drops, much too difficult to get up or down. The portage trail on the right hand side was well cut out, (mostly Albert's work) and less than half a mile long. It presented no problem for us. Bill and I carried the canoe over and Albert and Ole made two trips with the packs. From here on we panned for gold in any likely looking places. I got one good-sized chunk in a crevass in the canyon, but we never did find anything at all that resembled 'pay dirt'.

Fifteen miles above the canyon we left the canoe cached up on two logs and walked up McLeod Creek and over to Grizzly Creek and MacMillan Lake. While Ole and Albert sank some holes on Grizzly one day, Bill and I walked up the creek almost to the head. Here we branched off to the left and followed a small creek to its source near the top of a mountain. We panned in many places but not a color did we find except on Grizzly itself where we got a color or two in every pan. When we got back to camp the other two had sunk a hole down to the boulders and had only a few colors of gold.

At camp I said, "Well Albert, we'll head for your big creek and it had better pay off or we will have made a dry run of it."

Gus was away from his camp on MacMillan Lake, but Bill left the pail of lard in the tent, with a note attached. We were all relieved to get rid of that blessed pail of lard, as Bill had been guarding it with his life, and would hardly turn his back on it. I was almost going to throw it over a cliff once, but was afraid that Bill would go after it and perhaps kill himself on the rocks.

The next day we sloshed through rain and dripping bush back to the canoe. On the way two young moose just about ran over us, but we let them go, not wanting to carry meat to the Flat River.

Soon after passing Borden Creek we made camp where a game trail came out from Landing Lake, half a mile in from the river. I was delegated to hunt moose while the other three went back into the lake in hopes of finding some grub that had been left there some years ago. Sure enough, three hours later they returned with a three pound pail of lard and a four pound tin of jam. It was hard to tell what kind of jam it had been originally it was so sugary, but it tasted darn good anyway. The lard was so rancid it could hardly be eaten, but as we were short of grease, we used it for frying bannock. It is a wonder it did not kill us. It had been in an open cache for four years.

One more full day's travelling brought us twenty miles past Landing Lake, to Albert's big creek. Here we set up camp along the big spruce trees in an open spot almost smack on a well worn caribou trail.

Around the campfire the next morning it was agreed by all that the first consideration was meat for the camp. Albert was to take off on the game trail up the creek that led North into the granite range. I volunteered to go West into a valley across the river. We were to return to camp at night and keep hunting until we shot enough game to do us for a week at least. In the meantime Ole and Bill would sink some holes on the creek bottom in search of 'colors'.

Taking a packsack and my rifle I paddled the canoe

across the river, tied it up securely and took off to the West. The ground rose gently for about a mile when I hit a good game trail leading up into the hills. The trail crossed a small creek and very shortly started up a steep slope, zigging and zagging among the rocks, small spruce and mountain birch. Soon I was above the trees, there were just rocks and moss, and in places I could look straight down as the trail came perilously near the edge of the cliff. It surely was a goat trail, nothing else would be so stupid.

From the bottom of the climb I had noticed a fresh track on the trail, a cloven hoof that must have been a deer, sheep or goat. Very quietly now, tip-toeing along and still climbing I came over a hump and could look ahead along a hog's back for half a mile. The ridge had a shallow valley on each side where game trails wound through the ground birch and willow.

Here above the timberline there were patches of snow, and drifts two and three feet deep in places. I sat down to rest a while, roll a smoke and drink in the sheer beauty of the scene. Far below, the Flat River looked blue among the green spruce. Several grassy lakes nearby were a dainty pale green with fresh slough grass and new budding lily pads. There would be moose there, I thought, a good place to hunt if today proved fruitless. The mountains ahead looked cold and forbidding. "I'll not go much farther into the hills, the snow will be too deep anyway". Then my gaze rested on something white among the granite boulders on the ridge a hundred yards ahead. It was the head of a Dall ram, partially obscured by a tremendous set of curling horns. Moving very slowly I reached for the rifle, aimed and fired. I walked ahead and there was my ram. "Truly a beautiful set of horns", I thought, "they must be six inches through at the butt, and not broomed. We can't eat the horns so I'll cut them off and take the rest of him back to camp." This I proceeded to do, managing to stuff half of him into the packsack with the balance dangling around my back.

When I looked up again there were five big dark mountain caribou, standing in the valley close by, within easy rifle range. In my ignorance, I did not know the caribou would have been much better eating than the tough old ram. Rams, I found later, are very thin and extremely poor eating in the spring of the year. But this I had to find out later. The caribou trotted away, and I staggered back to camp. Getting the packsack, loaded with ram, onto my back was some tussle. A few times I had it up, then flop it would go and drag me down. If God had given me any brains, I would have left the damned thing there, shot a caribou and taken a hind quarter to camp.

The trail being so steep, I thought to make a detour around to the right over a talus slope grown over with moss. This was another mistake. The rocks were square, large and slippery, with the footing at all times uncertain. I took great care and very slowly edged my way along. When just about at the bottom, both feet took suddenly off for the south and with the weight of the ram up fairly high my body had a tendency to cartwheel. This it did, once or twice, I think. The old ram thought he had me now and headed for the deepest hole he could find. The next thing I knew I was upside down in a hole with my feet waving frantically in the air.

After considerable struggling and much grunting I managed to free my arms from the pack and get myself into a more dignified position. Now I thought, to hell with the ram. He can damned well stay in that hole. But we needed meat and Albert said sheep meat was the very best wild meat, and besides I hated to go back to camp empty handed. So I heaved and shoved and dragged the pack to the game trail a little distance farther on. I got it to my back again and struggled on. An hour later I was back in camp where Ole and Bill cheerfully informed me they had just shot a caribou that had wandered into camp. Albert returned in the evening; he had seen no game at all.

Around the fire that night we roasted and ate big chunks of caribou meat. I had skinned and cleaned the ram, but no one would venture to try eating it. "What's wrong with you chaps, don't you know how good sheep meat is?"

Albert grinned, "An old ram in May is like a piece of shoe leather, that old beast is as poor as a crow, it's lucky the boys shot a caribou."

Bill and Ole chimed in, "I don't think the ravens would eat it. It was more than likely dying of old age, and was too weak to run away when it saw you."

"Haw, haw, haw. So that's all the thanks I get for lugging it down the moutain for you three useless bums."

"You should have left the carcass and brought back the horns," advised Albert, "they must have been a good set." I wish I had, I feel sure they would have made the book.

"I don't believe you fellows, I think I will roast myself a nice slice of sheep meat." I did roast a piece all right, but could not eat it. It was just too tough to chew. The boys watched with chuckles as I gave up and threw it to the dogs. Even the dogs refused it for a time, but finally one of them got it down with a gulp.

"Bless me," said Albert, "do you want to kill the dog?"

Bill and Ole had sunk two holes in the creek bottom and had found no colors. Albert and I were all set to extend the prospecting operation on the morrow, into the surrounding area. Bill and Ole were discouraged and thought we should give it up. "After coming this far, it seems a pity to leave so quickly," I volunteered.

"We should go farther up the creek", Albert said. "It is just loaded with quartz from here on up."

"We're running short of fine-cut," Bill insisted, "and have to go back soon anyway."

Ole put in, "We've only got half a can left."

Albert knew from long years of experience, and I knew instinctively, that a disagreement among a party of men in the bush is the one thing to be feared and avoided like the plague. Hardship, misfortune and adversity in the bush can be overcome if there is co-operation and good fellowship among all concerned. Ill feelings, resentment or even a hearty argument between two or more men is like sand in the bearings of an engine. Three of us recognized this fact and took great care to keep all dissension to a minimum. If Bill had any shortcomings, one of them was a tendency to argue. Ordinarily this would not constitute a fault, but he did not realize that under these circumstances arguments should be avoided at all costs.

I looked at Albert and he looked at me. I am sure we were thinking the same thing. This was a chance of a lifetime to prospect this area. It was early in the season and there was no lack of game for food. When would we ever be able to get up here again? The tobacco habit could surely be relinquished for a time without harm to anyone. But, and this was the deciding factor, we had only one canoe for the four of us and we had to stay together. Nothing more was said for a while. Then Albert spoke: "O.K., we'll go back tomorrow."

It rained all that night and in the morning the river was up. The big twenty-two foot canoe had a light load and took the waves nicely. With the rising water and increased speed of the current we barrelled along. Albert was captain and sat in the stern with a big heavy steering paddle. He would stand up when coming to rough water and look ahead to pick out a channel among the boulders. Once in a while he would roar, "Give her hell boys," and the three of us would bend to the paddles and the big canoe would shoot along with Albert guiding it between the rocks. In twenty-four hours travelling time we came the two hundred and thirty miles back to the Butte. One of the kickers had a little gas left in the tank and we came around the corner of the Butte and pulled into the settlement under power.

Lodema told me they were eating supper when suddenly Vera heard the kicker, dashed out of the house and shouted "They're back." Lodema laughed and said, "I knew who she meant, she had been listening for days." Vera claims now that she has spent half her life in the North listening for motors. First kickers, then big engines when Don and I have been away with the barges. Then, latterly, airplanes; her husband's and her son's.

Here at the Butte we found several parties of men from outside, who had come in by way of Fort St. John and Fort Nelson, with home made boats, on their way to the 'gold fields'. 'Swift Water Joe' was here with a barge load of trade goods for various free traders on the Liard and Mackenzie Rivers. Some men had come this far with him and were now in the process of whip-sawing lumber for a scow to take them to McLeod Creek. Some turned back from the long hard boat trip through many miles of rapids and canyons with one portage, and a fifteen mile walk at the end of it all. Some made it all the way, staked their claims and returned.

All the while the controversy raged, in the cabins in the evenings, and around the campfires. Was McLeod Creek the place where the McLeod boys found their gold? Or was it Gold Creek, now renamed Bennet Creek? Had they indeed found any gold at all? Were the old sluice-boxes found on McLeod Creek made by the Klondikers or the McLeod boys, or by someone else? And most important of all, with the small pieces of gold scattered over this considerable area, was there a significant quantity of bedrock? And how far down to bedrock was it? And if it was a considerable distance, was it possible to get down through the boulders, some of which were as big as a table? It being so difficult to sink a hole to any depth, most stakers did as we had done, pan in the creeks and on the benches and in any likely looking spot. Some pans produced colors and once in a while a chunk big enough to drop in the pan and go 'clink'. Only two men stayed to sink a shaft. Gus Kraus and Bill Clark stayed a year or more and put down a hole on Bennet Creek. After a fantastic amount of toil they came up with about an ounce of gold, including one nugget the size of a bean. And to this day those creeks have failed to produce real 'paydirt'.

11

More Nahanni mysteries

Even as far back as 1930 the Nahanni legends were starting to take shape in the outside world. As mentioned early in the book Stan and I were advised to stay away from the South Nahanni River by one of my Tech instructors who had been in to Great Slave Lake a number of times and heard rumors that the Nahanni Indians had murdered two or more prospectors in that remote and mountainous country.

These rumours stemmed from the mysterious death of Frank and Willie McLeod in what was afterwards called Dead Man's Valley; probably in 1905 or 06.

The fact is that their bodies were found the following summer on the bank of the river two miles down from the entrance to the second canyon. One body was reported to be inside his bed roll or blankets; the other was said to have the bed clothes partially thrown off. Both the heads were alleged to be missing. Here you have a case made to order for speculation. In order to get an informed opinion on this tragedy, I asked Willie McLeod, who is one of the survivng nephews of the two who died in the valley. Willie maintains that his uncles starved to death, or possibly died from scurvy. He thinks that bears were responsible for the missing heads. It is common knowledge that bears will often

disturb the bodies of dead people. Willie speaks the language
of the Nahanni Indians quite fluently and has lived with the
Indians all his life, and is in a position to hear of any talk that
would lead him to believe there was a possibility that Indians
had killed his uncles. Willie rules out that speculation as
ridiculous. I am inclined to go along with him.

There is a hard-to-pin down rumor or theory that the
McLeod boys had a partner with them, and that he vanished
into thin air and was never from again. Albert Faille was
convinced they had a partner and that he disappeared with
four thousand dollars worth of gold. Linking this man to the
death of the McLeod boys is another thing, however, and a
matter for pure conjecture.

I have good reason to remember the night Bill Epler, Ole
and I camped in Dead Man's Valley on our way to the gold
creeks. We got started talking of the Nahanni mysteries when
looking at R.M. Patterson's map of the river. Patterson and
Mathews had trapped in the valley six years before and had
made a pretty accurate map of the river. Bill had got hold of a
copy of it somehow and had brought it with him on this trip.

From this the topic went to other trappers who had come
this way. Two men called Stark and Stevens had spent a
winter in the area and left the country soon after.

It is probably fortunate that we can in no way anticipate
what the future holds. In that case we would fear to make a
move. As the Irishman said, "I wish I knew where I was going
to die, for I would never go near the place."

As we sat around the fire that night little did we know
that one of us would soon be a part of the Nahanni mysteries.
Two years hence it would be Bill Epler who would disappear
and not be heard from again. Talking of McLeods I said, "Bill,
what do you think happened to them? What really caused
their deaths? Were they shot as some say?"

"Their heads were gone," Ole said. "But I think the bears
did that. And they were supposed to have had an Eno's bottle
half full of gold."

Bill spoke as he was rolling a cigarette. "Old Joe Hope
was the only one to see the gold, and they dropped it in the
river as they were passing it around."

"Sounds like a fish story to me," I said. "But if they
actually had some gold, I wonder where they found it?"

"That's what a lot of others would like to know" said Bill.
"Gerald Hansen, when he was at Fort Liard, had a map given

rnie Southerland at his beaver hunting camp
ear Fort Nelson, B.C., in 1920.

Ted Trindell with his wife Bella (at extreme
right) at their trapping cabin at Snake River
in 1930.

Starting off for an evening's beaver hunt in May, 1933, from the Lindberg cabin on the Long Reach. In the bow is Einar Pierson, who was with us on the abortive beaver hunt a year previously. Ole Lindberg is in the stern.

At McLeod Creek on Flat River, in Augu 1934, after staking placer claims. From le to right is Stan Turner, Joe Clark, a fur trad from Fort St. John, Boo Jodah and John No gaard. Stan and John had been living straight wild meat for the past two month

At the head of the Liard rapids, fifty miles above Fort Simpson, is Bill Clark and Jack Mulholland's power boat, in May or June, 1935. From left to right is Const. Stirling McNiel of the R.C.M.P.; Bill Clark, Jack Mulholland, man with pipe not identified; in the front of the boat is John Norgaard, Art George, Stan, Lodema George, Bill Epler, Nazar Zinchuk, Poole Field (with the big hat), and Charles Yohin.

Ole And Anna Lindberg at their cabin on the
Long Reach, with some of their winter fur
catch, about 1935.

At our cabin on the Long Reach in March,
1936, with Nancy, age one, in the carry-all.
The picture shows how a carry-all is fastened
to a toboggan.

At Art George's cabin on the Liard River in
May, 1936. From left to right is Ole Lindberg,
Boo Jodah, Hans Rorwick, Stan (with hands
on the shoulders of John Norgaard, Harry
Vandle (grinning), me (frowning), Joe Vandale,
Fred Turner (with Cap), Lodema Georfe, and
Art George.

Paddle Wheeler "Athabasca River" on the
Slave River in 1937.

Lynx.

Trapper's boat loaded with winter supplies, picture from the late 1930's.

Stan's wife Kay at their cabin on the Long Reach in March, 1938.

Dick Turner, his wife Vera, and their two
children, Donald, age two; and Nancy, age
four, in front of Stan's cabin at Long Reach,
Liard River, in March, 1939.

Albert Faille leaving the Lindberg Cabin for
his winter trapping grounds on the Flat River,
1939 or 1940.

Donald, myself, Nancy and Vera at our cabin on the Long Reach with part of our winter's catch in March, 1940.

Black bear swimming the Liard River.

Part of our winter's catch of furs at our cabin on the Long Reach, in March, 1940.

Stan and Kay's cabin on the Long Reach in August, 1940.

Vera with the dog team at Long Reach in April, 1941. She did not do ALL the trapping—I did some once in a while!

Our first barge, being pushed by the "Shooting Star," in 1944. We were loading fur to set off for Fort Nelson, B.C., 300 miles upstream, from Lindberg's cabin on the Long Reach. From left to right, Nancy, Donald, Jim Betsaka, Harry Tesou, John Vital and me.

rade goods and beaver pelts at our log cabin ading post on the Netla River in 1950. Some f the native hunters of the area gather around.

The "Come Later" on the Liard River in September, 1950. This tug was built at Fort Nelson in 1948, and for many years pushed a barge that brought our trading post goods from Fort Nelson.

Paul Tesou, one of the original Nahanni
dians. Taken at Netla River in July, 1952,
was likely seventy years of age at the ti
He was a hunter of perhaps twenty when
first Klondikers came through in 1897. He
one of the expert trackers that followed M
Field's cousin May when she was lost up
Nahanni.

The 'Beaver Dam' on the Liard River near
Fort Simpson, 1953.

Young horned owl.

A typical trapper's food cache. Tin is nailed to the four posts to keep animals from climbing up and getting inside. This one was at Nahanni Butte, 1954.

Bull moose

The author's cabin at Nahanni Butte in July, 1956.

The author, Dick Turner, at Nahanni Butte, March, 1968.

Virginia Falls on the Nahanni River, 316 feet high.

Black bear cub in a precarious position.

Trapper with pack dogs in the late 1930's.

My home-made river scow at second canyon
on Nahanni River in August, 1968.

**Repairing canoe ripped by grizzly bear at
Flat River, 1974.**

Delta of the Prairie River in Dead Man's
Valley.

Moose cow.

Second Canyon, Nahanni River.

Rabbit Kettle Hot Springs.

Beaver.

George's Riffle from downstream, on the South
Nahanni River. Corporal Ward and I were re-
turning form searching for the bodies of three
Swiss tourists in August, 1967.

Dall rams in the Nahanni Mountains.

Albert Faille.

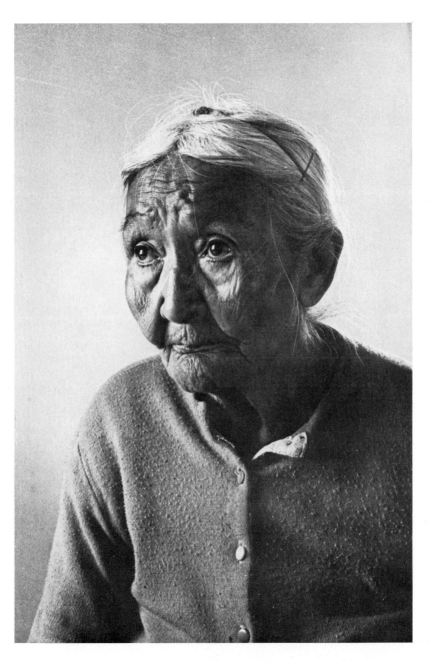

One of the familiar faces: Annie Macpherson, widow of John Macpherson, a long-time employee of the Hudson's Bay Company.

(Photo by Ont. Dept. of Lands and Forests)

This is the way a beaver trap is set by a trapper, throughout our Northland. Small trees are cut and placed around beaver house entrance.

(Photo by Leland Wooley)

Dead Man's Valley in May, 1972.

Hudson's Bay Company paddle wheeler "Distributor", one of the means used in years gone by of transporting goods in the North.

him by a priest which was supposedly given him by one of the McLeod boys, giving the location. Jack Stanier has another map with the same story behind it, but the maps are quite different."

"How come they drew a map when they were dead?" I asked.

"Their last trip was their second one," Ole explained, "and the gold that was seen was what they brought back the first year. But it still does sound strange. If they had found a good prospect it is hardly likely they would draw maps of it and go around handing them out to people."

"And making each map different, too," broke in Bill.

"They might have had a perverted sense of humor, and wanted to get something started," I chimed in. "Like the prospector in heaven who started a rumor of a strike in Hell, and ended up by going himself as he thought there might be something to it after all."

"Gus Kraus thinks for sure the McLeods found the gold on Bennet Creek," said Bill. "Jack Stanier is just as sure it was on McLeod Creek and Albert Faille thinks they found it on the Nahanni River and not the Flat at all."

"Well then," I said, "yer pays yer money and yer takes yer choice."

"Poole Field," said Ole, "is convinced that Jorgensen found the same thing the McLeods did, died or was killed soon after, and his cabin burned much later."

"What is the story on Jorgensen?" I asked. And between Ole and Bill they told me in essence what I have set down in Chapter Nine. They said they knew of no clues whatsoever as to Jorgensen's find, if indeed he had one. But why did he die? He was an experienced man and tough. And how did his cabin come to burn? Men alone in the bush take great care to see that their cabins do not burn down. A prospector does not set fire to his home and then walk outside the door and fall down and die. And there the matter rests to this day. That was number one mystery of a prospector whose death was coupled to the burning of his cabin.

Number two was the case of Phil Powers. He was a trapper and prospector who was discovered the summer of 1933, burned to death inside his cabin at the mouth of Irvine Creek on the Flat River. Identity was established by the gold in his teeth and his watch. Here also the results were found long after the death. Ole, Bill and I had all met Powers the summer of 1932 in Fort Simpson. He impressed us as a man of good character, a competent woodsman, experienced in the bush and well able to take care of himself in any situation. I have since thought that if a man of that calibre makes serious mistakes in the bush, then God help the rest of us.

As to the possibility of Jorgensen or Powers having been killed by someone, I have never heard an opinion expressed by anyone in this part of the north that it was at all likely, mainly for this reason: a person or persons bent on such homicidal tendencies cannot make themselves invisible. They would have to live, travel, eat and sleep in the country for an extended period of time. They would have to cut down trees, make camps, build fires and leave footprints here and there. Those of us who live and travel in the Nahanni mountains are almost certain when we see a cabin, a camp, a fire place, a trail or even an axe mark on a tree as to who made it and when. Up until the advent of helicopters there were so few people in the mountains that it was virtually impossible for one man to live there for even a year without his whereabouts and identity being discovered. To do away with the McLeods, Jorgensen and Powers he would have to have lived there for many years.

Phil Powers could be classified as one of the elite of the trappers and a story he told to Stan and me the summer before he died should be recorded. It is merely an amusing yarn but it serves to illustrate what trappers of that day discussed for the sake of entertainment.

He had been trapping the winter of 1931 and '32 somewhere at the head of the Beaver River. Besides his main cabin he had constructed several 'A' cabins along his trail at twelve or fifteen mile intervals, so that he could spend the nights in relative comfort on his trapline. In the month of January he lost his only timepiece, a pocket watch. Many hours of scratching around in the snow was to no avail in finding it. Soon after losing the watch a trip over his line was due, so he prepared a load of supplies for a six day trip and got to bed early to be up and away well before dawn. He awoke after a time, felt rested, looked out and thought he could see a faint light in the eastern sky. He got up, lit the candle, prepared and ate breakfast, loaded the toboggan and noted that it was still dark. "It will be getting light very soon," he thought. "I may as well hook up the dogs and start out."

This he did, and went on, mile after mile, expecting it to get light any minute, but it did not. He at last came to his first line cabin about twelve miles from home. "I'll make some breakfast," he said to himself. "It will be light by then and I'll go on to the next cabin." After a leisurely breakfast it was still dark. "I may as well amble along slowly," he said. "Surely it will be getting light any minute." And he did go on, and on, and on.

It was just breaking daylight when he came in sight of his second cabin. We laughed with him as he told us. "My God," he said, "I thought something must have gone wrong with the sun, and wondered what I would do if it never appeared at all. I must have gone to bed about five in the afternoon and got up about eight at night. After that I just waited for daylight, and to hell with it."

The fall of 1935 Bill Epler and Jack Mulholland opened a trading post at Nahanni Butte. Jack ran the trading post with the help of his brother Joe who had come up from the States to visit for the winter. Bill Epler ran their trapline by himself. It was a lot harder for one man alone but Bill actually liked work.

The trapline was not producing much fur that winter and along about Christmas Bill decided to pick up his traps and go up above the falls on the Nahanni to trap marten. He took Joe with him and flew up to Rabbit Kettle Lake in January. G.C. F. Dalziel took them in, and I have forgotten what kind of an aircraft he had at that time. They took traps, food, clothes and other necessary items. They also took enough canvas and paint to build a canoe to come down the river with in open water. Their plan was to come down the river soon after the ice went out.

Rabbit Kettle Lake is one of the best game areas in the whole Nahanni mountains as well as a very good fur trapping area. With plenty of wild meat to help out with the food problem they should have been 'fat'.

It was the last anyone saw of them, with one possible exception. Jack was still not too concerned when they did not show up right after open water, as he thought they might be hunting beaver on the way down. By the end of May when most of the trappers had arrived in Simpson, Bill's friends were starting to become concerned. It was all downstream from Rabbit Kettle, with one portage at the falls. The ice had been out for three weeks and they should have had plenty of time to be back. We all knew that Bill was inclined to be impatient and would not wish to wait around for anything.

Stan and the other trappers decided to organize a search

164

for Bill and Joe. I was not in town that spring but Stan told me about it later. Dalziel had the only aircraft in the country at the time, and both he and the airplane were in Fort Simpson. But Dal was having a small hassel with the law over some alleged game infraction, I believe, and the R.C.M.P. had grounded his aircraft. The Dept. of Transport and Dalziel had a few slight disagreements from time to time also and it could be that the R.C.M.P. were acting on instructions from the Air Services Branch. At any rate for some days the aircraft had been tied up and could not be flown.

Stan was in Simpson that spring hobbling around with crutches on a cut foot. He and another trapper, Harry Vandale, wrote out a petition asking the R.C.M.P. to release Dalziel's aircraft long enough to search for Bill and Joe. Stan and Harry took the petition around town and got the signatures of everyone. If I recall correctly Stan said everyone was more than willing to sign. For example, Stan told me of the two Catholic priests. He presented the petition for them to sign and they grabbed a pen immediately. Stan said, "Just a minute, this says that the undersigned will take all responsibility if there is a question of legality of Dalziel breaking the seizure of his aircraft, for the purpose of the search."

"Yes, yes," they said, "we understand," and signed right away.

Harry Vandale and Stan with his crutches hobbled over to the barracks and presented the petition to the Corporal. I do not recall his name but he did release the aircraft on the strength of the petition.

Dal took off with Harry, I believe, as an observer and flew the river to Nahanni Butte, up the Nahanni through the canyons, past the falls right to Rabbit Kettle. He flew just over the water, following every turn in the river so as not to miss the boys in case they were stranded on a sandbar. They returned to Simpson without seeing a sign of the lost men. Dal is an expert bush pilot and we all thought it extremely unlikely he would have missed the boys if they were anywhere to be seen. That was all.

There the matter rests, or just about. Certainly they never returned and their bodies were never found. We guessed. We assumed. We conjectured. What could have happened to them that one did not survive? Did they drown in attempting to walk home on the ice before breakup? Did they wait for breakup, build a canoe and then meet with a mishap on the way down? There was no reason in the world to suspect foul play. There was a coincidence, though, that set us to thinking. Their cabin was found burned to the ground with no indication that their bodies were inside. The traps were gone and there was no rifle or axe in the burned cabin. Did they come back to the cabin one day to find it had burned with most of their food and supplies? Did they try to walk out on the ice? This would have been suicidal under winter conditions. It was well over two hundred miles to the Butte through mountainous country with very deep snow and the river ice very unsafe.

Albert Faille was trapping on the Flat River and they may have tried to walk to his cabin, but they could not be sure just where he was; they might have had to go a very long way. And if their food had been burned up they could have had trouble getting meat. The spring of the year when the snow is very deep, is a poor time for hunting.

Certainly they died and one guess is as good as another as to the manner in which they perished. There is a possibility that wolves got them. It was close to Rabbit Kettle that wolves once almost nailed Albert. Bill Epler was almost without fear and might not have carried a rifle. That would explain why their bodies were not found, but it would not explain the burned cabin. There is a far out possibility that a grizzly got them. I suppose the most likely conjecture is that they went through the ice and were drowned. In thinking of this I have had some agonizing moments thinking of one of them going through the ice and the other coming to help, and both drowning. Bodies of drowned victims of the Nahanni do not always show up. Of three men who were drowned below the falls in 1963 only one body was recovered.

There is an interesting side light on the Epler and Mulholland disappearance that has given me a lot of thought and speculation. I believe that I am the only one alive who knows about it.

In January of 1938, two years following the Epler disappearance, I was in Simpson with the dog team for a load of supplies. I was sitting alone with Andy Whittington in the kitchen of his hotel. It was late in the evening and we were talking of trapping, prospecting and the Nahanni. The talk got around to Bill and Joe as it did so often among their friends.

Andy said, "Dick, I will tell you something I have never

told anyone before because they would probably not believe me anyway, and I don't want to stir up anything. If Bill is alive I don't want to jeopardize his safety. I knew Bill Epler as well as anyone. With that one eye and pug nose of his I could never mistake him. As you know, I was out in Vancouver last winter and was crossing the street one day when a taxi pulled up beside me and stopped to wait for a light. There was a passenger in the front seat beside the driver. He turned to look at me. I was face to face with Bill Epler. Just for a few seconds and the car was gone. I am sure to this day that it was Bill."

Andy could have been right or he could have been mistaken. Although his eyesight is very good and he is no fool, people have been mistaken before on the identification of some person, with tragic results. But truth is often stranger than fiction and Andy's story gives rise to some interesting thoughts.

Bill Epler had stood trial on a murder charge in the States when he was eighteen years old; that would have been about 1918. And he had the daylights scared out of him. At the time he was lost in the Nahanni he was thirty-two years of age. He was known to all as a man of good character, truthful, honest and intelligent (and an excellent bridge player), a gentleman and a true friend. Here is the story of his ordeal as he told it to me.

He was an orphan and had been on his own since he was eleven years old. He had been unemployed for a time and had beaten his way around on freight trains back and forth across the land. When he was eighteen he got into a hassel with the Greek owner of a small restaurant. The Greek accused Bill of something he did not like. They got into a scrap. Nothing further developed and no one was hurt. Bill went on his way. After a few blocks he came to a vacant lot where a group of small boys were playing baseball. As Bill stood watching, the ball sailed past him into the grass behind. He and the boys looked all around but the ball could not be found. "Hey, Mister," accused the boys, "you must have picked up the ball."

"No," said Bill. "Honest I didn't, you can search me," and he held his hands above his head. The boys did search him thoroughly, to no avail. The ball was later found in the tall grass and Bill walked on.

The next day he was arrested for the murder of the Greek who had been found shot to death.

Bill told us that never, absolutely never, would he go through what he had endured that month. He had no friends and no money. He had been seen fighting with the Greek and soon afterwards the Greek was found dead. What more could a prosecuting attorney wish for to make out a good case for conviction? The chap in the cell next to Bill's was found guilty of murder and was hung while Bill was waiting trial. Bill said he could feel the rope around his neck until the jury came in with the good news. The school boys who had searched Bill were brought into court, and Bill's lawyer made the most of their evidence, that they had searched Bill thoroughly and no gun was found. The jury had not long to deliberate. They soon brought in a verdict of 'Not Guilty'.

If something happened to Joe, say he was drowned or had met with some mishap that resulted in death, what would Bill do? I can still hear him say that under no circumstances would he ever face another trial. It was not likely but it was possible, if he had returned without Joe. He might have thought, "Australia for me, boy, here I come."

To my knowledge there is only one woman who has vanished in the Nahanni and she was a cousin of Mary Field. The only information I have on her disappearance is from Poole Field directly. I have never discussed it with Mary, his wife.

It happened when the Fields were camped on the Nahanni at what is now called Mary's River. It was about 1920 and Poole was with a group of Indians. They were Nahanni Indians, or as much Nahanni as any Indians were at that time. There were five top notch hunters among the older men. Their names now are legendary. There was Diamond See, Boston Jack, Yohe, Tesou, and Big Charlie. I knew them all and if they ever had other names, they were unknown to me. They were all very fine, decent men, and to consider seriously that any of them would have shot a white man for his gold is to me completely ridiculous.

The girl, May, was staying with the Fields and had been acting strangely for some time.

It was the month of July and the whole camp was working their way along the Nahanni from a winter's trapping. The bush was their home and they only went to a settlement to trade. Their diet was almost completely wild meat, with very little flour for bannock at odd times. The supply of ammunition was an important factor in their lives.

One day someone brought a report to Poole that May was missing and was nowhere in camp. A search was conducted in the surrounding bush and eventually revealed her tracks leading off up Mary's River into the hills. Poole and the five good hunters set off with light packs to track her down. They had a blanket each and rifles and shells.

The outcome was that they followed May for nine days and in that time Poole learned that he was a novice at tracking. May kept travelling and would only stop for intervals when she would stand and rest on her feet. Poole said he thought he was a cracker-jack of a hunter before this episode, and could track an animal as well as anyone. But he found he was completely out-classed by these Indians. She was wearing moccassins and her tracks were quite visible whenever she crossed a sand bar on the creek. But where she took to the bush and climbed the hills there was little sign that she had passed that way. Once in a while he could see a definite footprint in the soft moss, and when they came to rocky or hard ground even the Indians would lose the track. They would circle around far ahead and always one would give a call that he had found it again. To make it disconcerting for them all, the girl was apparently losing whatever marbles she had left. She would stop occasionally and divest herself of some article of clothing until Poole said she must have been stark naked. And with the mosquitoes so thick there was no way she could live for very long. Poole was pretty well without hope that they would ever find her alive. All she had on at this time were some moosehide thongs wrapped around the bottom of her feet to protect them from the rocks.

By now she had got into rugged country where she had to do some very steep climbing. She must have been without fear for she climbed some cliffs where the men were afraid to go and had to go away around and pick up her track on top. About the fifth day the hunters came to the bottom of a very rugged high cliff, which was actually the side of a five thousand foot mountain. Her tracks were visible at the bottom but they could find no sign that she had turned to the left or the right. Poole said there was just no way that any sane person could possibly have gone up that wall of rock. There was an indication that she might have tried for there was a narrow shelf-like ledge leading up for a hundred feet or so. Some of them went part way up but turned back.

Poole thought for sure they had come to the end of the

trail, but they worked their way around to the top and sure enough, there was her track again heading south and east. Sane or not she was heading in the direction of her home, which was Simpson. The search party was killing sheep and caribou for food and after nine days they only had six shells left among them. Just short of the canyons of Dead Man's Valley they abandoned the search and turned back for Mary's River.

A tributary of Mary's River is named after her, May Creek.

In recent years the Nahanni or Headless Valley as it is called now has never ceased taking a heavy toll of lives. Many are aircraft accidents, some are drownings and some are from starvation. One case sticks in my mind when three men out of a party of five perished. One killed himself, two died of starvation and two were rescued.

I think that it was in the fall of 1963, sometime in early October, when five men from Yellowknife flew into MacMillan Lake near McLeod Creek to prospect for the winter. I assume they knew that placer claims had previously been staked and given up on the nearby creeks. I did not see any of these five men and most of the information I have on this tragedy that was building up is from Gus Kraus, who was living in the village at the time, and Frank Bailey, the Game Warden involved in the episode.

Two of the five men involved were weathered in at Gus's cabin at Nahanni Butte on their way into the lake. I believe that the two men were Pappas and Webb.

According to Gus, this is what happened. There were three aircraft loads, two Beaver and one Otter, flown into the lake. The freight included a dog team and a toboggan. The men said that they all had prospectors licences and were going to sink some holes on the creeks to see if there was placer gold on bedrock. They were told by Gus, who was an honorary Game Warden, and said they knew already, that it would be strictly illegal for them to engage in any trapping activity whatsoever, for none of the five held a General Hunting Licence which was necessary to have before engaging in any trapping activities. In any case, the men said that as the holders of prospecting licences they were entitled to kill one big game animal each. Gus maintained that such was not the case and that the only condition that would permit any of the five men to kill a big game animal was if they were in dire need of food and were in danger from starvation. Gus told me they argued about it all evening, and after the two men had left for MacMillan Lake the next day Gus got in contact by radio telephone with Frank Bailey who was the local Game Warden in Fort Simpson, and asked him if there had been any recent changes in the game regulations permitting a holder of a prospectors licence to kill any animals other than rabbits and partridge. Mr. Bailey told him that as far as he was aware such was not the case; he knew of no recent changes in the regulations. He told Gus that he would check with the authorities in Yellowknife as regards the situation.

The next development in this case came in middle or late December when Mr. Bailey picked up Gus at Nahanni Butte with a Beaver aircraft and flew into MacMillan Lake to visit the five prospectors. Gus told me they found the remains of caribou bones and hide near where the dogs were tied. Two of the men were away and three were at the cabin on MacMillan Lake. Gus said that Mr. Bailey informed the men that they could not legally kill game unless they were very short of food and were in dire need. If they were short of food Mr. Bailey said he would take them back to Simpson on the aircraft as he had room in the airplane. But in the meantime he would have to take the bones and hide of the caribou back to Simpson as evidence for there was a possible question of legality as to the possession of caribou meat. The men replied that they did not wish to go back to Simpson as they had a considerable amount of beans, rice and flour on hand and had arranged for a company to fly in a load of supplies in early January. The Game Warden then issued them with a two dollar licence to enable them to kill rabbits and partridge but said they were not to kill moose or caribou unless they were in danger of starvation. There the matter ended for a time. A day or so later I believe that Bailey, Gus Kraus and the constable from Fort Liard flew in to MacMillan Lake again. The constable, whose name was Vic Werbiki, told me he had checked the amount of food the prospectors had at the lake and was satisfied that the quantity was sufficient for their needs for the time being. Vic Werbiki was cool headed, tactful, and was well liked and respected by all who knew him. He was stationed at Liard for two years and I thought he was of the best tradition of the R.C.M.P., a man who might overlook some minor items but with whom no one would care to tangle if he were investigating something serious. The

Game Warden, Frank Bailey, was a man of the same calibre as Vic Werbiki. They both had their jobs to do and would do them, but neither of these men would go out of their way to hurt anyone.

Nothing was heard of or from these men at MacMillan Lake for a considerable length of time. Gus Kraus and Vic Werbiki told me the foregoing and that is all I knew. That winter I had a Super Cub aircraft on skis and was doing considerable flying. I did consider going in to the lake to check up on these five men as it was only one hour's flight away, a hundred miles to the west. It would only have cost me fifteen dollars in gasoline plus operating costs and some hours of my time. But I decided against it and have regretted my actions to this day. I rationalized it this way: although it would have been strictly illegal for them to do so, perhaps they were trapping a few marten and might ask me to handle their fur for them. That would put me on the spot as it would be hard for me to say no. But I would not have bought or transported the furs for two reasons: first—it would jeopardize my whole livelihood by putting my trading permit in danger, and secondly Frank Bailey and Vic Werbiki were good friends of mine and in no way would I embarrass them and myself by doing such a thing as to even transport a parcel for anyone that might possibly contain illegal fur. I rationalized further that they might think I was being inquisitive about their prospecting activities.

So I stayed away and the following May we heard tragic events had taken place. On May seventh Chuck McAvoy, a flier from Yellowknife, had flown in to MacMillan Lake with a Cessna 180 on skis and had found only two survivors out of the five. These two were in a bad way from starvation but did recover. The aircraft that was expected in early January had not shown up and by the time the men became desperate the snow was deep and the game had disappeared. One man killed himself sometime between January and May. I understand that he became despondent, took a stick of dynamite, tied it to his chest and lit the fuse.

Pappas and Webb, I believe it was, started to walk overland to Nahanni Butte on April twelve. The snow was keep at that time of year and would be wet during the day. They were reported to have only a pound of salt and a pound of tea with them when they left MacMillan Lake. Their bodies were never found.

Later, I heard that the two survivors had instituted a lawsuit against the aircraft company for failing to appear, and that a settlement was made out of court.

All the rationalizing in the world will never ease my conscience in this affair. We all must conduct ourselves according to whatever set of moral values we hold. I happen to value highly the virtues of compassion and courage. And I believe that I should make the fullest use of whatever brains I have been endowed with. If I had used my intelligence, compassion and courage to their fullest extent I could have prevented this terrible tragedy. From that day I decided that if there was any possibility that someone in the bush needed help, I would first go and have a look and consider the consequences later.

12

Good catches

Soon after returning from the Flat River, I went on to Simpson alone to record the claims, perhaps sell one if lucky and get supplies for the summer.

The day I arrived in Simpson the *Distributor* had just arrived on its first trip of the summer. That evening I met a man who said his name was Crombie, and that he was the publisher of the Vancouver Sun. He was on the way down the Mackenzie River as a passenger on the paddle wheeler on a sight-seeing tour. An acquaintance I was with said, "Mr. Crombie has just bought a placer claim from me, and perhaps he would like another. Have you one for sale?"

"Yes, I have," I said. "I have just returned from McLeod Creek and have recorded the claims today."

I offered to sell two claims for two hundred dollars each, and Mr. Crombie gave me his cheque and we had the claims transferred to him the next day. He was obviously a man from the city who was buying something sight unseen. But we were all in the same boat and were taking a chance at spending our time and money on a tenuous claim. There was gold on those claims at that time and there still is. But whether there is pay dirt is another thing. If Mr. Crombie were alive today he might be interested to know that I have recently restaked several claims on those same creeks. I intend to keep them, they are not for sale. I still have faith there is pay dirt at depth somewhere on those creeks.

And don't say that I am like the prospector who went to hell, hoping to make a stake. I know it.

With the money from the sale of the claims I purchased food and supplies for the summer and headed back up river to Nahanni Butte.

*   *   *

On July 15th of 1934 Vera and I unloaded from the canoe the few scanty items of goods we owned onto the beach of the Long Reach and set up housekeeping in the tiny log shack I had used two years before. It was very old and small with a dirt roof about a foot thick. It was snug and dry and had enough room in it for a dwarf to swing a small kitten. We could sit on the bed and reach everything in the cabin from there. If someone went out in a hurry, the air was sucked out of the cabin and almost put out the fire.

It was going to be a lot of work to get the new cabin built before fall and I could not take time to roam about the bush hunting for the dogs, so I set out snares on the trails behind the cabin, for moose and bear. We checked the snares morning and evening and during the summer they produced enough meat to keep the dogs fat and healthy. I had found out the hard way that Mr. Renny was right when he said that you cannot run a trapline without a good dog team. For a place to keep the meat we dug a hole down to permafrost which was about three feet. We covered this with logs and earth. This cellar stayed at a few degrees above freezing and kept the meat fresh for well over a week.

There were no suitable logs for the cabin near the building site so we cut and peeled the logs a mile upstream near the bank of the river. Each day I would pull out a few, float them down and drag them out onto the beach. Then one by one I would carry them up the hill, fit them on and notch in the corners, laying moss between the logs for insulation. When the walls were up, the surplus moss was cut out and small peeled poles were laid in and nailed in the cracks. The logs were then clean and light with no moss visible.

The stove we had in the little cabin was just a small camp stove with no oven, and with no oven, baking bread presented a problem. But Vera had an idea. Stan had a B.C. Heater in his

cabin across river almost two miles away, and we could paddle
over and bake the bread in his drum oven. This we did. By
noon the bread was risen in the pans and ready for the oven.
We carried the loaves down to the canoe and paddled across.
The drum oven is a circular affair set in the stove pipe and
utilizes the heat going up the chimney. It bakes very well if
the damper is set properly and the fire tended expertly. I
think the oven took three loaves at a time, and in two hours
the bread was baked and we were home for supper. We both
noted the bread was all the better for its trip across the Liard
River and back. Both Vera and Lodema George used a drum
oven for years and the baking they did in them was the very
best. In later years we got a wood burning cook stove with an
oven and thought we were in clover. Finally we got a propane
cook stove, and the clover was higher.

But take my word for it, plant the clover first and get the
stove later. Starting at the bottom is no fun. When you do
manage to afford a long-desired labor saving device you are so
worn down and numbed that the capacity for enjoyment is
much dulled. You only want to sit and rest. I have read of the
pleasures of starting from scratch. John Goodall Sr. the first
elected member to the Territorial Council from our area, who
went through the same poverty we did, claims it takes so long
to make the scratch you have no strength left for starting.

We had some wooden crates and one bundle of ship-lap
that I brought from Simpson but we needed more lumber for a
floor and a door and so on. I had borrowed a whip-saw from
Ole Lindberg and now I asked Vera if she would like to help
me whip-saw several trees for lumber.

"I'm game," she replied, "but I don't know how long I'll
last at it."

"Nothing to it," I said cheerfully, "you can stand on the
top and pull the saw up. You will find it a piece of cake." I did
not tell her that grown men tremble at the thought of having
to use a whip-saw. I have heard men say they would sooner be
chained to a Roman galley.

The logs for the cabin were all cut and peeled and the
walls partly up when we started whip-sawing. We wanted the
boards to dry before using them. To make the saw-pit I chose
four trees in the form of a rectangle cut them off six feet above
the ground, notched in the tops and set in two cross pieces.
Then I cut down a spruce tree fourteen inches at the butt, cut
it off at sixteen feet and hewed it on two sides with an axe, so

that we would have eight inch wide boards. Lines were drawn with a straight edge and a pencil an inch and a half apart. Then the timber was hoisted up onto the platform and we were ready to go to work.

The whip-saw is shaped somewhat like a hand rip-saw only much bigger. It is about six feet long and eight inches in width. The teeth are all rip teeth and are three quarters of an inch in depth.

The cross handle at the top is permanent while the one at the bottom can be removed when you change cuts.

The sawing at first did not go too well. The saw was sharp enough, but the set of the saw was insufficient. It would cut coming down but was extremely hard to pull back up. Vera did not take kindly to this and said a number of words such as 'Damn' and 'Blast'. We took the saw back to the cabin and I set to work on it with a hammer, an axe and a chunk of steel rod. I gave it a wide set, sharpened the teeth again and from then on it went much easier. We eventually got four logs cut into lumber, enough for the floor and a door. Vera said she had all the whip-sawing she wanted and I cannot say that I blame her. It is some of the hardest work invented by man. The whipsaw is an instrument of torture that should be outlawed.

Roof poles for the cabin were made from small spruce, three or four inches in diameter, peeled and cut to eight foot lengths. Over this we laid moss and four inches of earth and topped it off with spruce bark. The bark proved very unsatisfactory and the following year we were able to replace it with rubberoid roofing. A sheet of celluloid eighteen by forty-eight inches was used for each window and the cupboards I made from shiplap. Wooden butter boxes with backs made for them did for chairs. I took a copy of a chair that Stan had made for himself and made one like it: an arm chair with seat and back stuffed with chopped moose hair. Vera washed the logs and hung curtains at the windows, and we were quite happy with our little cozy home. By fall I procured a B.C. heater with a drum oven.

Late one afternoon about August 7th we noticed the river was starting to rise and by bedtime it was running driftwood. There were still some peeled logs on the beach, well tied with rope and I did not expect a flood so late in the summer. In the morning when I came outdoors I could hardly believe my eyes. The Liard had risen about nine feet overnight and was running chockful of driftwood as we never saw it before or since. The canoe was floating in an eddy, but was still tied. Six of my building logs had drifted away. The river here is about a mile wide and was bank to bank with driftwood. Dry trees, green trees, old trees, young saplings, roots of all sizes and description. There were short logs, long logs, rotten logs and green logs, grave old plodders, gay young friskers. Chunks of roots that looked like whiskers. Crowded together from shore to shore, you couldn't have pushed in one stick more. Great gobs of foam like piles of hay, all dirty brown (or tattle-tale gray). (Apologies to R.B.)

Whole islands of driftwood went by that day, gobs that had been accumulating at the head of gravelbars for years were lifted free and carried away by the upward surge of water. The river water which had been clear and clean the day before was now a thick reddish-brown soup. It could not be used for anything, even washing dishes. All water had to be carried some distance from a small creek near the house.

After the third day the driftwood started to slack off and after ten days the river was back to normal, but it left a deep layer of muck along the shores that took a long time to dry.

Soon after the flood, I had to go to Lindberg's for some reason or other, and was away overnight with the canoe and kicker. On arriving home again I was a bit startled to find four quarters of meat hung up under the porch of the old cabin, with a smoke underneath to keep away the flies. I was puzzled as to what had happened in my absence. It looked like a professional job, and I could hardly credit that Vera had shot it and skinned it out, cleaned it and quartered it all on her own. The only gun she had at the cabin was a single shot .22 rifle. But she had, as she related to me in a matter of fact way, as if it was an everyday occurrence.

About four o'clock in the morning and getting daylight, the dogs started making a terrific racket. She went to the door and saw a black bear gallop by the cabin and start up a tree a hundred feet or so away. She took the rifle and fired at the bear's head and down he tumbled. She walked up and put a few more shots in his head to make sure he was not just stunned. She skinned it out and hung up the four quarters for our own use and cached away the rest for the dogs. The bear was as fat as a pig. The next day we stripped chunks of fat from the meat and rendered it down in a big pot. The rendered fat was slightly brown and stayed soft, but we put it away in lard pails and it kept very well. Vera used it for baking, and the dough-nuts she made from it were delicious. We did eat some of the bear meat, but neither of us were overly fond of it and as soon as I got a fresh moose, the bear meat went into the dog food cache.

In September and October we noticed fox tracks on the beach. Every day there were more and we soon noticed them trotting by. They were mostly reds with a few silvery crosses among them. In October they started coming to the cabin and stealing rags and old moccasins and looking in the window. Vera had some eating from her hand, and one boldly carried off the broom. We assumed his den needed cleaning out, but his wife must have taken a dim view of the matter, because the broom was found some days later not far away.

Although by now the Great Depression was well underway, the price of fur had held up surprisingly well and we were indeed happy to see the run of foxes. It boded well for a good fur catch, although I did not have nearly the amount of traps and snares I needed to make a good catch. I think by Christmas we had about seventy pelts, mostly fox with some lynx.

Early in October Stan came back from Great Bear Lake where he and Jack Mulholland had been freighting in the rapids on Bear River with a small boat. Freight was being moved in to the new Radium Mines on Bear Lake. Stan was getting ready for the winter's trappings so we had someone close to visit now. The Lindbergs were twenty miles away and we did not get to see them very often.

By November the Liard was running ice, and winter had set in, but as yet there was very little snow in the bush. Vera went with me on the line for the first few trips, as the weather could not become too bitterly cold until after Christmas. The three dogs pulled the toboggan with a light load. With but little snow, the trail was rough with stumps and roots and humps of frozen muskeg. The going was slow, and it took us five days to run our little line of thirty miles and back.

The first trip out, a mile or two from the first line cabin Vera was walking ahead of the dogs when she stopped and turning said, in a loud whisper, "Dick, a moose, a moose." She saw a bull moose close by and did not know that it was in a snare that I had set a few days previously. I snubbed the toboggan rope, grabbed a rifle and went toward the moose. Instead of using a toggle as we usually did, the snare in this case was anchored solidly to a tree. The bull was caught by one antler, and the ground was chewed up and the brush tramped down in a fair-sized circle. He was one mad moose. He was standing on the far side of the circle. When I went up toward him he came at me like a cyclone. I raised the gun to fire but I think there was a surplus of oil in the lever action for the hammer would not hold and the gun fired before I had it raised. I kept pumping shells in each time the gun fired. Three times this happened before the pin at last held, and I was able to aim and pull the trigger. In the meantime the bull had been brought to a sudden stop by the cable, and set back on his haunches with a thud. He was up immediately, striking at me with his front feet. They were slashing like knives and striking the ground with terrific force. His ears were back, his eyes were red with fury and he looked pretty mean. After I shot he still pranced around for a time before he dropped. If I was not trembling then I should have been, as I examined the strands of shiny steel that held him when he charged. I also thanked my stars that I had made a good job of tying the knots. I am absolutely certain if the cable had not held him he would have trampled all of us, including the dogs, into the ground and made mincemeat of us before he was finished.

We skinned him out and cached the meat there, but a tougher, bluer, leaner moose I have never seen. The dogs would hardly eat the meat.

This was the second time I had failed to use a toggle when setting a moose snare and resolved never to do so again. In September I had set a snare on the trail behind the house in a thicket of spruce. In the morning I went to check and found a big bull had run into it during the night and was evidently caught by his antlers for on the first lunge he pulled the tree out by its roots and kept on going. For some distance he took about twenty feet to a leap. I went home chuckling. It was extremely unlikely that the snare would catch on anything that would hold him and he would carry the cable with him until he dropped his horns in January.

I guess I should explain what a "toggle" is, and a few other trapper's terms as well.

13

Trapping gadgets

In trapping, as in other specialized occupations, there are numerous phrases that are intriguing but meaningless if one is not familiar with them. The word toggle falls in this category.

A toggle is any loose stick or part of a small tree to which a trap or snare is attached. For small animals such as marten or mink the toggle is more often than not a green spruce tree with all the branches trimmed off. For fox and lunx the trap is larger and the toggle heavier. A normal toggle is a sound pole about eight feet long and say three inches in diameter. The ring of the trap chain is driven on to the small end of the toggle until it fits snugly. Experience has shown that if a trap is fastened directly to a tree the animal will often pull out of the trap, whereas with a toggle there is a certain amount of "give" at all times. For a moose or bear snare the toggle should be a sound green log about eight inches in diameter and say twelve feet in length. This is stood up on end against a tree or bushes.

When I started trapping in 1930 there were only leg-hold traps in use. The so called 'humane' traps had not been invented, although steel snares were used extensively for some types of animals and usually killed the animal very quickly. At that time in the north, as I have stated in foregoing passages, there was almost no other way of obtaining the wherewithall to buy food and clothing except by trapping fur bearing animals for their pelts. I must admit that I came to love the life in the bush, the driving of a dog team, working a canoe up or down a rapids, the building of cabins out of fresh green trees, the smell of a spring morning when the air is heavy with perfume from budding leaves and wild flowers. I loved the never ending challenge of a wilderness life and the heart-moving satisfaction from an independent life. But I never did enjoy the necessary job of having to kill animals, with the exception of wolves and black bears. After the first years of trapping I grew to loath and detest timber wolves for two reasons: they took on the average twenty per cent of my fur catch, some years more; and I abhorred the cruel way in which they killed their prey. Toward the end of my trapping days, when other opportunities of making a living came to hand, the revulsion against killing any and all animals increased. Although I still roam the mountains for a few months every summer and carry a rifle with me at all times I have not killed more than a dozen house mice in the last six years. I have had chances to shoot timber wolves and black bears but could not bring myself to do it. I am all for introducing humane traps and would not own a rifle if I did not need it for protection from grizzlies in the bush. During our last years of trapping Vera walked over a short line to check some marten traps. She caught a marten, pretty little female, debated with herself for a time when she saw it in the trap, then killed it and cried all the way home. We had four children to feed and a dollar was a dollar. When she told me about it I felt as badly as she did.

That was when we were comparatively affluent. Back in 1930 we could not afford the luxury of sentiment. Our total effort had to be directed toward acquiring a sufficient number of pelts to buy the necessities of life.

The first winter with old Boo Jodah, Stan and I did learn a few of the basics of trapping. We learned that generally small pens or cubbys were built in the snow for marten sets and lynx sets. Bait or scent was tied to a stick at the back of the pen and twigs were arranged to direct the animal into the trap. Foxes generally would shy away from a cubby, so the bait and the trap were set against a root or a stump and nothing was disturbed to make the animal suspicious.

Mink will walk into just about any kind of a set, but the space must be confined or he will avoid the trap and go over or around it. Mink usually confine their wanderings to creek beds, and will investigate any hole in the ice or an opening in the bank of the stream. A chunk of frozen muskrat is a bait that a mink cannot resist. We would cut a muskrat up into chunks with an axe and secure it, hide and all, back in a hole. If a mink came by, he would never pass it up.

Beaver are trapped under the ice in the winter. Poplar or aspen is used for bait and of course the beaver is drowned immediately he is caught. Open water beaver trapping is a bit tricky. A pen is built on the shore-line at the edge of deep water. Fresh poplar is used for bait and a pen is constructed to direct him into the trap. The trap is attached to a pole stuck into the water in such a way that will drown him right away. We found the best was a sliding pole with nails (without the heads) driven in at an angle. A beaver will head for the deepest water, and the contrivance will not let him come back up. A trap for an otter must be set in the same manner except that meat or fish is used for bait. We found that over the years the best bait of all for any of the animals listed above is beaver castorium, mixed with the oil bags of a beaver which are right next to the castors when you skin a beaver out.

Much has been written and said about the infamous wolverine. The story books and the Disney films depict these animals in a very different light than I have found them. The amount of damage that wolverine have done to my trapline is minimal throughout the years. For the most part they go about their own business and do not bother a trapper. There is one thing about them, however, that a trapper must always remember. Any wolverine, by the very nature of the beast, dearly loves meat, especially tainted or rotten meat, so that a trapper with any brains at all will keep his meat and fish that he is using for dog food well away from his cabin and living quarters. If a wolverine comes within a mile of that meat he will head right for it and do his best to get to it, no matter how well it is covered. Wolverine will very seldom bother a cache where you keep fresh meat and bacon for your own use. I don't think a wolverine could be enticed into a cabin that was clean and smelled of soap and wood smoke.

I have always been pleased to see wolverine tracks on my line for their pelts were always worth good money and strange to say they are easy to catch. There again a trapper must have something more between his ears than a bone to hold his cap in place. Any wolverine that is on your trapline has likely seen many traps that were set in front of a pen, marten or whatever. He sees the trap and he smells the trap. It is obviously not good to eat and he might flip it over with his paw or simply go around to the back of the pen, pull down a stick and steal the bait. But if you set a trap behind the pen for a few sets, and farther along your line set some more a foot from where you normally set the trap, he will put his foot into it every time. But catching him is not to say you are going to hold him for very long.

It is almost useless to use a trap size smaller than a number three Victor with double spring. A number fourteen jump trap is excellent. Now he is well caught in a big trap. That is still not enough. He will chew down all the small trees within reach and will eventually get to the toggle. He will chew that off near the ring and away he goes. A very long trap chain is the answer to this. He will chew up the trees handy but has no idea the important one is some distance away. The only time I have ever lost a wolverine out of a trap is when they have stepped into a marten or a lynx cubby and been caught in a small trap. Even then some are still there when I come along. A wolverine is supposed to be a good fighter. I have never seen one fight with any animal but my work dogs. He makes a very loud ferocious roar, but the dogs have always come out of the fight without a scratch. After all, a sleigh dog will weigh up to a hundred pounds, whereas the biggest wolverine I trapped weighed forty pounds.

I conclude that the poor little wolverine has been much maligned.

There are many different sizes of traps used by trappers. Some are suitable for some animals and not for others. Until the Conibear traps came on the market the most popular trap was the Victor animal trap. These came in sizes from 0 to No.4. There was a bear trap that was much bigger but I never did use one that large. It was a horrible looking thing with jaws on it a foot long and ten inches wide with teeth in it. The No. 0 was for weasel and had a jaw spread of two and a half inches. The No. 1 was for marten and possibly mink and had a jaw spread of say two and a half inches. I have never used a small trap for mink. I had better luck with a No. 3 or 4. The No.1½ could hold a lynx or fox and the jaw spread was about four inches. The No.2 trap was exactly the same size as the No.1½ except the No.2 had a double spring. These No.2 traps were commonly used for lynx and fox. The No.3 trap had a five inch spread and the No.4 about six. The latter had double springs and were used to catch wolverine, otter, beaver and wolf.

An adequate supply of traps to run a proper line constituted a large expense for a trapper. Most full time trappers had from five hundred to eight hundred traps. Most winters a trapper would lose say five percent of his traps. On some the springs would break and some would be lost by being covered with water and freezing in the ice. Thus every year some traps would have to be replaced. In the forest fire of 1942 many trappers lost almost all their traps. That fire burned up my trapping area with a loss of over four hundred traps. I never did replace them all as I went into fur trading and the barging business soon after that.

When a trapper brings a pelt home his work is not over. First the animal must be skinned. The animal is held between the knees. With a sharp-bladed pocket knife, the back of the legs are split just through the hide, from inside the paw right to the vent. The hide is carefully worked off the legs with the fingers, just using the knife where necessary. Then the tail-bone is pulled out and the tube is slit so that it will dry. Then the animal is pulled inside out, again just using the knife where necessary. The front legs are pulled out and cut off at the paws and the hide is worked carefully away from the head, being careful to leave the eye-lids on the hide.

Marten and fox are easy to skin. The hide pulls away from the carcass quite easily, and so it does with a lynx, although a lynx is bigger and some are very fat. Wild mink are a headache to skin for there is a very tough layer of fat next to the hide and this must be thoroughly cleaned with a knife or the fat will tend to rot the hide, thus reducing the pelt in value. Wolverine are tough to skin. The hide is very difficult to pull away from the body and a knife must be used most of the way. On a wolverine the market value is greater if all four claws are left on, and this takes time and effort, to say nothing of a very sharp knife.

A timber wolf is the most difficult of all to skin, as they are so big and heavy. After the hind legs are skinned out it helps to hang them up to finish the job.

After the skinning is done, while the hide is still wet and fresh, it must be stretched. All the above animals are 'case' stretched. They are turned inside out and put on a flat board for mink and for others, a vee shaped set of three strips of boards that can be enlarged to suit the size of the pelt. All surplus flesh and fat must be removed before the pelt is allowed to dry. Also there must be no nicks or cuts in the pelt. If there are, the pelt is much reduced in value. On all cased pelts, with the exception of mink, the hide must be taken from the stretcher before it is quite dry and turned fur-side out. Then it must be replaced on the stretcher and left a day or two to finish drying. All pelts must be dried in a warm place and NOT in the heat. If they are dried too quickly they get what the fur trade calls 'grease burn' and are further reduced in value.

Beaver pelts are somewhat different. The hide must be cut off with a knife, every inch of it. The animal is first laid on its back and slit from stem to stern as it were. When the pelt is removed it is sewn on to a circular frame, tightened just so, and all the fat removed.

The last year we trapped I froze all the pelts on the trapline after skinning them and brought them home in a frozen state. Vera stretched most of them while I was away on the line the following trip. She did a hundred and twenty-five lynx, eighty-five marten, three wolverine and a few mink. I had no qualms about leaving her to buy fur in the store as she was pretty shrewd at sizing up a pelt. She knew the business inside out. (No pun intended.)

14

Dogs are important

That first winter in our new cabin on the Long Reach Vera and I had not more than forty traps and about fifty snares, which is only a fraction of the amount an established trapper needs. But with the foxes streaming into the country on what amounted to a migration, we had, by Christmas, around seventy-five pelts. Even if we had only three dogs to pull the toboggan the seventy mile trip to Simpson had to be undertaken in order to market the fur and bring home more supplies. But first we must have the traditional Christmas celebration.

At this time Stan was single and lived across the Liard from us. He came over with his team on Christmas morning (he too had a team of three dogs) and we had the best that we could muster in the way of a feast. Vera had a big linen tablecloth with china dishes and if I recall we had three silver plated spoons. She had made a pile of goodies that was amazing to behold. As long as Vera had some basic ingredients to work with she had a knack of making a variety of tasty dishes.

Ted Trindell, our neighbor who trapped eight miles down the river from us, also arrived that day and stayed for dinner. He had brought along his lead dog, Princess Charlotte, a beautiful husky bitch, with her six puppies. Ted asked Vera if she would keep Charlotte and the puppies for a month in exchange for her choice of two of the pups. This she agreed to and when Ted left for home Charlotte settled down with her family on a rug under the table of our little one room cabin and made herself at home. Charlotte was a lovely dog, gentle with everyone and a good mother to her family of hungry puppies. When the pups were small and could hardly stagger around with their fat little bellies touching the floor, our cat Midget would knock them over and roll them around on the floor with his paw. We were a little afraid he might hurt one. It was not many days when the tables were turned completely and the pups would maul the cat. Now it was his turn to yowl for protection.

Very naturally Charlotte ate vast quantities of food to satisfy those six big lugs that tugged at her. Vera would go out with the rifle every day and shoot a couple of rabbits, skin them and cook them up with rice and tallow or lard. When I was away on the line she had to leave them in the cabin unattended. All went well and nothing was ever touched or stolen until one day she returned and there was Charlotte up on the bed, away from the pups, with a can of butter between her paws, licking out the last of our last can of butter. Charlotte was such a favourite with us that Vera did not even scold her.

At the end of January Ted came and got Charlotte and the pups, leaving two as was arranged. Vera named them Laddie and Skukum and they turned out to be the best work dogs we ever had. They grew very large, were terrific workers, good packers and both had gentle dispositions. When they were nine months old I hooked them up with the three older dogs and from then on I had a good dog team. They did have a few faults. They were nervous, excitable and noisy. When I went out in the mornings to harness the team, these two would start to whine and bark and jump and tug at their chains in a frenzy to get going. They were so heavy and strong that I was often in a lather when they were all hooked up and ready to go. But that was the way we wanted it. There is nothing worse for a dog drive than to have to drag a protesting dog from his kennel or to have him out of the collar when you slip it over his head. In all my dog driving days I never carried a whip, as the story books have a dog driver do. The pictures show the driver waving a vicious whip at the team, and the fiction speaks of 'the crack of a whip' at every opportunity. As Ted Trindell maintains, and quite rightly, if the team is fed plenty of meat you will not have to whip them to make them go. Indeed, you will have trouble in holding them back. I saw Ted's team drag him a mile once before they would slow down enough to enable him to get on the sleigh. Our team (Laddie and Skukum were always Vera's dogs) used to take great delight in speeding around a corner and throwing me off then waiting with their tails wagging while I picked myself up and shook the snow from the back of my neck. Many times I would be standing on the tail-board resting and dreaming while they trotted along on a good trail. They would smell a fresh moose track or see a fox or a lynx in a trap way ahead. The toboggan would leave my feet and I would find myself flat on my back in the snow. If there was a lynx in a trap I would pick myself up quickly and hasten ahead to find the whole team in a pile with the lynx snarling and slashing and fur flying in all directions. I would grab a 'two hander' as old Boo called a club, and with some well chosen words proceed to break up the melee.

The dogs enjoyed these little set-tos immensely, and nothing I could do would ever break them out of it. In spite of diversions of this sort it was always nice to have a team that was full of pep. When we were hauling a big load and the snow was deep, I would have to break trail ahead with the snowshoes. Laddie would cry and whine in his effort to pull the sleigh up ahead of the other dogs, to be close to my heels. Often the leader would be so crowded he would have to step on my snowshoes and I would go sprawling in the snow. At least I knew they were always there behind me and did not have to call and coax them along. Sometimes the nose of the toboggan would catch on a tree and come to a halt. Then the team would lunge and leap and whine until they broke it loose or pushed over the tree. If they couldn't break it loose I would wade back through the snow and free the sleigh. Then all five would wag their tails, growl quietly, try to lick my hands and crowd in behind me again with Max, the 'wheeler', (the one next the sleigh), and Laddie pulling the whole load for a time. When the trail was good, they would start out in the morning on the dead gallop for a mile or so and it was a problem to hang on.

Toboggans are flat on the bottom and sleighs usually have runners, but throughout our part of the north either of the two words were used and interchanged when speaking of a toboggan. Part of the reason for this seeming ambiguity is that when the weather warmed up in the spring of the year many of us put runners onto the bottom of the toboggans and removed them again the following winter before starting out.

The rearmost dog of a team is probably designated a wheeler because if he is a smart dog he can guide or wheel the toboggan one way or another by throwing his weight to left or right as the case may be. The lazy-board is set up two feet from the rear of the toboggan and ropes are passed from the nose of the sleigh over the lazy board down to loops of raw-hide at the very back. The carry-all of tanned moose skin, a raw-hide or heavy canvas is held in place by the ropes. The space behind the lazy-board is termed the tail-board.

In the bush country the team of up to eight dogs are always strung out one directly ahead of the other, for most of the time the trails are very narrow and wind in and out among the trees. The best harness and tugs are made of latigo leather. The collar is padded and round and just large enough to slip over a dog's head. The collar should be soft and pliable so he will feel comfortable pushing into it all day long. Ted Trindell showed me how to make a home-made collar that was superior to the factory-made ones. It was made from tanned moose-skin and stuffed with chopped moose hair. The whole thing was soft and pliable and was very comfortable for the dog.

To run a successful trapline it was essential to have plenty of dog power. Most of the white trappers fed their dogs well for this reason alone, if for none other. Some of the Indians on the other hand had teams of skinny little half-starved whippets. In starting out they would have to be beaten to get them going. You would swear that they could walk right through their collars. Jack Mulholland would say that you had to line the team up sideways in order to see them at all. We often said that if the S.P.C.A. could see these dogs being so abused, they would have a fit. There were many dogs being treated in this fashion in the whole of northern Canada and people said that the problem was just too big for the S.P.C.A. to handle.

While many people mourn the advent of the snowmobile at least they have taken the place of the dog teams and have pretty well eliminated the suffering of thousands of work dogs.

I think the best dog team I ever saw belonged to Ted Trindell who was an experienced trapper, dog driver and woodsman. He had this team when he was trapping near us on the Long Reach. The leader of this team was Charlotte, and the wheeler was Nigger, a big black German Shepherd, the father of our Laddie and Skukum. He was as round and muscled as a Siberian tiger, was gentle with people and had the energy of a cyclone. The other three dogs of the team were brothers to Laddie and Skukum and were as full of life as they were. In the mornings Nigger would strain at his tie chain and open and close his mouth with loud whines in a frenzy of impatience to go. While the rest were acting in this way Charlotte sat on her haunches with a bored expression on her face and would step daintily to her place in the lead when called. When all were harnessed and Ted snapped the rope loose Charlotte came to life in a burst of speed and was off like a shot, with Ted hanging on to the lazy-board for grim death. Ted's dogs were all pets and he would often romp and play with them.

Some of the dogs in our team were getting old and as soon as we could we raised six pups to take their place. We gave two to Stan and kept four. When they were a year old I took them out one at a time to train them for the sleigh. I would place one pup on the wheel and the older dogs ahead. We would go for a short fast spin on a good trail, but not far enough at one time to tire the pup. After several of these trial runs the pup soon got the idea that whenever he was harnessed to the sleigh it meant he was to get out and go, and not sit around waiting for someone else to start the load moving. Another advantage to this method was that it taught the young dog to untangle himself whenever he got his legs over the trace. A pup will often get himself all mixed up in the harness the first time the team stops. He wants to go off and play or investigate something behind him. When this happens you signal with your voice for the team to take off, at the same time digging your feet in the snow and holding back. The poor puppy then gets flipped over and pulled along backwards or sideways or in whatever position he might be, ki-yi-ing loudly at the pain and indignity. After starting and stopping several times it is amazing how soon he learns to untangle himself. It is a lesson they never forget.

A good many of the dogs in the north were not trained in

this way and it was pathetic to see a so-called dog driver having to run up beside his dogs every time he stopped, to put all their legs back in between the tugs.

In later years when Laddie and Skukum died we had a team of six little dogs that were very fast. The leader was Muggins who was very clever at following a trail in the bush that was blown over with snow, had no bottom or feel to it and was hopeless to find. I don't know what kind of a sixth sense he had but on a hundred miles of trail, if he had every been over it before, he would follow it no matter how obscure it was. He was also pretty smart in other ways. Whenever we set off on a short trip of say ten or twenty miles he was all in favor of it and led off like he had been wanting to go for a long time. But if we started out on a long hard trip, say to Trout Lake, which was a hundred and twenty miles to my outpost there, he would try to turn back and dodge into every rabbit run he came to for the first few miles.

One problem that all dog drivers encounter sooner or later is fighting. Sometimes a team will get along well together and not quarrel or fight at all. This is often true of pups of the same litter that are raised together. But more often than not there will be one or two fighters in a team. Even one belligerent dog is enough to start something, as he can always find another to pick a fight with. Once the fight is well under way the whole team will get involved in the melee. This is most annoying to the driver for if the fight is allowed to continue one or more of the dogs ends up crippled. In all cases the driver cannot afford to lose a dog because every ounce of pulling power is needed. Consequently at the first sign of dissension in the ranks the driver grabs a willow (a whip is of no use here) and charging up among the combatants, lays about him manfully in an attempt to discourage such behaviour, with special emphasis toward the aggressor if possible.

At one of the first fights that Stan and I broke up among old Boo's dog team there was no willow handy and we attempted to dissuade them by pounding them with our fists. Dan and Whisky were engaged in mortal combat and we levelled some very forceful blows to their heads. The blows had little effect and we pulled them apart by sheer force, and jumped on them with our moccasined feet. We nursed our hands in pain while the dogs jumped up wagging their tails as if to say, "That was fun, let's do it again."

There seems to be a percentage of work dogs that love nothing better than a good fight and it is next to impossible to break them of it. When trapping, it is necessary at times to leave the team for a moment to attend to a trap or other things. It is extremely annoying to find on your return a mess of bloody dogs and perhaps one of them limping. One man I know who trapped for some years said that his team got into a fight once where there was no stick handy. He was so furious that he picked up the dog bodily that was the instigator of the row and bit its ear. Any dog driver will know just how he felt and will pardon the odd behavior.

One of the very few times my team got into a scrap occurred when I left them for a time to follow a fresh bear track in early November. The sleigh was snubbed to a tree and the leader was tied to a tree, and I thought they were strung out so they could not reach one another. Anyway they were tired and I assumed they would rest. When I returned in less than an hour two of them had been able to just reach one another and although the harness was not cut, both dogs were covered with frozen blood from head to foot. I was absolutely furious with them even as they wagged their tails and gave low growls to greet me. I felt sure that one or both would be crippled and with winter coming on I needed them badly. All seemed in order however and they trotted on home with no visible limps. In three days the swollen heads were down and things were back to normal.For some time after this I was fearful they would continue the battle and was afraid to turn my back on them when they were in the harness. If I could catch them at the start of a fight before it became serious and indicate to them in a definite manner with some carefully chosen words that I intended to join the fray with a hefty club and well placed blows, they would be deterred long enough for me to reach the scene of action. Then they would try to pretend that it was only some growls and snarls and really nothing further was intended.

Stan got two big pups from us that grew into big strong dogs and he called them Rack and Ruin for a time. Kay took a dim view of these names and they had to be changed. Ruin met with a premature end in some way, while Rack developed into a very good wheel dog. Stan had a team of six and the leader was a big red dog that had yellow slant eyes and could have been part wolf. Red was very gentle with people but he and Rack, (renamed Smoky), hated one another and would get into a scrap at the drop of a hat. This could have ended in death for one or both if a fight had been allowed to continue to a conclusion. They were both good workers and Stan was reluctant to part with either one of them.

One day on the line he happened to catch a glimpse of two caribou off to the side among the trees within rifle range. He was short of meat and the two caribou were just what he needed. He managed to bring the team to a halt, get the rifle from the carry-all and quietly walk to the head of the team to get a better shot. The dogs had not noticed the caribou and Stan felt sure of getting both of them. Stan did not notice Rack pull the load up to get at Red until Red wheeled around to meet the challenge. Stan was caught just below the knees with the harness at the instant he was ready to pull the trigger and found himself floundering on his back in the snow in the middle of flying fur and a snarling mass of fighting dogs. I will leave the rest to your imagination, but Stan came home without the caribou and without big Red.

Dog fights and frozen dog manure on the bottom of the toboggan, which makes the sleigh pull hard and has to be scraped off, are all part of the game to a trapper. The hardship cold weather brings falls into this category also. Oh, sure, you read about fifty below in the Yukon and picture a trapper bundled in furs riding merrily along in the carry-all with six beautiful huskies with tails over their backs galloping along on a well-beaten trail among snow-laden evergreens. At nightfall he miraculously comes upon a large warm cabin with a soft light glowing from the window. He throws the dogs each a frozen salmon and sleeps on a bunk laden with furs and an eiderdown robe. At night he never has to get up shivering to stoke the fire. At dawn he is away on the trail again with a large 'whoop' and a merry whistle. Writers in some fields pride themselves on being realistic but this does not seem to apply to many stories and articles on the Canadian north.

At one time all winter travelling was done by dog team and as might be expected there were good days and bad days. In very cold weather there were very few good days. For one thing toboggans pull very hard when it is forty below or more. The flakes of snow then are like grains of sand, very sharp and jagged. The sleigh moving over them does not melt and smooth the edges, thus there is a maximum of friction and the toboggan pulls like a stoneboat. Five or six dogs pulling a load of two hundred pounds can only go at a walk with many stops during the day. The effort required is that of six horses pulling a gang-plow. The driver must walk and if there has been a wind that has drifted in the trail he must walk ahead of the dogs with his snowshoes to break down the snow and make it easier for the dogs straining at the load behind.

Harry McGurran, who before the advent of aircraft carried the mail in winter from Fort Smith to Fort Providence, told me he would make a return trip each month, a total of six hundred miles. He had a 'forerunner', a young Indian lad who ran ahead of the dogs, and a team of five dogs. The trip was all on the Slave and Mackenzie Rivers and across Great Slave Lake. Harry said he almost never had a broken trail to travel on. He and the forerunner had to wade ahead of the dogs most of the way. The hundred and ten miles of lake surface was blown hard and drifted and they made good time on the lake. Everyone knew that the mail had to come through so they would wait for Harry to break out the trail. He said that once at Providence there were twelve Indian dog teams waiting for him to pass through, and they fell in behind like a bunch of timber wolves following the leader. Many times darkness would find him miles from a cabin or shelter, and the two men would struggle up the river bank some place where there was dry wood for a fire. Then there were two more hours of work to clear away the snow and make camp.

15

Stan has an accident

In January of 1935 when the pups were still small we had only the three adult dogs. The cache was full of fur but there was little food left so a trip to Simpson was in order to sell the fur and bring home a load of groceries. The trail was through the bush and was about seventy miles. The trail was good and I made Simpson in two days. I had a good eiderdown sleeping bag so I was able to stay warm at night in contrast to previous years. The return trip with a load of two hundred pounds was a different story. The weather turned bitterly cold and fell to fifty below. The load was more than the three dogs could handle so I helped them by pushing with a stick. Even down a slope the toboggan would not slide as it would have if it had been warmer. I spent two nights on the trail coming home and it was a slow struggle all the way.

In February I made another trip to Simpson and it was a repetition of the first one. The weather remained very cold and I was away a week. Vera was no happier with the situation than I was. She was alone at this time and apprehensive about what might have happened to me, as I had thought I could make the trip in five days instead of seven. It is actually more of a strain on a person waiting alone than it is for the one out on the trail.

In March the weather did warm up and we were catching a few lynx as well as mink and fox.

We were expecting our first child in May, and had made arrangement for Vera to stay with the Hansens in Fort Simpson and have the baby in the Simpson hospital. This was the Gerald Hansen who had been at Fort Liard when Stan and I arrived there in 1930. Gerald had recently gone back to Holland and brought back a wife. They were trading for the Northern Traders at Simpson.

I borrowed three dogs from Stan and took Vera in to Simpson in the carry-all. Again we spent one night on the portage, and this time the weather was mild and the trip was pleasant. Stan kept the two puppies and our cat while I was away. When I returned Stan said the pups were getting pretty rough. The only place he and the cat were safe was up on the bed.

The morning I set off from Simpson on the journey home it was blowing a gale from the north and it did not abate for three days and nights. The trail that had been a hard-packed rut in the snow was now blown full in places and partly full in others. It was hard to see and follow in the open places and was poor footing for the dogs at all times. I had a load of supplies for Stan and myself and the toboggan would not stay on the trail if I walked ahead, and without me walking ahead to break down the wind-packed snow it was more than the dogs could do to wallow through the snow and pull the load too. In a few places where the timber was large and thick the trail was protected from the wind to some extent and I was able to walk behind and rest, but for the most part I just slogged along ahead and came back to right the sleigh whenever it slipped off the trail. I was three long days in getting home and when we pulled into Stan's cabin we were a sorry and tired bunch, the six dogs and I.

In April I had to go into the mountains on a short prospecting trip. I went as far as the Butte in April and stayed with the Fields a week, then went on up the Nahanni River while the river ice was still safe. Poole had a trading post at Nahanni for some years but had given it up recently. A year before this, Jack Mulholland and Bill Epler moved their headquarters to the Butte and established a trading post. It was the spring of '36 that Bill was lost up the Nahanni and the following year Jack abandoned the post.

While in the bush for the next two weeks I tied up the

three older dogs at night but always let the pups run loose. They followed right at my heels during the day and never strayed away from camp. In the mornings they would be lying as close to me as they could get with their noses pushed inside my bedroll. I built a raft to cross a miserable raging creek one day and the pups unhesitatingly plunged right in behind me. The three older dogs walked up and down the bank of the stream for a long time before getting the courage to swim across.

I arrived back at the Butte the first week in May and stayed with the Fields again until Jack and Bill Epler came along on the way to Simpson with their boat.

Poole was fifty-six years of age at the time and had spent most of his life in the bush. As noted previously, he and Mary had come from the Yukon about ten or twelve years before. He was born in Winnipeg, had gone west as a young man, and found his way to the Klondike in '98. Since then he had trapped, traded and prospected to make a living. He spoke Cree and Slavey fluently, and the Indians told him he was a better woodsman than most. To my mind he was the best. He had been in the R.N.W.M.P. as a young man, and later some claims he staked near Dawson City during the rush turned out quite rich and he was worth a hundred thousand dollars at one time.

When I arrived at their place at the Butte early in May, the ice was still in the big river and I had no way of getting home. I was also completely out of food. Poole and Mary treated me like a long lost son. After we had supper, when we sat talking Poole said, "Mary, dear, do you think perhaps we could have one little jug of wine that we were saving for Bill and Jack?"

Mary laughed and said, "I was thinking the same thing myself." She set upon the table a jug of home-made wine and two glasses. It was very good indeed and was soon gone. Another jug appeared upon the table, and after that I lost count, as Poole and I were deep in a discussion on philosophy. Soon after midnight Mary said, "Well, I am going to bed, there is a kettle of water on the stove and a tub in the kitchen, Dick, if you would like a bath before you go to bed." I suppose I answered something like, "Shanks, Mishus Field, Itsh ullbe no shtrouble at all, I mean shanks for the shtrouble, a bath would shure like me, hic."

I can remember no more of the evening, but I think I had

a bath, because in the morning when Poole went into the kitchen to light the fire I heard him laughing and he was still laughing when he went back into the bedroom and spoke to his wife. "What in hell is so funny?" I thought, feeling my head. I had to see, so I staggered to my feet and went out into the kitchen. The tub of bath water was still in the middle of the floor with a little water left in it, but most, I am afraid, was scattered all over the room. The floor was soaking and there was even water on the table. It was a long time before I lived that down.

The next day Mary said to me, "Dick, your moccasins look pretty well worn out, here is a pair we would like you to have," and she handed me a beautiful pair of moccasins that she had just made.

"Good Heavens," I said, "these are too nice for me, and besides I have no—I mean I can't."

"Don't be silly," Poole said. "We want you to have them, they're yours."

Jack and Bill showed up a few days later and we took leave of the Fields and went on down river. We stopped at Stan's for a day or two and got into Simpson on May 16th, just as the ice was moving out of the MacKenzie. When we pulled in Dr. Truesdell was on the bank to greet us. "You have a daughter, Dick, three days old, they're both doing well."

Over at the Hospital, Vera said, "The doctor has been wonderful, and the sisters are very kind indeed. Do you want to see your daughter?"

When the nurse brought her in, I looked and said, "The poor child, she looks like me, why does she have to look like me?" Vera and the nurse laughed.

"That is what everyone says, but she'll get over it, she might even be handsome some day. She's sweet, isn't she?" We named her Nancy Jane, Nancy for Vera's mother and Jane for mine.

We got home to our cabin with our new baby in July, and during August I got out logs and built an addition on to the house for a bedroom. When that was finished we thought it a good idea to clear some ground for a garden to have ready for planting next spring. The soil seemed suitable for growing vegetables, the only problem was that it was covered with a mass of roots, a layer of moss and numerous trees up to ten inches in diameter. Fortunately there were no stones in the ground and the roots were mostly horizontal in the first eight inches of soil. I had an axe and a round mouth shovel and with that I went to work. It was back-breaking toil.

Our new baby had to be the cleanest baby in the world to go by the amount of water Vera had me carry for her washing and baths, and if the Liard water was a bit too murky she had me carry water from the clear little creek behind the house.

Trapping season rolled around again and I found while fox and lynx were not so plentiful, the marten and mink seemed to be on the increase. Though we had a fair to middling grubstake that year the January trip to Simpson had to be made to ship out the fur before the price dropped, as we were always fearful it would.

I wanted to build a small scow for my kicker and Stan said he would help me whip out some lumber. (Vera excused herself this time.) Stan had some very fine spruce trees near his cabin so we decided to build a pit and cut the lumber there. On April 15th, a fine cool morning, I went across the river to Stan's and we started to prepare the pit, which should by rights be called a platform.

We sharpened our axes to a razor edge and went out to work. We were both chopping away when I heard, "Damn it, Dick, I guess I've done it!" I looked over to Stan and he was on his knees with blood all over the snow. I went over to him, he grabbed my arm and got to his feet and I followed him over to the cabin. He had cut his foot across the bottom over half an inch deep and was bleeding like a stuck pig. In the cabin he took off his moccasins and socks, and I said, "How about sewing it up?"

After a minute Stan said, "We have no sterilized needle or thread and it might get infection in it. I think we had better bandage it up tight and hope for the best." This I did, with what white cloth I could find. Round and round, over and over, but it still bled. He lay on the bed with his foot tied to the ceiling, but it still bled, drip-drip-drip, through the bandage and into a basin. Eventually it did stop and we let the foot down, but what a mess. "What a hell of a time of the year for this to happen," I thought. "To get him to Simpson to the doctor now would be a real problem. The trail through the bush is out, and the ice through the rapids will be rough with lots of open water."

Around supper time I went home to let Vera know the

situation and then went back to check on Stan. Two days later we took off the bandages. The wound had stopped bleeding but the gash was wide open and the foot was swollen. We soaked it in salt water and wrapped it tightly again. Day by day it did not seem to improve and looked dark and ugly.

Stan had previously planned a beaver hunt with John Norgaard who had trapped the last winter with Ole Lindberg. About this time John came down from Lindberg's by dog team, set out some beaver traps on the creeks and helped me whip out the lumber for the boat. On April 25th John and I moved Stan over to our place. The cut still looked bad. The foot was swollen but so far there was no sign of serious infection. We held a conference that night and considered trying to take him to Simpson on the river ice. By morning Stan had decided not to attempt the trip by dogteam as it was possible that we might not have been able to get through the rapids, with the breakup coming soon. John was game though and would have gone with me. The next day John slugged home through the water and we settled down to wait for open water and hoped the foot would get no worse. In the meantime I worked on the boat.

By May 10th the ice was out and piled high along the shores. The foot was no worse. The swelling had gone down some but the cut still was dark and wide open. Instead of going to town right away, Stan decided to go up to Art George's in the boat with me to meet our brother Fred and Harry Vandale and Milt Campbell. Vera and Nancy went along as far as Lindberg's and stayed with Anna. It was not until the end of May that Stan got into Simpson and to the doctor.

Stan and I picked up John and Ole and went on to Art George's cabin to meet Milt, Harry and Fred who were coming in by scow from Fort Nelson with a placer washing outfit.

It had been known for a number of years that there was flour gold off the gravel bars of the Liard River. Lately the bars had been checked and some bars were found between Liard and Nahanni that seemed to be worthwhile working. My brother, Fred, with Milt and Harry, built a scow and with two small kickers brought in a load of supplies—pump, engine, hose, iron rods for grizzlys, food, gasoline and oil and tents. With three other trappers they planned to get working as soon as the river dropped enough to expose the sandbars. They were able to commence in early August; they would work one bar then move the camp upstream to the next one and so on. A pan of gravel taken from the right place would show a good streak of gold, but the stuff was so thin it would almost float and it took a good lot to make an ounce. At the end of a day they took the black-sand with the gold dust, and with the use of mercury, separated the gold. At the end of the season the gold bannocks (the residue after the mercury was burned off) were sent to the bank, and the total vaue was seven hundred and fifty dollars; about ten cents an hour each for their time. It was not nearly enough to pay for their equipment so the operation was terminated.

It was at this time that Stan and Harry Vandale got the search underway for Bill Epler and Joe Mulholland.

A year or two later Vera and I saw enough nuggets and coarse gold reported to have been taken from the upper Liard to make our eyes pop. Two prospectors who were strangers to us stopped at our cabin overnight on their way to Simpson. After supper they produced a one pound baking powder can and a two pound jam can both full of gold nuggets. There must have been three or four pounds of the stuff. It was the real goods all right, no doubt of that. The men said they got the gold from the streams at the head of the Liard.

It is said that gold is where you find it. We did not enquire too deeply into the matter. In the morning they left for Simpson and we heard no more of them. In the north you don't go poking into other people's business: if they wish to volunteer any information that is well and good, but if not you let the matter drop. Anyone who is too nosey gets short shrift.

Eventually the beaver season was opened to white trappers to a limit of fifteen the same as for others, and a special permit was required each year by each trapper before he could take or sell beaver pelts. The issuing of the permits and the stamping of each and every beaver pelt was in the hands of the R.C.M.P. To be eligible for a permit one had to be the holder of a general hunting licence and the head of a family or a widow depending on hunting for a livelihood. This seemed at least half fair at first glance but what happened was this: some trappers and many native widows would get a permit and not bother to hunt beaver at all. Some couldn't and some wouldn't. So it became a general practice to sell a permit to the highest bidder. The game authorities must have known what was going on but seldom if ever prosecuted an offender. They reasoned, I believe, that those who would not or could not hunt beaver got a good chunk of the value of the fifteen pelts anyway which they would not have if the bootlegging had not been in vogue.

What it meant to a full time trapper was that he had to get about forty-five pelts to equal the price of thirty. It also meant that you had to cache the pelts you had in excess of the amount of fifteen. You never knew when someone would squeal on you or more likely some game authority would get the idea to make an example out of one of us. I had reason to suspect that I might be a candidate for such an office, so I took great care to keep any surplus beaver pelts well hidden. As stated above all beaver pelts had to be stamped with a spiked steel mallet by the R.C.M.P. before they could be offered for sale.

Beaver are much harder to trap than most other animals and some knowledge and experience must be gained before a man becomes a successful beaver hunter. After a year or two of trial and error and some instruction I became fairly proficient at it. After you know the technique it is just a matter of getting out and working very hard. When the ice is on you have to cut many holes through two feet of ice and sticks, making sure the holes are in the right place. In open water you have to travel many miles, often carrying all your supplies and equipment on your back. Some of the beaver creeks are a mess of windfalls, thick willows and bogs. In the afternoons and evenings the mosquitoes are out in force. When you get a beaver you cannot leave it unguarded for a moment for fear a black bear might sneak off with it.

16

Hardships of winter

The worst feature of dog team winter travel was without doubt the necessity of 'camping out' on a cold night, and I am thinking of the nights I spent out in the open at fifty-five and sixty below. There is not always a cabin handy to spend a warm night and it is often not practical to carry a canvas tent and a stove with your. While a big roaring fire of dry logs and trees make it bearable while drying the moisture and snow from parka and moccasins and while preparing and eating supper you must sleep and the fire soon goes out. After many hours of terrific exertion encountered during the day the body must rest and eight hours sleep is mandatory.

Even the best bedroll is none too warm on a sixty below night in the open. And if you have little or no bedding you are indeed in a bad way; you can but sleep for a half hour or so and then jump up and build the fire up again. Inside the best of eiderdowns it is never too warm on a bitterly cold night. If you have had a good hot meal before going to bed you might sleep warm for three or four hours but long before it is time to get up you turn, squirm and shiver, making sure the robe and tarpaulin are tucked tightly all around. The you huff and puff in an effort to get enough oxygen.

Very often someone (you hope it is your partner) has to get up to answer the call of nature, and a roaring fire must be made to warm up before going back to bed. A few nights in succession of camping out in the extreme cold and you feel as if you had been pulled through three knot holes and poked in the eye with a sharp stick.

Once Raymond George and I travelled on the Mackenzie River for two days in bitter cold, trotting behind the dogs all day and barely able to keep from freezing solid. I had a woolen balaclava over my head under my parka hood and even then froze my mouth and chin a little. Raymond pinned a blanket over and around his head. On arriving in Simpson we were told it was sixty-two below with a twenty mile an hour wind. We both felt glad we didn't know how cold it was when we set out.

Coming home from Simpson one winter at New Years an Indian and I camped out in the bush one night and found later that it had been sixty-eight below that night. It was bad enough to be driving dogs at this temperature but to have to camp out is a bit too much. During the day we had found it difficult to stay warm even bundled up as we were, wearing everything we owned and walking. A fog from the dog's breath hung over continually and crossing the lake or a slough the fog was so thick I could barely see the lead dog. I had heard that both men and dogs would freeze their lungs in such weather, but neither we nor the dogs were bothered by this respect although we made a point of not hurrying but just kept plodding along. The first night was fifty-five below and we were able to camp in a tent with a stove in it. The inside of the tent was coated with a thick rim of frost all the time even though the stove was going full blast, but it was warmer than outside and with all our clothes on we were comfortable. During those two days the small spruce trees that we cut down for brush for a camp would shatter in our hands at the first blow of an axe.

We were on the trail the next morning before daylight hoping to make the forty miles home by night. It got colder during the day and with the heavy loads and the slow progress we soon knew that we would have to camp out another night. We halted at noon as usual to build a fire, get warmed up, gulp some hot tea and food, (stew warmed up in a fry pan), and home-made biscuits thawed before the fire.

About four in the afternoon it was dark and I noticed that Billy's team was not behind me as he had been all day. When he caught up to me he said that he had just about frozen his feet and had stopped to build a fire.

I was having a difficult time to stay warm myself, and knew this was a night we would need lots of firewood. At six o'clock I stopped at the place I had in mind and started to make camp. Billy came along a few minutes later. After spending twenty minutes at shovelling away the snow for a camp, we felt that the weather was warming up. This was pure self-deception as we felt warm only from the exertion. The full moon was out, the air was very still, fog hung around us from our breath and the touch of a dog chain felt like fire to a bare hand. Our mitts were off very little that night, even while cooking, eating and sleeping we kept them on. We were able to fell several big dry trees over the spot where we wanted the fire, dragged in some more, split kindling and got the fire going. The flames were six feet across and four feet high but we had to keep turning around before the fire to stay warm. The frozen fish for the dogs we put beside the fire would thaw on one side and freeze again when turned over. We finally got some tea and hot food inside us without either burning or freezing our hands. It was nine o'clock when we finished eating and rolled out the eiderdowns with a tarp tucked under and over them and wondered if we would be warm enough to sleep. Billy, an old hand at winter travelling, had insisted we scrape away all the snow right down to the moss and put down a good bed of spruce boughs. Because of this we were able to sleep for six hours. We both woke up at three. I called to Billy and suggested we both get up before we became too cold. We hopped from the robes and felled and dragged in some trees to warm us before the fire got going. We were in a comfortable state after we got some coffee and food inside us, and were on the trail again well before six. I was home by noon and Billy went on to his cabin eight miles farther.

I saw Stan as I passed his cabin and he said it was sixty-five below at noon. Our own mercury was right down in the bulb and we knew it must be chilly.

Camping out in such weather is strictly for the polar bears. If a man is alone one mistake could mean disaster for him. On this trip Billy told me that some time before he had got a real scare when camping alone somewhere near Bischo Lake in northern Alberta. He was travelling with a dog team when it got dark, and he was tired and could go no farther. It was useless to go on as there was no shelter within forty miles. It was bitterly cold and he was chopping at a tree to make a fire when his axe-handle broke and the blade of the axe went spinning off in the snow. "By God, it was cold." Billy said, "I just had to find that axe, it was pitch dark and I was cold without a fire. If I couldn't get one started I would be dead cold. I scratched around in the snow for a good two hours searching for that axe head. Feeling for it was what I did for I could not see a thing in the dark. I did find it at last, but I was sure scared before I found it."

"What did you do for a new handle?" I said.

"I chopped one out of a birch stick," he replied, "then burned out the old axe handle."

Billy convinced me that he had been near to panic and thought he would have frozen to death without a fire.

Poole Field told me once that he might on occasion leave his rifle behind but never his axe.

Thinking of the scare that Billy had brings to mind a question that is often asked of me and others that live in the bush. The question is, "Have you ever been brought close to fear when alone in the bush?"

The occasions are rare but they do happen. Fright I would say is fairly frequent; fear would be rare and if fear results in panic then the chances of survival are limited.

One time when I was crossing the Liard in an old rotten canoe and a strong wind came up, I think I was near to panic. I had bought a canoe at Fort Liard for two dollars. It was pretty rotten and had not been used for many years, but it was all I could afford and I thought it would get me down to the cabin on the Long Reach where our good canoe was. I stuck a little tar on the rotten canvas so the contraption would float, then lay an old board or two on the bottom and bent in some willows to keep them in place. I had very little in way of a load anyway and the thing floated well enough if I bailed constantly. The river was in flood and the sandbars were covered. At the head of the Long Reach a breeze had blown up and I thought I should cross right away before the waves got any bigger. So I headed across.

The river here is well over half a mile wide, and as I was quartering the waves in a head wind I was slow in getting across. When I was halfway over the wind increased and I started to get into whitecaps and waves four feet high. A wind on a swift-flowing river does strange things and the waves were close and choppy with no regularity. The shore looked to be too far away for comfort, and the one behind me was farther yet. Right then I thought I had bought the farm. There was no way that old canoe should have held together. It should have broken in two the first big roller I encountered. All I could do was to keep quartering the waves and bail with one hand every few strokes of the paddle. Then for some odd reason I hit a calm circular patch of water. Immediately I swung the canoe to quarter the wind. I could feel the movement of the waves become less violent as I went with them. I knew then I might make it and soon I was near shore where the water was far less violent. My throat was dry and I gulped water from the bailing can. I was so scared that for three days I could not get over my good fortune at having escaped drowning.

Another time I fell out of a canoe at Trout Lake in the mouth of a river while looking at a fish net. It was the October 14th and snowing. There was a freezing wind and I was dressed in heavy clothes with moccasins and rubbers. It was a small canoe, twelve feet long, and very narrow. It was hardly big enough for a small dwarf, let alone a grown man.

I reached out too far for a big fish in the net and I was in the water just like that. The first thing I thought of before I started to struggle was stories I had been told by fisherman of men falling overboard; the buttons of their clothes get caught in the net and the more they struggle the quicker they drown.

I was floating pretty high and I thought I would move very slowly and if I was caught in the net I would get out my pocket knife and cut the damned thing away. On moving carefully I found I was free of the net and foolishly took time to try to right the canoe which was upside down. I thought I could roll the water out and get aboard. Thirty seconds was wasted in this futile effort, then I gave up and headed for shore. Fortunately I had not far to swim, possibly two hundred feet, but I found my arms and leg movements getting slow and sluggish as I pulled myself onto shore. Then I discovered I was on an island and there was one narrow channel to swim to get to the mainland. Thankfully I found the water was shallow and I only had to swim the last few feet.

208

Dragging myself up the steep bank was a bit of a task as my legs were refusing to move. The cabin was half a mile away and I trotted along as soon as my legs would function again. My outside clothes were soon frozen stiff in the cold wind but the inside of my body was fairly warm. Once inside the cabin I wasted no time in getting a fire going. Stripping off my clothes and getting into dry ones I noticed my skin was beet red. "Better red than dead," I thought, but I did not laugh too loud or too long.

Another fright I had of a different sort happened one spring when I was hunting beaver. Our youngest child, Martha, was five years old and was always wanting to go with her dad on a trip as the older children did. So this time I took her with me on a two day beaver hunt. I had her sit in the canoe, right up in the bow where she could not fall out and would not be in the way. We were on a small river; it was nine o'clock and getting dusk. I shot at a beaver, missed it and had to chase it for some time before I got a shot at it again. Eventually I got it and heaved it into the canoe. By now it was long past her bedtime and Martha was sound asleep. It was no use to wake her, I would paddle back to camp and call it a day.

We drifted along quietly for a few minutes. I looked at my watch. It was eleven o'clock! No wonder it was getting dark, no wonder she had fallen asleep. The shooting of the small rifle was a common noise to her and she had slept right through it. But I had not realized it was so late. I glanced at the dead beaver. Funny how different things look in the dark. I thought I had set the beaver in the middle of the canoe and now it seemed to be farther toward the bow. I kept my eyes on it. "My God! It's moving, it's crawling toward the child. It's not dead, only stunned, it's head is now only a foot from the child!"

I recalled Carl Arhus saying a beaver had bitten right through his hand in one last dying effort. I knew a beaver could cut off a tree the size of the girl's leg in a few swift chop, chop, chops, faster than you can say it. By now I had a grip on Mr. Beaver's tail and noticed that his head was now right between her feet. I pulled but could not budge him. I pulled some more, I braced my feet and with both hands I pulled, and still he would not come. He was holding on to something for grim death and wouldn't give an inch. I dared not release my grip for an instant for fear he might swing his head over and bite the child's leg. With one hand I must manage somehow to kill it. I ruled out trying to shoot it and the paddle was the only other thing I had. I got the paddle in one hand and by jabbing straight down I was able to kill the poor beast.

We had been drifting down stream all this time and were now near our camp. I woke up Martha, took her to the tent and came back down for the beaver. He was stone dead all right, but his jaws had a grip on one of the ribs of the canoe that I simply could not release. His teeth were sunk into the rib and when I eventually yanked him free, two chunks of rib came away in his mouth. When I went to bed, after a cup of coffee to steady my nerves, I was still wondering how I would have released his grip if he had bitten into Martha's leg instead of a rib of the canoe.

Another time I was very badly scared was during the second year of trapping on the Long Reach. I was about twenty miles out from home cutting trail in the bush, toward the end of the moose rutting season. I had a pack on my back and one pack dog with me. It was snowing just a little with a skiff of snow on the ground. The trail led through some scattered bushes in a muskeg at the edge of a small lake. I could see there were some very fresh moose tracks on the trail when the dog became excited and looking over in the bush I saw a bull moose standing not more than fifty yards away. There was another behind him partly obscured by some small spruce.

I had not seen many moose at this time but knew that there was something odd about this one. One antler appeared to droop toward the ground in a singular manner. It had either been broken recently or had grown in that strange position. H is head was lowered to the ground, his ears, which are normally very prominent on a moose, were laid back and he looked to be in an ugly mood. For all my inexperience I felt that here was a situation that had all the earmarks of having unpleasant consequences.

There, obviously, stood a beast that looked as if he had been in a scrap recently, who still was in a bad humor and seemed anxious to meet anyone more than halfway who wished to challenge him. I had only a .22 rifle with me, one that shot in circles and was of less use than a pea shooter. If there had been any possible way of doing so, I would have conveyed to him the certainty that I had no intention of disputing his territory or the right to his harem or in fact anything at all he wished to dispute, and would order an immediate and abrupt withdrawal of all forces at my command.

This last I did indeed proceed to effect in a summary manner. In other words, I got the hell out of there with as much speed and dispatch as could be mustered. Fortunately my lone pack dog was of the same mind and in less than ten seconds we were far away and making good yardage. In the distance I saw a large dry poplar tree, and perched on a limb twenty feet from the ground was where I fervently wished to be right then. I stood at the bottom of the tree for several minutes listening intently for the bad old moose to come crashing through the bush. If a squirrel had moved in the bush about then I would have been up that tree and on the branch in one leap. However all was quiet and peaceful and I continued on toward the house, hoping the bull moose would be taken up with other activities more worthy of his time than molesting a poor defenseless trapper.

That was one of only two mad moose I have ever seen. It was a miracle he did not come at me with feet flying. I could only have made two jumps before he would have had me ground to a pulp in the muskeg.

Afterward I called that lake, Teepee Lake because of some burned spruce that had fallen together in the form of a teepee. That winter about Christmas I was coming home again, this time wearing snowshoes and following behind my dog team. Well, a one-dog team to be truthful. If one dog can't be a team then I was following behind my dog. Anyway, I had this one dog harnessed to a toboggan, and I was crossing Teepee Lake and pushing on the toboggan with a stick to avoid coming to a complete halt. Other times I walked ahead pulling with a rope. Mostly I preferred the going behind method, as when going in front, on looking around I would observe my dog riding. Yes, riding, he was a smart dog. I did not mind him riding so much, why should I? It made no difference to the pulling. Then he took to dragging his feet which made the pulling a bit harder. Finally I looked around and he was curled up on the sleigh sound asleep. I immediately went to him, lifted him upon his feet and placed him on the trail ahead of the load.

"Old dog," I said, "in this world and at this particular time and place, we must all pull our weight," then took up a position behind.

Stan would say, "What the hell you got that stupid dog

for? He never works, all you do is push him."

Now you know the old saying, "Love me, love my dog." No one likes to have anyone make fun of his dog. Although he was a useless mutt I had to defend him.

"I have him to make a trail for me." I replied. "That's it, the sleigh makes a trail for me and he pulls the sleigh."

"He pulls what?" said Stan. "You're pushing the sleigh yourself most of the time, and the rest of the time you're pulling it."

"So what, so what, it makes a good trail, and besides he is a very fine dog, look at the nice tail he has, did you ever see such a nice tail?"

"Oh, Harrumph," said Stan.

We had just crossed the lake on this cold winter morning when I looked back and saw six black timber wolves scooting along the shore parallel to the trail, and acting a bit strange, I thought. They seemed to crouch low on their bellies, then go like hell, then stop again.

I still carried that .22 rifle that shot in circles. It was somewhat similar to the dog; it looked like the real thing but was not too serviceable. I did not feel brave enough to stop and join the battle with those six black monsters and judged the next best thing to do was put on a bold front. So I shouted at them with the manliest voice I could muster, interspersed with descriptive adjectives that came to mind.I threatened all sorts of dire consequences if they dared to come a step closer. Then I turned and departed homewards as swiftly as possible banging on the sleigh with a stick and whistling whenever I could find enough breath.

I had lunch at the cabin on top of the ridge and then headed out on the last lap of ten miles to home. It was rarely I caught a pelt that winter (I should have stood in bed for all the good I did). The few traps I had along the trail were all in good working order and needed no attending to so I plodded right along.

It was almost dark when, still about two miles from the river, I gave the toboggan a bang with the pushing stick to stir my old dog along. I wondered what button I had pushed, for there arose behind me and off to the right the most blood curdling chorus of howls you would ever expect to hear. It sounded as if forty wolves were within sixty feet of me and all of them intent on scaring me to death. I began to give them the same verbal treatment I had given at Teepee Lake that morning, but somehow what I had in mind did not emerge from my lips in an overly confident manner and I decided to save my breath for more effective action.

"Lad," I said to my dog, "this is no place for a God fearing Christian, nor is it any place for me. Let us herewith instantly and hastily depart." And would you believe it, new life came into that old dog's limbs and into my own legs and we took off like a hired man toward the dinner bell.

I do not know if the last bunch of wolves were the same ones I had seen at Teepee Lake or not, if they had improper designs on my flesh or if they were chasing a moose or merely having a bit of fun at my expense. They did sound to me rather unfriendly. I found it uncomfortable running north and looking south, but finally made it to the warm light of the cabin and Stan's gruff voice seemed even kindly, and I almost embraced him.

17

Harry's adventure

We had not been in the north for many years before the writing was on the wall signifying the approaching demise of the dog team era. Aircraft were making scheduled mail runs from Edmonton north to the delta. In summer time the aircraft were equipped with floats and in the winter the floats were exchanged for skiis. There were two air services operating: Canadian Airways and Mackenzie Air Service. Both were started and operated by returned airmen from the first World War.

Vera and I were expecting our second child in March or April and in January we got Archie McMullan to land at our cabin with his big Bellanca and pick up Vera and Nancy and fly them out to Edmonton, and on to my folks in Calgary. Archie took them as far as Fort Smith and Wop May (of World War I fame) took them on from there with a Wacco.

After Vera and Nancy left, the cabin seemed desolate and lonely. I had to stay out of the house and keep busy every day to keep from going nuts.

Early in April my sister sent us a message by the C.B.C. Northern Messenger which was as follows—"Donald James born March thirty, both doing splendidly." So now we had a son. There were four of us now.

In June I went to Simpson to await the return of my family. Early in June Stan MacMillan flew them in from Edmonton. On his arrival he said to me, "Did I bring the right ones?"

I looked them over carefully and replied, "No, it is a different bunch than went out, but I guess they will do." Nancy was not yet two and had been away for six months but came to me quite willingly when I stepped on the floats of the aircraft to greet them.

We stayed in a cabin in Simpson for a month before going home to the Long Reach. With Stan and his wife Kay and John Norgaard and his wife Rose we gathered our supplies together and with two scows and kickers we set off up the Liard again to our homes.

Stan and John Norgaard had just returned from Edmonton and Calgary where each of them had got married and brought their brides north to their trap lines.

In June Harry Vandale and Alf Lewis arrived in Simpson from above the falls on the Nahanni River. Harry of course had been in the country for several years, and had trapped in the Nahanni before. Alf was a young man from Alberta who had always wanted to see the Nahanni and now had seen all and more than he cared to see and was headed back outside at the earliest opportunity.

Harry had gone into Rabbit Kettle Lake the fall previously to trap marten for the winter, with the intention of coming out by aircraft before break-up. Alf, who was a neighbor of the Vandales in Alberta, flew into Nahanni in January and got a ski-equipped aircraft to fly him into Harry's camp. Harry had only a tent at his base camp at Rabbit Kettle, he had no idea that Alf was coming, and he was away on his line at the time. Alf unloaded his stuff anyway and made himself at home, to await Harry's return. He knew that Harry had no dogs, was back-packing on the line and kept watch up the trail every day for his return.

The day that Harry did show up, Alf said at first he thought it was a grizzly. Harry's eyes peered out from a tremendous patch of beard, his hair was long, he was bent over with a pack upon his back and he was covered with frost and snow. It was Harry all right, but a different looking Harry from the one he had last seen in Alberta dressed up and swinging his heels at a dance. Harry said that Alf's eyes bugged out about a foot.

They put in the rest of winter trapping, and by March their food supply was running low. One big sack of supplies that Alf had brought in with him and that he thought was food, turned out to be clothes and other personal items belonging to Daisy, Jack Mulholland's wife, that had somehow been put aboard the airplane by mistake in place of the bag of groceries.

As time wore on and the days got warmer Harry decided to build a raft and float down to the Butte. It was a hundred miles to the falls where they would have to portage and build another raft below. The Nahanni was very high that year with driftwood running continuously. They fully expected to get game, moose for sure, as they were drifting down the river. But as so often happens, when you need meat badly, luck seems to run against you, and they saw nothing. They portaged the falls and went on below for several miles to find timber to build another raft. They had a pack each with their food and clothing, axe and gun, a sack containing Harry's hard-earned marten and lynx pelts and the sack of Daisy's clothing, which Harry said he felt obliged to bring along; altogether they had more than enough to carry. By the time they built the second raft the river had risen more than ever with the amount of driftwood increasing every day. Harry had never seen the river so high. With the waves and rollers they must navigate the raft was continually awash with water, cold, muddy water. In consequence everything was at all times wet, including the sack of fur and the bundle of Daisy's clothing. If they had stopped to dry things out, all would have been soaking again after hitting the first wave. There was nothing for it but to keep on going as they were getting very short of food.

The river was in such a swift and turbulent state Harry felt apprehensive about running George's Riffle. (In high water the Riffle is spelled with a capital R.) They pulled ashore at Dry Canyon in Dead Man's Valley and walked down along the mountain edge to have a look at it. The water was black, the foam was grey and it looked like a boiling mass of trees and logs going through that they could hear slamming into the cutwall at the foot of the Riffle.

Harry said they were both thankful they were seeing it from above and not from aboard the raft. Without another word they went back to the raft, crossed to the far side of the stream, and let the raft go. Hungry or not, they chose to walk through the bush and over the hills instead of trying to run the canyon. The walk of twelve or fifteen miles to the foot of the canyon was going to be no fun at all so they looked over their load to see what they could leave behind to lighten their packs. The sack of fur was heavy with water. They dumped it out on the ground. Every pelt was slimy with rotting tissue and river mud. Daisy's clothes were examined. They were wet but otherwise O.K. Harry still could not bring himself to throw them away so into their packs they went.

Harry told me through all the adversity they had met with thus far, Alf struggled to stay cheerful and optimistic, but after pushing through the bush and fighting off the numerous mosquitoes that assailed them, he felt a head of steam was building up. During one of the stops to rest and ease their shoulders, Alf dug into his pack to get out a pair of leather gloves he had been guarding jealously on the journey thus far. Harry moved away a few steps when various items began to appear from the pack with somewhat more emphasis than was necessary. After a few tense moments Alf straightened up with one glove in his hand, threw his cap to the ground and with an emotionally charged voice gave vent to an opinion that had been gathering force for some days. "It seems," he said, "a man is not supposed to have a God damned thing in this blankety blank, miserable blankety blank, cursed blankety blank, useless, good for nothing country. You can take the Nahanni River and the falls and Dead Man's Valley and George's Riffle and this bush and these blankety blank mosquitoes and put them in such a direction, such a position, in such a place, and I hope to never see them again." End of quote.

Harry assumed from this outburst that one glove had been left behind and Alf felt one glove only was not sufficient to meet the requirement which, in this case, was to keep the mosquitoes off and protect his hands from rose thorns. In telling about it, Harry said Alf's dissertation emerged with such clarity, calmness and oratorical fervor that he, Harry, was about to applaud, but thought better of it.

Glove or no glove, they eventually fought their way through the bush to the foot of the canyon, built another raft and arrived at the Butte a day later. Poole and Mary Field were away, Jack Mulholland was also gone and the only person at Nahanni was Daisy. She did not seem too happy about the state of the clothes the boys returned to her, but made them a cup of tea anyway. Daisy said that perhaps they should not stay to the night as she was alone. Harry blinked his eyes and looked at her incredulously and said nothing. They borrowed a small canoe from an Indian and with one glove yet, paddled the fifteen miles up the Liard to Netla. Old Boo made them welcome and a fresh pot of booyaw tasted very good. That was Harry's tale as told to an appreciative audience in our cabin in Simpson.

In late August, with Stan and Kay, we were once more back at our cabins on the Long Reach. Our cabin now had two rooms. I later built on another two rooms and we then had a four room house.

During these later years on the Long Reach we had a very good team of dogs. We added to the supply of traps each year, cut more trail to extend the line, built more cabins and eventually ended up with a man-sized trapline.

Beaver season was open at this time to May 20 so we could take them in open water. Then the regulations were abruptly changed again to restrict the season to one month only in the middle of winter, and the limit cut to ten. Marten were restricted in the middle of winter, and the limit cut to ten. Marten were restricted to two on one side of the river and fifteen on the other. (Naturally everyone trapped both sides, or at least said they did.) This was after a new Game Department was set up to advise on game regulations and administer same. This was a good idea in itself if it had been conceived with any degree of intelligence. To all of us who lived in the bush and whom the game regulations concerned most vitally it truly seemed the regulations were formed in complete ignorance of the reasons for fur and game cycles, and also a thorough and complete disregard of the welfare of those most concerned, the trappers themselves. There was no sport hunting in the Territories at that time and the only people who took wild game, moose, caribou and fur bearing animals in particular, were the trappers.

In our opinion some of the bright ideas concerning the restrictions came from wide-beamed chair warmers in Ottawa who supposedly had some degree of academic education, but whose ignorance of conditions in the bush, including the reasons for the fluctuation of animal population, was colossal. More than this, they proved they had no concern whatever for the settlers, both Indian and white, who lived in the bush. For example, two regulations were introduced in the early forties prohibiting the use of snares for the purpose of catching animals (rabbits were excepted). The Indians had used snares for catching animals long before the white man arrived on the scene and it was puzzling for them to hear that it was forthwith prohibited. Also for a time the regulations prohibited the killing of all moose with the exception of one male moose to the holder of a General Hunting Licence who was also the head of a family. The Indians have traditionally been strictly meat-eating people and moose meat is the principal item of their diet in this vast area.

Several years later when Government biologists began going into the field to study wildlife, one of them told me they simply did not have enough information and knowledge to formulate a definite hypothesis as to what caused the fluctuations of different species of wildlife. They suspected that it depended on such factors as the available food supply, climatic conditions, disease and predators. Wildlife biologists for many years could not definitely say how large a part man, as a predator, played in the control of wildlife species in the sparsely settled areas of Northern Canada. Caribou was the one exception. They felt fairly sure the high powered rifle in the hands of irresponsible hunters was playing havoc with the migrating herds of caribou.

How then, with such careless abandon, could officials in Ottawa or Fort Smith be justified in formulating restrictive legislation that practically took the food from a trapper's mouth, purely on the basis of hypothetical conclusions?

The answer I think is twofold. Firstly, these people in the Game Department were drawing, I assume, substantial salaries and possibly felt they should do something to earn their money even if it were the wrong thing.

Secondly, it was felt that certain species of fur bearing animals were being depleted. What could be simpler than to restrict the hunting of them by trappers? Whites especially, if possible. Indians were wards of the government and their welfare would be taken care of in any eventuality. If the white men were discouraged from trapping so much the better; there were too many of them anyway. They trapped too intensely and left little fur for the natives.

A few things were forgotten. One was that any legislation that is generally felt to be overly restrictive and unjust by those concerned is extremely difficult to enforce. This should be obvious in regard to game regulations in an extremely sparsely settled area such as the Territories were at that time.

Another point is that natives as well as whites were being hurt, and along with whites and Metis, protested. A third point is that the trappers, both native and white, were savages. Whatever color of skin they happened to have, they wanted the same things from life as others who were engaged in perhaps more congenial activities.

Stan and I followed the progress of the restrictive game laws partly because we had been politically oriented since our childhood and took an interest in all public affairs, international, national and local, but mostly because trapping was our bread and butter and the regulations concerned us vitally. Consequently we were vociferous in our opposition to the current game laws. We became unpopular in certain quarters and among people who had only heard our opinions second hand.

About this time we started to send outside for our supplies and had them come north on the Hudson's Bay Company's barge. One or more of the traders complained about this, thinking we should buy our goods from them. I applied for a trading permit and got one and have bought all our supplies wholesale ever since. One evening I had all my goods piled in front of my tent in Simpson ready to load the next day for the trip home. One of the young R.C.M.P. constables came along to sit and chew the fat for a minute. He was a very decent chap, but sharp of eye. He noticed a roll of fifty feet of one inch steel cable that I had neglected to cover up, among my freight. Other trappers were sitting with us. The constable looked at the cable and said, "Say, Dick, what in the name of heaven are you going to do with that tremendous chunk of cable?"

I just about fell over. "Christ, Turner," I thought "when will you smarten up? You are stupid to leave that moose snare cable right out in plain sight."

"What cable?" I said, "oh, that bit of cable, well, mmmmm, uuuu, well, Andy, you see that boat of mine is so darned heavy and water-logged I am continually breaking the rope when I pull it out each fall, so I thought I would get something that would hold for once." (The cable was big enough to pull the paddlewheeler *Distributor* out of the water.) Noting the size of the cable again I felt I had to keep talking. "I ordered quarter inch cable, and they sent me three-quarter inch," (It was one inch cable that I had ordered and received) "but I guess it will do," I added lamely.

The other trappers helped me out. "Oh yes, yes," they said, "rope will never hold a boat the size Turner has, you have to use the cable. This is really not too big, it should hold all right."

I had to get the subject changed but quickly, and then get out of town with that boat-pulling cable.

That winter in December who should come along to our cabin one night on the R.C.M.P. dog patrol but the same Andy. After supper we sat talking and smoking and Andy said, "By the way, Dick, did that cable hold without breaking, when you pulled your boat out last fall?" He laughed so hard I was afraid he would choke. I swallowed twice then joined him in laughter.

"Yes," I replied, "it stretched a wee bit, but it held all right." He knew the situation completely and no other explanation was called for.

At this time I was running a line of a hundred and twenty miles in the form of a circle or loop. Although I had four of the best sleigh dogs in the country, still and all it was a hard gruelling trip to make every ten days or so; usually five days around the line and five days home. I could not possibly have done it if I had not had dog food cached on the line.

My sister Donata who had come in from Calgary in August to stay the winter, was visiting us that year, and we persuaded her to baby sit for us while Vera went on one trip with me over the line. It was February, the days were lengthening and the weather was not cold. Our load consisted of thirty pounds of meat for the dogs, our grub box, bed roll, axe, gun, two pair of snowshoes and packsack with spare clothes, etc. I said we would try and make the trip in four days if we did not get a storm. We took off on the trail through the bush to the first cabin at Birch River, sixteen miles down river, before daybreak in the morning. We took turns riding on the sleigh and walking behind. The dogs, as always, kept up a fast trot, until we hit Birch River and the one of us walking behind had to step right out to keep up.

At Birch River we turned South toward the high country and the head of the Blackstone River. It was all lynx country we passed through to this point and so far no lynx had been caught although one or two had passed by the pens but had not been enticed to the bait. At two in the afternoon we stopped at the twelve mile cabin to brew a pot of tea and have lunch. The dogs were getting weary by now and were glad to lie down, lick the hard packed snow from between their paws and rest.

A mile past the cabin I noticed the dogs sniffing the trail, then looking off into the bush. "Stop a minute," I said to her, "I want to look ahead, there is something on the trail." I walked to the head of the team and there in the inch or so of fresh snow on the trail were wolf tracks. Walking on ahead of the dogs I noticed the wolves were making a detour around every set they came to. Then I could see, where they had spread out, that there were three of them. Stepping off the trail I fell in behind the team and said to Vera, "It looks like an old one and two pups; they are just ahead of us. If they don't leave the trail they will clean up everything on the line."

We had left the lower ground and heavy timber behind us and were coming out into muskeg and small black spruce, old burns or brules, with strips of small jack-pine. This was fair to middling marten country and I had possibly two hundred marten sets in the next fifty miles. There had been marten tracks here all winter and I had picked up a few here every trip.

By now it was pitch dark. The dogs were tired so we were both walking. I held the nose rope and Vera came behind. We talked as we ambled along and were laughing about the unusual sensation of walking on a humpy trail in the dark. You did not know whether the next step would up a foot or down a foot. The trail was forever dropping out from under your feet and then when you least expected would be a foot higher than you anticipated. We were both tired but the walking kept us warm and comfortable. Then the humpy trail ceased and we emerged into a half mile of heavy spruce near a small creek where the cabin was.

Soon the dogs stopped, and I could make out the outline of the cabin in the dark shadows close to the trail. I undid the wee door, went in, lit the candle and with shavings and dry wood piled handy I soon had a fire roaring in the little tin stove. Then I heard Vera's voice from outside. "How in the world do you get into this thing? I've walked around it twice and there is no door."

"Please do not call it a 'thing' I replied, It is Uncle Frederick's cabin, he made it, and it is a very nice, cosy, warm little cabin, and for your information, there is no door, so, we're comin' in the window." I put out my head to direct her into the proper channel, and there she was with a somewhat puzzled look on her face, staring at the little square of candlelight, with my head blocking most of the opening. "It is a mite too cold in here to take off my cap, and space is somewhat restricted for a proper bow, but if you will overlook the absence of those welcoming gestures, I herewith bid you enter."

"Thank you, good sir," she replied, "you are more than kind and I would in troth accept, but alas I have walked a weary mile this day and—"

"Nothing to it," I broke in, "just put your left foot up close to your right ear, now tuck your head in close to your abdomen, lean forward—" And with a leg up and a hand out she was inside.

"There you are," I beamed, "safe and sound, as snug as a bug in a rug, albeit a bit rosy of cheek," I added on seeing her flushed face. "And look," I continued, "there is or should be, a Pat. pending on the door to this—er—domicile. I do not think there is another one like it in the world." I picked up a board, put it in the opening, turned two knobs and the door was closed. "Isn't that neat?"

I unharnessed the four weary dogs, prepared a bed of boughs for each of them and gave them each a chunk of the meat they had hauled from home.

In half an hour the tea was made, the stew, (not booyaw, God help me) was sizzling in the fry pan, the home made buns and can of butter and plate of doughnuts were warming on the shelf. Parkas, sweaters and moccassins were hung behind the stove to dry. The cabin was warm and cozy, the fresh boughs on the floor smelled fragrant. We sat on the bedding spread out on the bunk and ate our stew and buns and jam and doughnuts and cake and drank multi cups of tea. When the pangs of hunger were somewhat assuaged Vera volunteered, "It is a nice little cabin, but a person thinks twice before going in or out."

As we had only twenty miles to go the next day, where I had a tent for a camp, (due to the lack of timber large enough for a cabin) we did not pull out until after daylight. The dogs were rested and full of pep once more. There was more snow on the trail now and some drifting in the open places. The wolves were still with us and were taking the bait from the marten sets. I was hoping against hope they would come upon a fresh moose track, be induced to follow it and thence leave the trail. But no such luck. Soon after leaving the cabin we noticed a disturbance and mess in the snow at a marten set ahead, a marten had been caught, the wolves had eaten it, hide, hair and all just leaving the toes in the trap. "There is the first thirty dollars down the drain", I said as I put the sticks back in place and reset the trap.

Ten miles out we turned off the trail to pick up two night's dog food from the cache of meat. The cache was a platform eight feet off the ground. The wolves had spent some time there, pawing and scratching in the snow, but had not been able to reach the meat. Here we turned and headed West to join my main line twenty miles farther on. We were glad to see the tent at sundown as we both had been walking all the way from the cabin. Just past the tent I had a 'set' where the wolves had eaten another marten, and that was three so far.

We had a comfortable night camp at the tent, although it required more stove wood to keep it warm than a cabin.

The following day we caught a nice big marten the wolves had somehow overlooked, or was caught after the wolves passed by. One pelt to skin and put in the bag that night, anyway. Before nightfall we found they had eaten three more, and I was feeling a bit perturbed, you might even say slightly annoyed with those loathsome creatures. If I had caught one in a trap about that time I planned on breaking every bone in its body with a club before I killed it.

We ate our supper in the new line cabin on a jackpine ridge, a few miles from the Blackstone River. Vera said, "Is there no way at all to get rid of those so and so wolves that are eating up the fur?"

"I've tried everything I know of," I replied, "traps, snares, meat bait with lye in it, fish hooks, and razor blades. I do get an odd one but am never able to get them all." I added, "You see how they avoid all the sets I made for them, and the fish hooks and razor blades I put out in a bit of frozen meat, they gobble up and look for more. They must have a cast-iron stomachs."

The load was light the next morning as we set off the thirty-five miles to the home cabin, and we could ride a bit here and there. The trail wound through numerous thickets and jackpine ridges where I had lynx traps set. There were some scattered lynx tracks and on top of the ridge ten miles from home a lynx had been in one of the traps and of course was gone, eaten right down to his toes in the trap. The wolves did leave a few small scraps of hide that they disdained to eat. At five o'clock we pulled into the home cabin, and Donata was just a bit surprised to see us. "Stan thought the trip was too far for you to make in four days, and I did not really expect you until tomorrow."

"The trail was good," Vera said, "and I was able to ride perhaps a third of the way, but I think one trip will do me for this winter."

Within the following few years legislation was introduced restricting the legal take of marten and beaver, and moose to one only. The snare legislation was brought in about 1940 too. One summer in Simpson we were able to meet with a Mr. Cummings who was a member of the advisory council of the Northwest Territories at that time, and was visiting some of the northern settlements. He seemed a little surprised the trappers were unhappy with the game laws and suggested we form an organization in order to submit, with one voice, a request for suggested changes. Mr. Cummings said that an organization of trappers and prospectors in Northern Ontario was able to procure good legislation by this method.

Later that summer we did form a Trappers' Association in our area, and had about sixty members. Not one trapper refused to join and most were very enthusiastic. Then we heard that the Superintendent of Game, a Mr. Oldum, was coming through Simpson and we thought it would be an opportune time to have a discussion with him. There were five ringleaders in the Association, John Goodall Sr. (later our first member of an elected Territory Council) Fred Sibbeston, Ted Trindell, Stan and myself. We called all the trappers to a meeting. Everyone came, Indians and whites. The room was packed. We proceeded to draft a petition to the Northwest Territories Administratin to present to the Superintendent of Game, Mr. Oldum. We were unanimous in our list of grievances and our suggested remedies and requests. John Goodall and Stan had some knowledge of business procedure and we made certain all was legal and in order. We suggested registered trapping areas similar to the British Columbia regulations, that would enable a man to take game when the conditions warranted and to protect his supply of beaver where he thought advisable. This would enable a trapper to utilize his area much as a fur farm. We pointed out the very unsatisfactory consequences of having the moose restricted.

The petition was drafted about ten o'clock one evening and we sent a delegation to request Mr. Oldum to attend the meeting. Surprisingly, he showed up, with two of his henchmen. I was the chairman of the meeting. I welcomed the game officials, introduced them to all, told them the purpose of the meeting and said we were desirous of discussing the petition point by point, hoping to get approval or criticism. Mr. Oldum was agreeable so I read out the petition and the trappers took it up point by point. I felt that Mr. Oldum was a bit shocked to find the present regulations had produced such a militant attitude amongst the trappers. Slim Jones quietly said, during the discussion. he was having to break the game laws every day in order to make a living.

I took this to be my cue, and soon after, I stood up and addressed Mr. Oldum thus: "You can see that we are perturbed about the situation regarding the current game regulations, as we have listed in the petition. There are many trappers in this one area, who, in the winter time, are scattered over the country far and wide. As it is now, we are all, without exception, having to break the game laws every day if we are not to starve. You will not find a trapper here who does not deplore this fact. It is a sad thing indeed to have a situation like this develop, and to put a stop to it you would have to have a game warden in every trapper's cabin. Even then half of them would be for the trapper. We would like to join you in recommending regulations that are practical and that we can all honestly uphold, where we will be the game guardians and your work will be made much easier. As it is now, it is either good for you nor us."

Mr. Oldum instantly replied, "I agree with you." Then he paused, "We will submit your petition to the administration, and I will recommend most of your requests and perhaps we can come up with something better."

The trappers all applauded and the meeting came to a close.

We all went home immensely cheered and heartened. The air had been cleared and I think we had gained Mr. Oldum's co-operation.

Mr. Oldum was as good as his word. The regulations were soon changed for the better. We got registered trapping areas and the restriction on moose was removed. The legal take of beaver was restricted for some years, however. One R.C.M.P. officer who came to Fort Liard soon after this said to me, "These Indians around here are sure poor hunters, none of them get more than one moose a year."

"They have been trained to lie," I said, "and it will take some time to undo the damage."

A year or two later when we had four elected members on the N.W.T. Council (somewhat corresponding to a provincial government) and the beaver were still restricted to the amount of fifteen, I wrote a sharp letter to the Council, through our member, Mr. Goodall. I complained about the beaver quota and suggested the season be opened. To my surprise the season was soon opened to a fair limit, and I put it down to coincidence.

The following summer, 1942, I met L.A.C.O. Hunt in Fort Simpson. He had previously been the Bay Manager in Simpson and was now the Commissioner of the N.W.T. "Hi, Laco," "I said, "how's everything?"

He replied, "Fine, and how's the family?"

"Great, growing fast, as everything does here in the North."

"By the way, Dick, that letter you wrote to the council did some good, it woke them up. Are you happy with the regulations now?"

"Yes, I am," I replied, "everything is just wine and roses."

From that day to this the game laws have been legislated with reason and common sense and administered with, I would say, 98% fairness which in this day and this world is better than par for the course.

The present administration, in the seventies, I think is the best we have ever had, partly due to a good commissioner and a good game superintendent and partly because we now have elected members on the council whom we the electorate can reach. And too, things are changing fast. The professional trapper is disappearing and there are few part time trappers, while the population of the north is increasing with those who are interested in hunting for sport and not in trapping for a living. This changing condition presents a different set of problems than we had in 1930, which I have no doubt will be solved in a sensible manner.

18

Spring of 1940

In the spring of 1940 I had again taken that trusted blade of steel in hand and forced myself to whipsaw enough lumber for a thirty foot boat. Vera refused to help me, darn it, and I had to get someone else and it was Stan. This time we did not cut his foot.

I got the boat built and installed an old car engine that Stan and I had bought from a traveller for one hundred dollars. It was a four-cylinder Star and was ideal for a boat engine. It worked many years for me without trouble and was eventually sold at Fort Nelson when I built a bigger boat. I named it the *Shooting Star* and hoped to do a little freighting with it. A friend of ours, Bert Nielson, had a contract to transport by river twelve hundred barrels of fuel oil to Fort Nelson for the construction of the Alaska Highway. The river was very low that year and the bigger boats were having trouble in the rapids above Fort Simpson. The bigger boats could hardly get through empty. For a mile there was only eighteen inches of water. Several smaller boats including mine worked there for about a month, dribbing the barrels of fuel oil through a two-mile stretch of water.

The weather had been hot and dry all summer; we had not a drop of rain for four months. The bush was actually tinder dry and there were small bush fires in all quadrants. A week before I started to work in the rapids the chinook wind started to blow—a hot dry wind from the West. Stan and Kay with their young son John were away in Simpson and Vera and I watched from our cabin with apprehension as the fires got closer, and the smoke got thicker and the heat grew greater every day.

The third day of wind it really blew. On the opposite side of the Liard, where Stan's cabin was, there were big spruce trees for miles both up and down the river and for a mile back in places. About noon I said to Vera, "I think we should go over and get the old placer gold pump engine going and wet Stan's yard down a bit." So the four of us jumped into the *Shooting Star* and felt our way through the smoke to Stan's cabin. After some trial and a lot of error I got the engine started but was only able to get a feeble trickle of water up from the river into the yard. The water that came out of the hose just seemed to disappear as it hit the ground. After an hour or two we decided to go back as I was afraid we would be caught like rats in a trap when the flames came through. We had no sooner got home than we could look across river to the other side and see the flames coming. Then it got dark and very hot, the wind increased and we said, "What's that? Thunder by God, it's going to rain. Man, what a blessing."

Then the wind came, and made the river such a mess as we had never seen before. The wind was cross river to the current and there were waves six feet high going in all directions. It was lifting the tops of the waves and carrying them in sheets of spray. The thunder continued. Very soon it dawned on me that it was no thunder we heard, it was spruce trees igniting in explosions!

You have to see and hear this to believe it. I have read about forest fires but this one impressed all of us as nothing else would. In fifteen minutes all was quiet again. The wind was gone, it was terribly hot and the smoke was suffocating. There were ashes and burned spruce needles falling all around. I went to the house. Vera had the table set for supper and I said to her, ":Maybe if we go over now, we can save the cabin. I don't think it has burned yet for I have heard no shots and Stan was sure to have a box of shells or two in the cache." Again we got in the boat and tore across river. The smoke was clearing and we could see the cabin. The fire had passed by in the tops of the spruce overhead, there were small fires all over in the underbrush, but the cabin looked safe yet.

We dashed up the hill and looked about. The moss in the cabin was burning in several places, the woodpile was on fire and there were small fires here and there in the yard. Vera went to put out the small fires with the water that was available. I got Kay's big wash tub, put it at the top of the hill and set Don and Nancy to work carrying water up the hill in small lard pails. Vera and I got gunny sacks and keeping them soaked with water put out the fires that were starting from falling debris and then worked at beating back the encroaching fire from the bush. Don was five years old and soon tired of carrying water up the hill. I told him, "Have a rest then, once in a while, but you have to keep at it." We soon had things pretty well under control and could slack off some. About ten p.m. we heard a kicker coming and Stan and Kay pulled in from Fort Simpson. We were glad to see them and they were glad to see us. In a few minutes Stan manipulated the engine to get a decent stream of water from the hose and by midnight it was safe to go to bed and leave things until morning.

Some of the wild animals must have caught merry hell in the fire. The green patch around the cabin contained many rabbits. They were confused and frightened and would run back and forth in and out of the burning bush where the hot coals and ashes lay six inches deep. I think most of the moose got away into wet places and sloughs that did not burn. Weeks before the fire we noticed the foxes had moved their dens out to the bank of the big river where they were safe. So the casualties were mostly little animals like squirrels and rabbits that could not escape.

Our side of the river had not burned as yet, although there were fires all around behind the cabin, eating their way slowly along and I knew it was only a matter of time until our home would be in danger. There was very little spruce behind the house. The timber was mostly birch and poplar with some small spruce and I felt there would only be a ground fire moving slowly. As I had to leave and go to work in the rapids very soon, I dug a trench about two feet wide through the moss and roots all around behind the cabin hoping this would stop the fire. The creek was just above the cabin some hundred feet or so and I back-fired on the other side of the creek, to protect the up-river side. I dropped a match and away she went. I have never seen the bush so dry.

We brought the placer pump and engine over from Stan's, set it up and instructed Vera in its operation. Then I took off for work and hoped for the best. Sure enough, several days after I left the fire came. It burned more fiercely than I had thought and Vera and the children had an interesting time of it. She had the young ones out of the house and on the beach while the fire was at its worst and she was able to save the house. The spruce trees did go up with more fury than expected. Even the small trees were so dry they exploded when the fire hit. The fire burned for many days in the ground where the moss and roots were a foot thick. When I came back I pumped umpteen gallons of water on the moss and yet it smouldered for days after. There were some spots in the bush where the fire did not go completely out until winter set in. I later heard that this fire of 1942 was the biggest in the history of North America.

It is an ill wind that blows nobody good. Because of the unusually dry season the rivers were very low and consequently I was able to get work with the little boat for a month in the rapids. Stan worked on a rapid boat too and Kay cooked at one of the rapid camps. My job was in Driftwood Bay, in the middle of the rapids. The larger rapid boats would bring the barrels of fuel oil as far as the bay and I would load four at a time and take them through the shallows as far as Scotty's Creek, where the scows loaded them and took them on. These barrels of fuel weighed four hundred and fifty pounds and we got pretty expert at hefting them around in and out of the boats. Not that we tried to lift them bodily, which was a bit too much for an ordinary man. You tilt them and roll them, edge them along the gunwhale and ease them down. What ever sheer lifting had to be done was done with the legs and not the back.

By the time trapping season opened we knew the fire had burned most of our traps and line cabins and made the trails impassable. I thought I could perhaps salvage some traps in the wet places, but alas, the trees that were not burned completely fell over and made the bush into such a tangled mess it was impossible to follow the trail at all. So the trapline was written off to profit and loss. The winter wood pile was also burned up; I could not even see where it had been. Ah, well, these little things are sent to try us I suppose, and they usually do.

19

My canoe destroyed

After the snow came I went upriver a few miles and wiggled and squirmed my way through the bush to the Blackstone River about twenty miles out. The fire had left patches of green timber here and there and I was able to avoid the worst of the burned area. This line produced some lynx and mink during the winter. With some short lines from the home cabin, we had as I recalled about fifteen hundred dollars worth of fur by the end of March.

Near Island Lake near the end of my old line there was a very good beaver country. But as the old farmer said, "You can't get there from here." The portage trail to Simpson was still being used after the fire by going in a roundabout way, and I decided to approach my beaver country by the back door, via Simpson and the winter road to Trout Lake. The price of beaver pelts seemed very good and if I made a good hunt I wanted to take the family outside to Calgary for the summer and also to bring back a trading outfit; trading supplies to last a year. Trapping itself was not producing much of an income and something else had to be done. On April 12, leaving Vera at home with the two kids, aged 5 and 7, I headed out for Simpson by dog team. I was two days getting there having to wade some creeks to the knees. The weather was warm and the creeks were starting to build water. It looked like an early spring.

Poole and his family were in Simpson that winter and as he had nothing else on tap he and his son Richard agreed to come with me and hunt beaver together. Richard was seventeen. He was known as Sonny then, and is to this day.

We left Simpson with two teams and supplies for a month. We intended to canoe down the Muskeg River to Fort Liard and be home by the end of May. The second day out the snow was almost gone and we were having to wade the creeks. At Island Lake we left the sleighs and dog harness and went on with packs on the dogs. At Moose River we established a camp, got out canvas and paint and started making two canoes. I had just enough paint for the bottom of my canoe and used beaver fat for the rest to keep it water-proof. Never again will I do such a foolish thing.

For ten days we hunted up the creek and then headed back down to the mouth of the creek at Trout Lake. In the early mornings we would check the traps and shoot an odd beaver perhaps. During the afternoons we'd skin the beaver and stretch the pelts. Skinning a big beaver takes half an hour to make a good job and the stretching about the same. The pelt must be sewn to a circular frame with stitches every two inches. After about twenty-four hours of good drying weather the pelt is ready to come off.

We had forty-five beaver by May 20th and were ready to head home. The Blackstone River was swift and rocky all the way and cannot be canoed except during the run-off for a few days. Now the creeks were starting to get low but we expected a rain to bring them up before long. The Indians at Trout Lake told us they canoed down the Muskeg River every spring to Fort Liard, and we thought that by going via Trout Lake and the Muskeg River we would be able to canoe most of the way.

One early morning when we were camped at Moose Lake, Sonny and I took the canoe down the creek on a hunt, while Poole was working on some skins. It was cool and very quiet, robins and blackbirds were singing, the sun was just coming over the trees and the water in the creek gurgled and murmured. A rabbit scampered in the bushes, a squirrel chattered. We dipped our paddles noiselessly, waiting to see a beaver. I sat in the bow of the canoe with the rifle ready; if you saw a beaver you had to shoot right now or he was gone.

There were few quiet bends in the creek, the water was slow and the small riffles made only a subdued trickling. No sign of beaver yet. Then, just ahead on the right bank was a small dark spot and I could see a slight movement. Sonny saw it too and kept the bow of the canoe pointed directly at it. Yes, it was a beaver but only a small one, we would let it go; a baby beaver was of little value. We were perhaps sixty feet away when something big and dark flashed off the bank directly behind and above the young beaver and carried it into the water. It was an otter. The rifle was aimed and ready. The otter would get his due; this time, I felt sure, I just couldn't miss him at that distance.

In the next few short seconds we experienced a sight that seared itself in my memory like a hot iron. The otter had the small beaver by the throat and the water was churning with the struggle. The two would sink and appear, sink and appear, again and again, going over and over like a paddle-wheel. Every time they came up the beaver would cry. That crying pierced us to the heart. It was the cry of a child, filled with terror and desperation. I must have been half paralyzed, for I did not shoot, or thinking that if I shot at the rolling mass I might hit the beaver. Surely the movement would cease; for a fraction of a second the otter would hesitate and I could not miss. The bow of the canoe was only six feet from them when the otter saw me and dived with the beaver before I could pull the trigger. I cursed myself for a fool, to have waited. We searched carefully in holes in the bank and every possible hiding place, but to no avail. We did not see them again. Hours later we paddled back to camp and related the incident to Poole.

"Yes," he said "nature is very cruel, otter kill many small beaver, wolves kill beaver, bears kill them and lynx do the same. We kill them too for money because we have to eat. There is no use to think about it."

"I know it," I replied. "I am not excusing myself at all, but, damn it! Otter are supposed to eat fish, not beaver. No book I have ever read on animals ever mentioned this."

"True enough," said Poole, "people who write articles and books about animals are usually motivated by the desire to present the animal in a good light and are not too concerned with the truth."

"I think a lot of them do not know what they are talking about," I said. "Do you notice, Poole, that most stories picture a trapper, any trapper, as a low-browed, brutal almost sub-human creature, and the fur bearing animals he catches in the most kindly light?"

Poole nodded, "Yes I have. Trappers, Indians and half-breeds are always the villains. The hero is a wolf, an otter, a policeman or a missionary."

"I think I will renounce this uncongenial activity, and take up the cloth, instead," I said.

"Better wait until this trip is over, Dick, we still have to kill a few rabbits before we get home."

One afternoon when we were camped on Moose Lake number three, I paddled across the lake and walked a short distance to a pond to get another beaver or two before we started down the ten miles into Trout Lake. Poole and Sonny went the other direction around the shore of the lake. The pond was a quarter of a mile from the end of a narrow inlet that widened to the bigger lake. I sat on a hump near the big beaver lodge and waited for the beaver to appear. Usually they come out late in the afternoon to feed and swim around all night and go back into the lodge for the day. There was a small breeze off Moose Lake and I felt the conditions were good for getting a couple of beaver here anyway. Nothing showed up at all until six o'clock in the evening, when one big fellow came up in the middle of the pond well out of rifle range. He swam back and forth with his nose in the air, dove and swam under water to the lodge. Fifteen minutes later two more came up in the same place and they also dove and quietly disappeared. No splashing of tails, no playing around. They sure were acting strange, as if they had been hunted recently, but I was certain there had been no one here this spring. About seven thirty I gave up. They had not appeared again and it was very unlikely they would come out again that night. Beaver have an excellent sense of smell and depend on it to save their lives. Unless the coast is clear of all unfriendly odors, they refuse to stay out to feed. Whatever it was that made them wary, my beaver hunting was over for that night.

I ambled back to where I had left the canoe in the buck brush. I could almost see it from where I sat as there were no big trees in the way. I got back to the canoe but where was it? The poles of the frame and the ribs were scattered around and what were those strips of canvas in the water? "Good God, my canoe, it's been all torn up by something. What in the world was miserable enough to do that?" There was no meat in it to attract an animal, in fact I had left nothing in it but the paddle. Nothing could have done this but a bear, I thought. I looked around; yes sir, fresh bear tracks and bear droppings. Why did I not see him from the beaver pond? I bent over with my eyes about the height of the bear and could then see he would have been just obscured by the low brush. If I had not been so intent on the beaver I might have glanced over and got a shot at him. So, what now? There was a great inlet both to the right and to the left that ran back for miles into some sloughs and I was not going to tackle an all night walk through the bush. There was always the old reliable bush signal—I would have to call on Poole and Sonny. I walked along the shore where I could see across the lake to our camp. In the light of the setting sun I saw Poole's canoe enter the opening of the creek and disappear. They had returned to camp so now for the signal. First a fire to guide them. I gathered brush and sticks, built a good fire and got it smoking well. Then I took rifle and fired two shots in quick succession, a pause, then two more quick shots. I put down the gun, sat down beside the fire and looked across the lake. A few minutes previously when Poole and Sonny were paddling into camp I could see the flash of the dipping paddles, a slow rhythmic stroke that moved them along well without hurrying. Poole very seldom got in a hurry. He always said you must take it cool if you wanted to stay alive in the bush. About thirty seconds after I had shot, I saw the canoe come out of the mouth of that creek like a robin at a worm, their paddles going dip, dip, dip, flash, flash, flash, just as quick as that. My goodness, I thought, they look like they are going for the doctor, I had better stand up so that they can see I am all right and not hurt. As they came closer and could see I was all in one piece they slowed down and came into shore at a more leisurely pace.

"Whatever happened?" Poole said, "we were worried for a time until we could see you walking around. I told Sonny, his arms must be all right or he could not have fired the shots so quickly. But we thought of a broken leg or a cut foot."

"It was the most unlikely thing," I replied. "You would never guess. A blankety blank black bear tore my canoe all to hell. It's a total loss."

"Where is it?" said Poole, "let's have a look at it."

We paddled into the inlet and fished out the canvas and looked it over. Poole at last ventured, "I think it can be sewn up. It is all here, torn badly, that's all."

"Looks pretty hopeless to me" I replied, "but if we have enough gilling twine, it might be done. That blasted S.O.B. of a black bear."

"What possessed him to rip up the canoe?"

"We should have known. It was the beaver grease you used. Anything that smells of beaver will attract them. If there are no dogs around the bears will come right into camp and take beaver meat, hides and all," Poole said.

The following day while Sonny and I hunted ducks and rabbits for food, Poole sewed at the canoe. It took him all day, but at least we had sufficient twine and he at last had it finished. We put it back on the frame, almost as good as ever.

Our food supply was getting more than low and we had to make tracks for Liard and home. We thought, a day to Trout Lake, two days down the lake to the Indian camp, one day on the portage to the Muskeg River and two days of canoeing should bring us to the Liard River, eight miles below Fort Liard. One more day by boat and we would be home.

As we started down the creek from the lake we knew that something was not as it should be. The creek, that was actually named Moose River, and was a fair sized stream all summer, was now a mere trickle among the boulders. The ten miles to the mouth of the so-called river took us a day and a half. Most of the time was spent in walking among the rocks, pulling the canoes behind. At last we came to the winding dead water and pulled in to Johnny Lomond's camp. Johnny was an old Indian whom Poole had known years ago. Johnny had a fine cabin, with factory windows and chairs, lumber on the floor and rubberoid on the roof. He had a well-built cache full of dried meat, dried fish and some white mans' grub. Many large, fat and noisy dogs were tied at their houses. He had a twenty-four foot canoe he had recently completed, which was a work of art. It was built exactly like a factory-made canoe except it had higher sides and was higher in the bow, to take the waves on the big lake. This location is ninety miles from Simpson and all supplies had been brought in by dog-team in the winter, since there is no navigable stream into Trout Lake.

Johnny told us that the level of the lakes and the creeks had been very high during the run-off but all were dropping fast, even the lake level was receding. Then it dawned on us that the fire the preceding summer had burned off the protective cover of moss and roots which normally soaked up a good deal of the melting snow. As a result the whole thing drained away at once like water on a tin roof and there was nothing left to feed the creeks. The only hope now was for a two-day rain to bring the creeks back up.

There was no ice in the lake as far as we could see when we set out to paddle along the Northeast shore to the Indian village thirty-five miles away. I went ahead with my canoe to shoot beaver or moose or caribou if any should be so indiscreet as to get within rifle range. Poole and Sonny stayed behind with the dogs in the bigger canoe so the dogs would not frighten any game that might be seen. There was no wind, the surface of the lake was smooth and the beach was sandy with rocks here and there. The day was lovely, the air warm and the sky clear. A mile paddled was a mile gained for there was no current to overcome. At noon we went ashore to have lunch. There was tea, dried meat, a small bannock and nothing else. "Looks like we'll have to get a moose, Poole, or it's going to be another one of those starvation trips."

"You know," Poole replied, "I have lived in the bush all my life, I've gone real hungry at three different times, once for nine days, and each time I swear it will be the last. Then it happens again. It seems you get to depend on something that does not turn out."

"I suppose the only way to avoid it is to stay home near the grub pile, or live in a town or city."

"I don't think we could stand city life," Poole replied, "whenever I am out for a week or two I'm more than glad to get back to the North. The hustle and the bustle and the rushing around and the stink of the cities is more than I can stand."

"There is one thing about going hungry," I mused, "you certainly learn to appreciate food. I wonder how the Muskeg will be? It must be a hundred miles down to the Liard."

"It is all of that. If it rains we'll be O.K. We should be able to get enough rabbits to keep us going anyway, when the bannock runs out."

"That will be very soon," I said, "there is damn little flour left now."

Later in the afternoon I noticed a timber wolf trotting along the shore in search of dead fish washed up on the beach. He had not noticed me at all.

I was a good ways from shore and it was a long shot. I very quietly pointed the canoe straight at him, to enable me to shoot over the bow, then gave a low whistle to attract his attention and get him to stop. I took careful aim just over his back and fired. The wolf dropped right there, squirmed a little and lay still.

"That is for you and your relatives who have been robbing my traps," I said, and paddled on. There was no bounty at that time, his hide was useless and a dead wolf is a good wolf and I let him lay.

An hour later, in a little sandy bay, as I paddled very quietly along I noticed a black bear standing on the beach right at the edge of the water facing me and not moving at all. He was over a hundred yards away, and a facing shot is not a good shot with a small rifle like the little .25-.20. There was no time to waste, he would be gone in half a second. The canoe was pointed right at him. I took aim over the bow for just under his chin and fired. Well, sir, I have seen many black bears and killed a lot of black bears and this was the strangest, the funniest result I have ever seen on shooting a bear. As soon as dammit after the shot, the bear was going the other way. He did not turn to the right or to the left. I had my eyes on him and he was absolutely never in a sideways position. But he was going away, he was receding in the distance with great dispatch. I think he thought of something he should have done last week and decided to do it right now. How he got turned around I will never know. He must have gone up and over, 'ass over tea-kettle' as we used to say when we were kids. He had a hundred and fifty feet to go, up a sloping sandy beach, to reach the trees. He went like a fox, through the air just off the ground. His hind feet were ahead of his nose in the attitude of a blind man reaching for a door with both hands. Once in a while his feet would reach down and gently touch the sand, then were tucked back up again. At the top of the gentle incline, instead of going on into the bush, he turned sharp, ninety degrees to the left and went north. Before and after he turned his speed did not slacken at all. It seemed to increase if anything. Just as he got nicely settled on his northern course he was going south at the same velocity. I had to assume he continued his journey southward for he did not appear again.

"I must have nicked his ear," I thought, "and he has got clean away. If that is the bear that tore up my canoe I hope he has a nervous hemorrhage from his fright. I think I will go ashore and look at those tracks."

Stepping onto the hardpacked sand beach I pulled the canoe up and went over to where the bear had been. There were two great gouges in the sand and nothing more. Wait, there were a few drops of blood and some broken hairs. I must have hit him after all but I sure was not going to follow him until Poole and Sonny came along with the .30-.30. Soon their canoe appeared and they came into shore.

Sonny said, "We heard your rifle, what did you shoot?"

"I shot at a black bear and I think he is wounded. I was waiting 'til you lads came along with the big gun."

Poole and I followed the tracks through the bush with great care, as wounded bears have been known to take a swat at you if you stumble over one. In less than a hundred yards, there he was as dead as a mackerel.

We opened it up and got about ten pounds of lard from around the kidneys, and discovered the bullet had gone through the lower portion of the heart. "Blow me down," I said, "how could he have run so far and so fast when he was shot through the heart?"

"A heart shot does not kill instantly," Poole explained, "they'll often go quite a ways."

That night we got within five miles of the Indian village when we had to take to walking and packing. The ice was jammed into the south end of the lake and we could go no farther with the canoes. We folded the canvas of each canoe and put it into a dog pack. Sonny and I carried the beaver pelts and most of the other supplies were put on the dogs.

Walking the bush from there on we reached the camp the next morning. We stayed at the village all that day and had a good feed of trout. The Indians talked to Poole and Sonny in Slavey, telling them of the country we had to pass through and details of the portage trail to the Muskeg River. Then they spoke of the river, where the best spot was to build the fresh canoes, and details of the river from there down to the Liard River. One thing they did not say was that there was to be no rain, the river would be almost dry and we would have to walk all the way.

One day's walking on a fair trail brought us to the Muskeg. It was cloudy and dull with an east wind the day we started to work on the frames for the canoes. We felt it was certain to rain as there had been none for a month and we were due for a storm. By now our food was almost totally depleted. We had tea and salt, a few cups of rice, and flour for perhaps two more bannocks. Until we shot a moose the poor little bunny rabbits would have to provide us with sustenance.

Although most of the bush had been burned with the previous summer's fire there were some green patches of timber and underbrush. Each evening and early morning Sonny and I would take our rifles and head out to these green patches, and did not dare come back to camp until we had at least one rabbit for each of us. We got nine rabbits most days but it used up a lot of time. A bush rabbit is a small animal; in the Spring there is no fat on them and Poole said we would starve to death on rabbits eventually, but they would keep us alive for a time.

For the two days we were building the canoe frames it was cold and windy, but it did not rain. One morning we launched the canoes and set out. After two hours of dragging the canoes over the rocks we gave up and went on with packdogs. It would be more than a hundred miles following the river, taking in all the bends and curves. If we tried to cut off a bend we would end up in a mass of burned windfalls. The Indians had a summer trail to Liard that crossed the Muskeg at least once. When we found it we weren't sure it was the right trail, so we kept to the river, as we thought it safer in the long run. A long run it proved to be. We were eight days steady slogging. There was one good feature about the walking conditions. The river being very low (in fact almost dry) either one shore or the other presented good walking. The shores were gently sloping and covered with goose grass, small rocks and sand. When we did come to a cut bank the opposite shore was good and we just walked across the stream without even wetting our feet.

Poole was sixty-four years old at the time, and in spite of our half-starved condition held up as well as Sonny and I. Sonny was seventeen, and this was his first long tough trip, but he never complained. Poole had a light pack and a walking stick in his hand and stayed behind the procession to see that the pack dogs did not wander away. Laddie and Kukum never left my heels but the others sometimes took a notion to go off on a private hunt of their own. I could not blame them when they did, for all the dogs were getting to eat were the heads and guts of the nine rabbits per day. At night we had to camp early for we had to shoot our supper before we could eat. While two of us were hunting, Poole would cut some brush for the camp and build a fire and make a pot of tea. (We still had tea and salt.) I got pretty sharp at hunting rabbits on that trip. I would look around for a green island of poplar and willows (island in the burn) with small thick spruce close by, or a good tangled mess of blown-over spruce that presented cover for rabbits. Sometimes we would not see a rabbit in the whole day's walking and I found they were hidden in thick heavy growth.

I would approach the thicket and proceed very, very slowly, taking perhaps ten seconds to take one step. The noise you made did not matter much. The only thing they are wary of is swift movement. Now the eyes must be used to advantage, peering here and there and everywhere, especially under low-spreading trees. Ahh, there is one about twenty feet away and blending well with bush. Very slowly I raise the gun, turn slightly and shoot it in the head. (A body shot is not to be considered, for the meat then tastes of half-digested bark.) Now I stand stock still, there will likely be another one not far away. If not, I move slowly on again, picking up the dead rabbits when I had my quota. If we were lucky we would get three for supper and three for breakfast. Poole told me that if you can hunt rabbits in these conditions, you can also hunt moose. The same technique is used for both.

Whenever we were gathered around the fire or stopping for a rest during the day, Poole kept us entertained with stories of his younger days in the bush. He had travelled with the Indians a good deal and had many yarns concerning them. It took our minds off our troubles and kept us from getting despondent.

Once in the goldrush days of the Klondike he and a partner had staked a claim on a creek just below some pretty rich ground. The two of them spent all winter in freezing down holes ten feet apart to a depth of eight feet to bedrock clean across the stream bed. In theory the idea of freezing down is this. If in one night the bottom of the hole freezes down say six inches, you thaw from the top and dig out only four inches. Thus you work your way to the bottom without letting the water come in. Anyway they found no colors and abandoned the claim and moved on. Later another man restaked the claim, sunk holes between theirs and hit paydirt four feet wide and six inches thick right on bedrock.

He told me of three different times he and a group of other trappers had run out of food completely and were five, seven and nine days before they killed meat. Once they found a cabin that contained grub and the other times they hunted until a moose was killed. Then they camped right there and feasted all night on roasted meat. Talking of this we both thought it was an odd thing that a dried up shrunken stomach could stand a sudden influx of meat without ill effect; whereas other foods, especially rich foods, had a reaction that could kill.

He told me of trappers who had made a pet of a small beaver. When they first brought it into the cabin they supplied it with a pile of poplar branches to eat, and the beaver proceeded to build a dam across the room. Soon it became friendly and could be petted. It took possession of a corner of the room under a shelf. It would go out of the cabin and bring in a chunk of green poplar. When the bark was eaten off it would take it out and exchange it for another one. The animal never dirtied in the cabin and always went to the door to ask out to do his business. He grew large in time and when a stranger came to the cabin he would proceed to slap his tail on the floor.

Many animals, even carnivores, make nice pets when they are small. Bear cubs are cute little fellows but get to be a regular nuisance when they grow up. I heard of a trapper who had a bull moose calf for a pet and he let it come into the house for snacks. When it got big and grew a large set of antlers getting in and out of the house presented a problem. At Wainwright Park in Alberta there was a full grown bull moose that would come to the door of the Park Warden's house and eat from the hand of a four year old girl.

Vera and I once had a pet weasel. He lived in the cellar and would come to the kitchen to drink milk from a saucer. Another time a pet weasel brought her young ones into the kitchen to show us. They were scrawny, ugly little things, but we admired them anyway.

The Lindbergs had a wild duck once that followed someone home and took possession of the house. When Ole went to the kitchen it followed him and when he went outside it pursued him. "By Jove," Ole said, "it must think I'm its mother." Another time they had a tame grouse and it would scare the daylight out of Anna when it flew up onto her lap when she was busy fancy-working.

Poole had given me his share of sugar for some time now, so I quit smoking and let him have what tobacco I had left as he was a confirmed smoker and tobacco did not mean much to me. But the second last day he ran out of tobacco completely and was reduced to scraping the bowl of my pipe for a cigarette.

I used to think it was ridiculous that people would get a bit frantic when they ran out of tobacco. What is tobacco anyway? It is mostly habit, I thought, but later I was convinced that nicotine must be a very potent drug. Later at Trout Lake an Indian and I were waiting for a plane that did not show up with our load of supplies. We were living in a tent and had nothing but trout to eat and the last week we ran out of tobacco. I caught myself crawling around the stove searching for butts among the spruce boughs. Being out of tobacco seems worse when you have to spend most of your time waiting.

We were starting to think this stupid Muskeg River was like time: it went on and on forever. At last one evening we hit a trail and saw some fresh rabbit snares. The trail was well travelled and we knew we must be near the Liard at last. A mile more and we came out to the big river, smelled smoke and saw the tents of the Indian camp. "Strange looking Trout Lakers," they said as they greeted us. We told them of our hunger and in five minutes the women were cooking and the men were bringing us food. Soon Sonny and I were busily gobbling up fried meat, biscuits and jam. Poole smoked about a pack of cigarettes before he would eat anything. I accused him of eating the cigarettes and he laughed and did not deny it.

The Indians took us to Liard the next day where we sold the beaver pelts for a good price to The Bay. I borrowed a boat and a kicker from the Bay manager and it was a swift pleasant trip down the Liard the hundred and forty miles to home. Come to think of it, I don't think I have eaten a rabbit from that day to this. I tried a snared rabbit once again but gave it up. It almost made me sick.

Poor Vera had almost given me up for lost as it was the eleventh of June and we were long overdue. She did not know who I was when we pulled in with the boat and refused to wave to me. She said I was a bag of bones and looked like death warmed over.

We were thinking of moving to Metla to start a trading post and before our trip to Calgary I went to Simpson to make application for a trading post license for Netla. At that time it was necessary for all such applications to go through the R.C.M.P. office.

The officer in charge of the Fort Simpson detachment at that time was not a particular friend of mine. It sticks in my

244

mind that he might possibly have been told of a conversation I had with a constable one day. It went something like this.

We were joshing one another as we all did at every opportunity. I told him that I felt there were three requirements to be met to be accepted into the R.C.M.P. and those were a size five hat, size fourteen shoes and something in between to hang a uniform on. He replied, "Ah, too true, but at that they are superior to a trapper who carries his brains in his ass which is always frozen."

I did however enter the office this summer day of 1944 and made known my desire for the necessary application forms. He handed the forms to me saying, "I cannot recommend this application of yours for a trading licence for the village of Netla."

I bridled immediately, "And why not, Sir?" He hesitated and fumbled around a bit then came out with it.

"Because away up there at Netla it will be harder for us to keep an eye on you." This man was either disarmingly frank or was guilty of colossal ineptitude, depending on the point of view. Possibly both. Anyway it made me instantly furious. I stood up trembling.

"If you don't mind, Sir," I said, and the Sir was pure sarcasm, "I intend to take this matter further, above your head if I may."

"Go right ahead," he said. And he was not smiling.

Once again I came away from that little building mumbling to myself in an unhappy manner. I vowed, "If that man ever comes to our cabin on a patrol I will put sand in his porridge or salt in his tea or maybe go so far as to make faces at him through the curtain." I soon got myself back into a better humor. "Mustn't let the guy bother me, there is always a rotten stick in the forest. Maybe he IS right. Perhaps I am a bad actor and a rotten egg. All the same I still have to make a living and had better get after that permit." And I paced firmly down the road to see Dr. Truesdell.

Over a cup of tea I explained my troubles to him. "Art," I said, "do you think you can help me get that permit?" Doc laughed, he was a bit amused at my discussion with the good corporal.

"Sure, Dick," he replied. "You get a petition signed by all the Indians in your area stating that they wish you to establish a trading post, I will include it in a letter to the Deputy Commissioner and I think I can come up with your permit."

This was done and in the fall, when I arrived back in Simpson, as I was walking by the barracks the corporal came out and handed me the permit, signed by the Deputy Commisioner. "Thank you," I said. And I do not remember ever speaking to him again.

20

Trip to Fort Nelson

In planning our trip outside Vera and I wondered what our reactions would be after being away from so-called civilization for so long. It had been ten years since Vera had come north and thirteen years for me. Nancy and Don, who were nine and seven, had never seen a car or train or neon lights or the bustle of traffic in their lives. After seeing it all again we all agreed that the civilized world was not much more civilized than the north.

We took four days with our little power boat to reach Fort Nelson. The Fort Nelson River was in flood with water near the top of the banks. It was almost chocolate colored with the sand and sediment carried with it.

At Fort Nelson an airport was under construction and contractors and bridge gangs were busily engaged in building the Alaska Highway. Fort Nelson up to this time had been an isolated trading post of a dozen white people. Now it was being invaded by swarms of soldiers, airmen, truck drivers and construction workers.

The local trappers had all made a good catch of land fur plus the spring beaver hunt. Beaver were bringing up to fifty dollars and some had sold their spring catch for six thousand dollars. Prosperity had hit them and they were spending money right and left with reckless abandon. One man paid two hundred and fifty dollars to go to Fort St. John by taxi. Whisky was bringing from twenty to forty dollars for a 26 ounce bottle. People were paying twenty-five cents to cross the river one way, to see the village. Some trappers with boats made as much as forty dollars a day doing this.

We went by truck as far as Dawson Creek and the winding road, the steep hills and the heavy traffic just about scared me to death.

In those days Dawson Creek, at the end of steel, had to be one of the dirtiest towns I have ever seen. The mud and filth were disgusting.

At Dawson Creek we boarded the train for Edmonton. The train crew must have been working by the hour and wanting to get in overtime, for they surely did take things easy. If we had been in a hurry we could have hired a horse and wagon. Besides, the food on the train was very good. Many others thought so too. It took just exactly four hours for the four of us to get to the diner, have a meal and get back to our seats. In the thirteen years since my last ride on a northern train I thought there might be some improvement in the trains and the train service. I was sadly disappointed. I thought "Perhaps the road bed is unsafe or the engine lacking in power or the engine driver has lost his way," as I noticed he was backing up most of the time. The old steam engine at least had a healthy whistle that was a joy to hear. It brought back nostalgic memories of the prairies. Once we got on a down grade into a river valley and the engine driver could not find the brake pedal: did we ever whistle along! We must have been doing all of fifteen miles an hour when we hit the bridge. On a good trail my dog team would have put them to shame.

Edmonton at last! People scurrying around like ants, apparently with no objective. They were pushing and jostling one another with grim determination. There were as many going north as south. Those going west were bumping into those going east. Apparently there were more than us having a hard time finding their way around. I said to Vera, "In this jungle, the first thing we must do is to hire ourselves a good guide."

We did survive, however. The two children seemed to take all the new sights in their stride and did not seem surprised at anything. Unkind people said our brains were atrophied from being frozen.

We were back in Fort Nelson by the middle of August, with our grubstake and a trading outfit. I had a bit of everything: groceries, dry goods, and hardware. There were about ten tons of freight to take home.

I bought lumber from a local mill and built a barge forty feet long, with a ten foot beam and four foot sides. I used rough lumber and caulked the seams with oakum and tar. By September 2 the barge was in the water loaded and covered with a tarpaulin. The *Shooting Star* was fastened solidly behind to push the load and we were away on the three hundred mile journey home.

The Fort Nelson River was a different stream entirely than we had seen in the spring. Now it was low, with gravel bars sand bars and piles of rocks in every bend. While the river bed was wide, in many places the channel was very narrow against one bank or the other with very shallow water spread over the rest of the width of the river. In the one hundred and ten miles to the junction with the Liard River we ran aground three times. Twice we had to unload part of the freight in order to float free. Vera helped me unload and load up again, as we had to relay the freight to shore with the tug. Three days of this and we were out of the woods and on to the Liard where there was at least enough water to float the barge.

We were all glad to see our little cabin on the Long Reach.

Early next spring we moved, lock stock and barrel, up to Netla River. There we lived for ten years and ran a trading post. I built a bigger tug and a barge and worked on the rivers in the summer, mostly for oil companies who were doing geological work in the search for oil. Don helped me in July and August when he and Nancy were home from school and from the time he was sixteen Don operated a tug and barge on his own. I think he was twenty when with one helper he took a tug and barge to Fort McPherson and worked on the Peel River during the summer for Imperial Oil Ltd. Vera always said I drove myself too hard and expected too much from our sons and when I look back on it now I think she was right. But others were doing the same. In those days we were all hooked on the 'work ethic' and thought there was no other way of making a nickel.

During the ten years at Netla our last two children were born, both at Fort Simpson: Thomas Rolf in 1945 and Martha Ruth in 1948. When Rolf was born Vera went in to Simpson by boat. With Martha the trip in and out was by aircraft. It seems that the four children have grown up with dog teams and aircraft; the most advanced and the most primitive methods of transportation. As I write, the dog teams have almost disappeared and along with pack mules and plow horses are a thing of the past.

All four children took correspondence lessons at home with Vera instructing. From grade nine on, they went to High School at Dawson Creek, B.C., and were able to board at the dormitory there. It was rough on all of us having them away for ten months of the year but we could see no alternative. While we were trying to make a living in the north the kids just had to get an education and it was fortunate for us that they were able to board at the dorm. Boarding out at a private residence would have cost us much more. Leaving home with the boat every fall to go back to school Don and Nancy would be very quiet and sad. Coming home in June for the holidays on the barge, they would chatter, chatter, chatter. In later years we had an aircraft and brought the two younger ones, Rolf and Martha, home for Christmas which made a break for them and a change for Vera and me.

During the years at Netla I tried to establish an outpost at Trout Lake, trapping there and trading with the Indians during the winter months. I found that transportation was the killing factor, and it was impossible to supply the post by aircraft or dogteam and keep the cost within reason. Vera ran the post at home and did as good a job as I could have done.

One year in October I made arrangements to have an aircraft bring in a load of freight from Fort Nelson to the lake on November 25th. With a dog team each, an Indian and I set out from Netla the first day or so of November and were at the lake in a week. It was a hundred and twenty miles to my outpost on Paradise River. We had to walk ahead of the teams all the way as there was no trail to follow.

At the lake we set out a short trapline and set several fishnets under the ice for trout. The marten were plentiful and the line did well. Trout Lake lived up to its name, there were ten to twenty big trout in the nets every morning. On November 25th we were all prepared for the airplane. It did not show. Day after day passed and it still did not appear. The weather was perfect and I could think of no reason to cause the delay. (It had broken down and did not appear until February.) We kept waiting and waiting, thinking it would be along any day. Soon we were out of all food except fish, and the tobacco ran out too. By December 20th it was obvious we would have a pretty hungry Christmas if we stayed at the lake. It was a long way home, the snow would be deep and it would be a rough trip with nothing to eat but fish. At least the dogs were all in good shape and we could take fish for them to eat. When we went by the Indian camp they gave us a bundle of dried trout, a small bundle, as they were in short supply of food themselves.

It took four days of steady slogging on the trail to Netla. The snow was deeper now. Over a foot had fallen since we were over it, and it was drifted in. At meal time we had tea, without sugar and boiled fish. A fine trout steak, rolled in flour, and fried with plenty of fat would have been very good indeed, but we had no fat, and so had boiled fish. We had boiled fish and more boiled fish, and the next day had boiled fish until I hated the damned stuff.

The last night camping out we had something different. The supply of fresh frozen fish had given out so we dug into the sack of dirty old dried fish. Never at any time was it intended for human consumption, but under the circumstances these humans tried to consume some. It was forty-five below that night and felt like it. We sat by a big fire and tried to keep warm while we chewed this awful stuff. It tasted not bad actually, and went down all right except for the sand. Trout Lake sand is coarse red sand, and these fish had evidently been sprinkled well with it as they were drying. It felt as if I were chewing glass. I gave up in disgust, rolled into my sleeping robe and tried to sleep.

We were up and away before dawn and at noon we hit a good trail. It was hard and smooth with fresh dog tracks, the dogs perked up and began to speed and we jumped on the tailboards and rode. Something went whurrrr-cluck, cluck, and two prairie chickens flew up and sat on the trees. Harry pulled out his .22 and shot both of them. He was happy. "We'll build a fire, Dick, and I'll show you how to cook them."

He skinned them, hide, feathers and all in two seconds, opened them up, pierced the meat with two short sharp sticks to keep them flat, and gave me one on a long pointed stick. "Roast that and see what you think of it." The chicken was fat and I held it close to the fire where it sputtered and sizzled to a nice golden brown. I turned it and did the same to the other side. Then I ate it—every bit of it except the bones. It was delicious. Prairie chicken meat is dark meat and the bird is twice as big as a partridge. I felt as if I had had a meal.

"Harry, the day is saved. I think we will make it home." In fact, all we had to do now was to hang onto the sleighs. The dogs knew they were headed home and sped right along. It was four o'clock when I pulled up to the cabin. Vera was in the store, but she shoo'd away the customers and dashed into the house. As she had so many times before she wondered if I were ever coming home. Tomorrow was Christmas Eve, a tree had to be cut and decorated and things would be busy at the store. She was glad to see me, and I was glad to be home.

Vera set the table right away and as soon as the dogs were unharnessed and fed, I came in and sat down and ate and and ate. I ate six times a day for weeks and gained twenty pounds in twenty days. We had a case of canned Devon cream and I think I had cream on everything including potatoes. In February the airplane arrived and I went back to the lake. This time, believe me, I took enough food.

The Trout Lake venture had to be abandoned later, as in the fall when I returned to the lake there were a lot of goods missing. In June I went into the lake and found the cabin literally cleaned. Trade goods, clothes, blankets, scarves, socks, mitts, food, dishes, pots and pans, saws, axes, traps, gas lamps, and stove.Eventhe window had been taken out. The Indians at the village all blamed the other members of the tribe and each one said he had taken nothing himself. I gave up in disgust and went home.

Trading in the early days was fairly simple. The goods you had to carry in stock were the basic things that people living in the bush required. Items such as tea, sugar, flour, baking powder, lard, tobacco and matches did for groceries. A certain amount of clothes for all ages was required; a lot of print and yard goods, blankets and tents. In hardware, one carried guns and ammunition, traps, knives and axes.

If a trader wanted to build up a continuing successful business he paid a price for the fur that allowed him to make a fair profit. Some traders, both Company and independent, would take advantage of a rising market to pay a lower price than they should have. A reputation in the North travels like wildfire. News soon got around, and a trader who consistently paid the best he could got the business. Still and all, over a long average I feel it is true to say the natives did not get a fair deal from the traders.

The problem of fluctuating fur prices was something that all in the fur business had to face. A fur dealer could sometimes make up his losses, a trapper by the nature of his business never could. A number of free traders have gone broke by buying fur when it was high and having to sell some months later when the bottom had dropped out. I took a very heavy loss one spring in the fifties, when the beaver market suddenly went for a slide. I was able to make it up in after years by having friends in the wholesale business who carried me on the books.

One of the most unpleasant aspects of trading that we found over the years was dealing with customers in varying stages of drunkenness. I very soon conveyed to them in no uncertain manner that I did not wish to have them on the premises at all when they were under the influence. I found it often necessary to reiterate these rules, and it was one prime reason why we eventually quit the trading business.

One ruse that the natives pulled more often than they should have been allowed to led to disgust and despondency on our part but was so simple and succeeded so often it was unbelievable.

The situation would be like this: 1. There was a policy of no debt, no credit, no 'jawbone' given out at all until a month before trapping season opened. 2. All debts must be paid before the close of trapping season. (If some rules were not followed they would take your whole stock before trapping season and you wouldn't ever see a cent of it.) O.K. so far. They knew this and reluctantly accepted it. They should have been able to get by, for the Department of Indian Affairs gave out rations during the summer months. Now, about August 10 or 15, Jimmy or Joseph would come to the store and the following conversation would ensue: Jimmy—"Dick, I got no stuff, no tobacco, no tea, no grup, (they cannot pronounce the 'b' sound) my kids hungry."
Me—"Jimmy, I just gave you your rations for this month, also your Family Allowance, that should have done you until next month, is it all gone?"
Jimmy—"All gone, Dick, all gone. My kids no grup, you give me little jawbone Dick?" Jimmy would smile sweetly, a shy friendly smile.
Me—"Goddammit Jimmy, you know there is no debt, 'til fall, you should make your rations last until the end of the month."
Jimmy—"I know Dick, maybe I catch lots of fur, I pay sure."

Me—Maybe, Jimmy, maybe you catch lots of fur and maybe *not* catch lots of fur. Trapping long time away. Big debt no good."

Jimmy—"Yaw-aw, I know. Just a little bit now, my kids hungry Dick." (Jimmy and I are about the same age and have grown up together in the bush, sharing many a camp-fire.)

Me—"O.K. Jimmy, I'll give you little bit of flour, lard, rolled oats, milk, that's all. No more until fall you understand, no jawbone until trapping starts."

Jimmy—"Merci, Dick, you good man."

I look at Jimmy with a grim, beat expression and mumble under my breath. "I'm a stupid weak fool, nothing else." I get out the counter check book, give him the stuff and mark it down—twenty-five pounds of flour, can of baking powder, a pound of tea, a pail of lard, sack of rolled oats and maybe five pounds of Trumilk.

Jimmy happily stuffs the groceries in his pack and turns to the counter again. In his hand there miraculously appears a five dollar bill. Jimmy speaks aggressively now, "I want raisins, sugar, yeast, I pay."

Now I look at Jimmy with mixed anger and amusement at the way he has put over the old trick. He had the five dollars all the time. He knew that I would never give him brew material on debt or 'jawbone' as they called it. And he also knew that we would give him credit if he and his family were in need. So instead of spending his cash on groceries he got them on credit thus having the cash left for brewing material.

The first time they pulled this stunt with Vera she came in from the store with tears of exasperation. "Their kids are hungry, and dirty and ragged, I gave him food on credit, then he pulled out the money for brewing material."

"Well, don't let it bother you. We have our own family to look after. We can't take on the responsibility of feeding their kids too: it is no use feeling sorry for the poor little scamps."

"Yes, I know," Vera replied. "They had little Mary Joe with them today. My, she is a sweet pretty thing. I'd like to take her and clean her up, but oh, what's the use?"

"Exactly," I said.

About this time the demand for different types of goods started to change in the store. Previously the natives had all worn moccasins and rubbers; now they were starting to ask for factory made boots and shoes. A big headache it was, trying to get the kind and sizes they wanted. Some of the young men would come into the store in the winter time wearing boots with only one or two pair of socks.

"Good God," I said, "you'll freeze your feet, you idiot. Your wife got no moose-hide for moccasins?"

"No kill moose," was the answer. "No moccasins, I want heavy boots." And he would indicate to me that he wanted the rubber bottom, heavy, lined flight boots.

"No, I do not stock that stuff. They are no good for the trapline and besides they are high-priced, they cost much more than moccasins and duffle and are not near as warm."

I could have saved my breath to cool my porridge. They saw these boots in the catalogue, they saw oil men and pilots wearing them, and they had to have them. Paying for them was something they could care less about. They would buy on credit and pay later or never.

Then they wanted bicycles, and Hondas, cowboy boots and cowboy hats, battery operated record players and rock records. Transistor radios and tape recorders were in big demand. Clothes—nothing but the latest fashions, tight pants and flashy colors. "No, not red or brown but a purple blue, like I saw in Playboy Magazine." Most of this kind of customer did not know where his next meal was coming from.

It seemed to us somewhat amusing that the white men coming into the North all wanted to buy moccasins and the Indians were wearing cowboy boots.

The fur trading posts of the old days are fast disappearing, when the Indian hunters came in from the bush with a bundle of pelts, would sit smoking and talking with the trader while a leisurely deal was made. Trading posts are called stores now and merchandising is the big thing. The wild fur business is taking a back seat and represents a very small percentage of the total business of a retailer now. Tea billies, ice chisels, skinning knives and other trapline items are not stocked in some of the Northern stores anymore. So passes an era.

21

New innovations

About 1948 we could see that the north was in for some changes. Oil exploration was creeping north, aircraft were seen more frequently and there was talk of helicopters: strange flying machines that lifted straight off the ground.

If the country was going to develop the rivers would have to be used as highways for some time yet and I thought perhaps we could make a dollar or two with a tug and barge. One spring I took twelve hundred of our hard earned dollars and bought a forty-two h.p. Gray-marine gas motor. At Fort Nelson I sold the old *Shooting Star* and my new .30—.30 rifle to pay for lumber for the tug. Don and I made a little money with this boat and went on to acquire two fairly good outfits at last.

So my life as a trapper and dog driver was nearing an end, and fifteen years as a riverman was beginning. I was late in getting back from Fort Nelson with the new boat so Vera instantly dubbed it the *Come Later*. Don and I built a bigger barge for this tug to push and most of the time it did indeed come later. Our good friend Captain Walter Johnson claimed that if the boat came much later it would not come at all.

The first trip of the summer for the *Come Later* was a trip to the falls with a group of American tourists. I was doubtful if the new boat could cope with the fast water of the Nahanni as it was not a speed boat but just a tug. However we did make the hundred and twenty miles to the falls in three days.

I engaged the services of Fred Sibbeston, an expert riverman from Fort Simpson, for the trip. The third night out we were camped in a little sandy bay two miles below the falls. There were five of us sitting around a campfire on logs and stones, busily engaged in eating our supper. One of the tourists, I have forgotten his name, spoke.

"Say, Dick, now that we are up here just where is the gold that can be picked up in chunks out of the gravel?" He was not smiling. He seemed to be in earnest. His friends too were watching me with seriousness and interested looks. I glanced at Fred: he was grinning broadly, wondering what I would reply. I swallowed some tea before I choked on it and put down my cup. Surely he must be joking.

"Eh, what's that?" I replied. "Did you say something about gold that can be picked up with the hands from the gravel?"

"Yes, we have read accounts of placer gold near the falls where gold nuggets are large and plentiful. Fear and superstition keep the natives away. They say it is guarded by headless men, and we would like to see it."

"This is very interesting," I managed, "if such a fabulous place exists we would certainly like to see it too. Have you heard of this Fred?" And I turned to Fred Sibbeston who was chuckling away to himself.

"I have been in this country all my life, spent a good deal of time on the Nahanni River and know the Indians very well, in fact I speak Slavey fluently. The stories of gold nuggets and headless men is pure trash, written to sell magazines, that's all. The Indians have many superstitions in other matters but none in regard to headless men."

"That is just the size of it," I said. "There are dozens of men like Fred and myself who know this Nahanni area very well, and if there was any place such as you mention, any number of headless men and all the superstitions in the world would not keep us from that gold. I for one would dearly love to get my grubby little paws on just one big nugget, to say nothing of quantities that can be shovelled into pails and sacks."

Later on when we were alone I said to Fred, "You know, we must look pretty stupid for these chaps to think we would guide them to a gold mine and watch them scooping up multi dollars while we stood around shuffling our feet. They must take us for aborigines."

"They have just read too many sensational yarns, Dick, about the Nahanni, the McLeod gold and headless men and have come to believe it."

For the next three years the *Come Later* was busy in the summer months of open water, pushing barge loads of supplies and gasoline for helicopters, down from Fort Nelson and distributing the loads to different points along the rivers.

One spring day in the beginning of May when the ice was moving out of the river I was working on the boats getting them ready for launching. We heard a single engine aircraft approaching. It came over and circled low. We recognized it as CF—IOD, the Imperial Oil Beaver their geological crews used. They were on wheels and there were no airstrips within many miles and of course they could not land. They circled again and came over very low and fairly slow and we knew they were going to drop a message. I stood in an open spot and held out my arms. The aircraft shot past and down came a coffee can with a ribbon tied to it that missed me and hit the ground four feet away. (With an aim like that who needs a Sperry bomb sight?) The can contained some chocolate bars to give it weight and a note asking if I would take one hundred barrels of Avgas from Fort Nelson to points on the Liard River soon after break-up. If the answer was in the affirmative I was to wave both arms. If negative I was to wave one arm only. The Beaver circled once more and came over low. I waved both arms, the aircraft acknowledged with a dip of the wings, and away they went.

"Who was it?" Vera asked.

I looked at the note again, "Darned if I know, it is not signed." I handed the note to Vera. She read it and laughed.

"So you undertook to do a job, for an unspecified amount, at an indefinite time, and you don't even know who it is you are working for."

I laughed with her. "Yes, it is funny. But it was the Imperial Oil Beaver, I assume it was some of the boys we know, I assume the job is for Imperial Oil and have reason to believe the payment will be satisfactory."

"I suppose you are right," she said, "but the way you were waving your arms I thought they would come off, or perhaps you were trying to get airborne."

"Hardly—haw—haw, ver-r-r-r-ry funny," I said, "but I would have waved four arms if I had been so equipped."

From then on for several years I had many contracts with Imperial Oil and a very happy relationship existed with all the geological and field crews.

In the winter time at Netla we were occupied with trading post activities. As the days lengthened and˙ the weather warmed toward spring, I could hardly wait for the snow to go so that I could get the boats ready for launching to get to Fort Nelson with the barge, get the fur out to the auction sales and bring home a load of supplies. I was always fearful that the fur prices would drop before the winter's accumulation of furs were sold on the June sale. It was very seldom I could catch an aircraft going by to ship out the fur. I kept thinking it would be a good thing to have an aircraft of my own, so I could ship out fur for each monthly sale and bring back needed trade goods.

In the meantime I had to keep working with the barge to bring in some of that folding legal tender to facilitate the purchase of an aircraft. Each fall the tug and barge had to be pulled from the water out of danger of the spring break-up ice.

The freeze-up of the rivers in the fall and the break-up of the ice in the spring of the year are the two most important and interesting times of the year. The rivers are the highways and open water was necessary to move freight and supplies into the North. In this day it is still true but not to the extent as previously for aircraft have taken over much of the transportation with the exception of heavy freight.

The warm weather of April, the amount of rain or snow, the temperature of the nights, the amount of run-off of the small creeks and rivers (which precedes the break-up of the big river by several days) was watched anxiously, for if high water was to induce the river to break up and move while the ice was still solid, ice jams could take place with consequent flooding above.

One year the ice did jam below Netla about twenty-five miles. The ice was still solid and blue when the river rose fast and the push from above forced the ice to start breaking up. About eight hours later the current slowed down when the river rose almost to the top of the banks, nearly thirty feet above the normal level. The ice, mingled with trees and logs, brought in by the run-off of smaller streams above, was forced together in a slowly churning, heaving, crunching, grinding mass. Although the level of the water itself was just to the top of the bank, the level of the moving ice was six feet higher. Soon most of the ice had stopped moving with the exception of a channel down the middle about two hundred feet wide. This continued to move along and never did cease to move entirely. All that night the river continued to rise very slowly until it was very near to the cabin. All night long the subdued thunder of the river was in our ears, and I was deeply concerned lest a further rise of water would allow the ice to flood inland, carrying trees, cabin and all before it. The ground behind the cabin was level for a mile back and there was absolutely no place to which we could escape. I brought the canoe close to the cabin door, hoping the four of us (Don and Nancy were outside at school) could get back into the bush on the rising flood, ahead of the ice.

For forty-eight hours the river stayed at about the same height with the grinding and snapping still coming from the slow moving stream of ice and logs in the middle of the river. At long last, and it seemed an eternity to me, the river dropped two inches, hesitated for an hour, then dropped a few inches more. Inside of twelve hours it went down two feet and the whole mass of ice started to move again. The jam below must have broken for the current did not slow again.

The sight and noise now was something to see and hear for there was much solid ice moving down. Some big slabs a hundred feet across and two feet thick were upended ten and twenty feet in the air, then would tip and snap and come crashing down. Great black wet logs would reach into the air with the force of the churning ice. Often they would snap and break and sometimes slip quietly back and disappear. We had never before seen such a great amount of driftwood go out with the ice. There were many tremendous green trees going down, recently torn from the banks of the river above. We stood on the trembling ground and marvelled at the force of the great relentless stream, that was at other times our calm placid Liard River.

Right then I made up my mind we would move from this spot. Where I did not know, but somewhere there was high ground to escape to in case of another flood. Preferably someplace off from the main Liard. We later decided on Nahanni Butte, at the foot of the five thousand foot mountain.

That July the kids and I cut and peeled fifty big spruce trees along the banks of the Liard, for building logs. There was too much to be done to move that summer, so a year later the move was made. I hauled rough lumber, plywood, doors and windows from Fort Nelson with the barge, the first trip of the Spring, and while Don and I were busy on the MacKenzie River with the barge, I hired two men to build a frame stove on the new building site, well back from the banks of the river this time you may be sure.

At the end of September when the barging season was over, Don and I set to work to build our new log house. By October 3rd all the logs were rafted down, winched from the river and up the bank to the site about three hundred feet from what we thought was the high water mark.

We did not realize how much junk we had accumulated at Netla until we moved it all by barge to Nahanni. Years before when Vera and I built our little cabin on the Long Reach we had nothing but the clothes on our backs. When we moved to Netla we had a barge load. The move to Nahanni constituted several barge loads. A large part of this was, of course, food and trade goods which are at all times valuable, even indispensable, you might say. Dishes and cooking utensils must be taken. Chairs, tables, beds and other furniture, while mostly junk, we had to have. There were two heaters and a cook stove, the gramophone, stacks and stacks of books. The kids' toys, (boxes of them they had out-grown but would not do without) boxes and bundles of clothing and bedding, odds and ends around the house that nobody would throw out. Then there were such important things as tools, shovels, picks and axes and saws, (mostly broken and worn out, but I might need them) empty barrels and kegs, pipes and elbows and rusty pieces of iron (that might come in handy) and many other items that were of absolutely no use at all (such as old rubbers and pails and tin cans,) unless you happened to need them for a repair job. If you throw anything away you are sure to need it the next day. I once made a stern bearing for the *Come Later* out of the heels of a pair of old rubbers, and it lasted out one season, which is better than the factory made ones do.

But still and all, as we carried this vast conglomeration of assorted odds and ends down the bank and onto the barge, doubts assailed me as to whether it was worth the effort of carrying it all up the hill again at Nahanni. Vera and I have agreed if we ever move again we will simply put on our hats, pick up the axe and walk away.

There is a story I like about putting on your cap, picking

up the axe and walking away, that may as well be told here. It will only be appreciated I fear by those who have had some experience in camping out. In the morning, you know how it is, you gather up the food and the dishes, roll up the bedding, put the spare clothes and oddments in the packsack, take down the tent, stow away your axe and the guns, then check for any items hidden in the grass. At last you depart and worry for an hour or two about various things that might have been left behind. I have even heard of people who have returned for many miles to retrieve a forgotten item only to discover that it was in the load all the time. Sometimes you wish there was not so much stuff to gather up.

Jack Mulholland and Jim Macauley built a raft on the Nahanni River one spring to float down to the mouth. Like other people in similar circumstances, they were returning from an unsuccessful beaver hunt. They had not killed any game and were more than a little hungry. Also they were in a hurry and did not wait for all the ice to move out. Somewhere in the Splits they ran into an ice jam, leaped ashore on what turned out to be an island and saw their raft devoured by the ice with what little equipment they had. All they had time to grab was the axe. Another raft to enable them to reach the mainland was put together out of driftlogs and by that time darkness had set in.

Jack finished the story with, "We gathered in a big pile of driftwood, built a tremendous fire, lay down, pulled our coats over our heads and went to sleep. In the morning we got up, put on our caps, picked up the axe and walked away. It was the easiest camp I ever broke."

For my part, leaving Netla was the most and the biggest camp I ever broke. We did at last get it all moved down and piled in tents and under tarps until we got the house built.

When we were ready to start building the new house I got up one morning and found a foot and a half of wet snow on the ground. It was somewhat depressing to find winter was setting in so early when we needed at least a month of good weather yet.

Winter or no winter, come snow, blow or high water the cabin had to be built and although the weather might slow us down it could not stop us. We had decided on building a big cabin this time, no more building on in a jerry-like manner. It would have five rooms. The forty foot logs, some sixteen inches at the butt, looked too huge to lift; but they were partly dry and Don and I were able to roll them up and fit them into place without too much trouble. Notching in the corners took a lot of time and the log had to be lifted in and out several times to assure a decent fit. I had talked so much of 'Moss Chinked Hovels' that both Vera and I thought we would try a different material for chinking. I had a supply of oakum of the type used for caulking barges and this stuff proved to be the answer for caulking between the logs.

In a week or two the Chinook winds had taken away most of the snow and on November nineteenth we moved in and had our first meal in the new house.

April 1st Don and I built a saw-pit on the island among the big spruce and started whip-sawing lumber for a new tug. The planks in the *Come Later* were getting a bit rotten and we wanted to build a bigger tug powered with two Graymarine engines. The barge we had now would hold twenty-five tons and was too big for the *Come Later* to push. Day by day we kept at it and at last got eight trees done into about fifteen hundred board feet. We needed only enough lumber for the hull as we had enough commercial lumber for the ribs and finishing.

After the boards were brought across the river ice and piled on the bank to dry, I built a long bench and set out to hand plane each board, as for the hull the boards must be true and straight to fit closely together. This necessitated planing each board on both sides and both edges. My evenings and spare time were well taken up. I finished up with a pile of shavings a hundred feet across and two feet deep.

By May 31 Don and I had the two engines installed in the new tug and were on our way down the Mackenzie River on a summer's job for Shell Oil. We were home by the middle of September.

The new tug had to have a name and when someone dubbed it the *Go Easy* it stuck. It had eighty-four horses and lots of muscle so I did not feel too badly about the name. It was decked in with plywood, had a galley and pilot house and was fairly comfortable on a cold day.

The following summer Don operated the *Go Easy* and barge with a deck-hand to help him. As his outfit was out on contract all summer, I built another barge and put another Gray in a small boat and named it the *Wee Three*. That little tug would scoot right along and I made three trips to the falls with it.

After moving to Nahanni Butte we saw more of our old friend Albert Faille. Every summer he would stop in for a few days on his way up and down the river on his annual trip to his country above the falls. Vera would make a batch of cinnamon buns for him whenever he came along and we would sit and hash over the latest developments on the Nahanni River, how the prospecting was and especially how his search for placer gold was progressing.

Albert was now seventy years old and he was as yet hale and hearty; but still and all the years do take their toll. He had hurt his back during the First War, and again twice since that. Once he lay in his cabin for many days before he was able to move around again. He could stand fairly straight when not moving, but when walking he was always bent over with his hands near the ground. It may be imagined how we felt to see him that way, but he was a proud man and we dared not show pity or sympathy toward him in any way. The portage at the falls was getting to be too much for him. One outboard motor, gasoline and other supplies had to be back packed up a steep four hundred foot hill and over a three-quarter mile trail above the falls. He needed supplies to do him a month on the upper river.

We did not relish the thought of Albert setting off alone on these trips. He was a typical northerner and did not take kindly to advice even from friends. We held our counsel, waved him goodbye and were very glad to see him return safely each fall. He had by this time ceased to spend the winters in the bush and each fall returned to his little house in Fort Simpson.

One particular summer he was later than usual in leaving Fort Simpson on his journey to the mountains as he waited for the Liard flood stage to abate, for the rapids in the Liard are nasty in high water. He had the usual uneventful trip for the hundred and twenty miles to Nahanni, with as much gasoline as his little boat would carry, about a hundred gallons.

About a week after Albert left us at the Butte on his way to the falls, I set off for Fort Nelson with the *Wee Three* to bring back a load of groceries for the store. Martha, who was nine years old then, was with me, as the two young ones were always wanting to come on a boat trip and it was her turn this time.

The first day we made it to Fort Liard and camped aboard the little covered-in tug. Ready to make an early start next

264

morning I awoke at six o'clock and found the weather had
turned sour with rain and a cold wind, so went back to bed for
a time. By eight o'clock I had the gas stove on full blast, the
coffee pot on and the bacon sizzling. I was just going to get my
daughter up for breakfast when I heard someone tramping
along the deck of the boat. It was the new R.C.M.P. Constable
who had come to relieve the other one for the summer. He was
not at Liard long and I cannot remember his name.

"Dick," he said, "I was hoping to catch you before you
pulled out. I have some bad news for you. Albert Faille has
swamped his boat in the first canyon and is walking out. Jim,
the forestry warden, sent a message by his mobile radio last
night from Dead Man's Valley."

"Good God!" I replied, "where did Albert upset, how long
ago was it and why isn't Jim looking for him?"

"Jim and Joe Donta left the Butte yesterday on their way
to the falls and they found Albert's boat upside down on a bar
in the Splits. Ten miles or so farther on about the middle of the
canyon they saw his camp with a note written with charcoal on
some birchbark, left by Albert saying he had swamped, lost
everything and was going to try to walk back to the Butte. It
has been eight days now since he swamped."

"What is Jim doing?" I said. "Did he go back down the
river looking for Albert? He should be along the river
somewhere."

"Jim sent the message last night from the valley and I
understand he is going on to the falls today," the policeman
said.

"One of the girl school teachers at Nahanni Village picked
up the message originally and passed it on to me. There are no
men at Nahanni right now, Phil Howard is away and Jack
Norcross has gone flying somewhere." (These two men are
missionaries at Nahanni Butte.)

The policeman continued, "I thought you should know
about this as something should be done I guess."

"You're right," I said, "someone should be looking for him
right now. He is an old man, apparently he has no food and he
has to climb four thousand feet to get out of that canyon before
he can start walking back to the Butte. But, say, the police
Beaver is here tied to the dock, I notice, can you get that to
search for him when the weather clears?"

The constable shook his head, "I'm afraid not, as the
inspector is here on his way to Aklavik to look for some

Eskimos lost on an ice floe and he wants to leave right away."

"So. Mmmmmm," I replied. "But surely you could have one quick look, you might spot the old man and drop him some food and in the meantime we could be on our way to pick him up."

"I don't think we can take the time. But his age bothers the inspector."

"Yes, I would think so. Well, OK, if that is the case I will have to do something: but it will take me two days to get back to the Butte, get organized with gas and supplies and get up to the canyon. Christ, that would be ten days for him and tough as he is the old man cannot last for ever."

"Well, let me know what you decide on." And the constable left.

22

The 'chopper'

Martha was up by then and we ate breakfast. Martha said, "Dad, there is a helicopter here. Would they go maybe?"

"That is not only a good idea, it is an excellent one," I replied. "I think I know the party chief, he was at our place with Keith Williams last summer. You scoot up to Mrs. Radcliffe, the teacher's wife, tell her what has happened, and stay there until I get back. I could be an hour or several days."

A few minutes later I went up the hill, and along the bank among the trees to where the geologists' camp was. Among the tents I spotted the one with the stove pipe, shouted "Hello" and entered. The cook and the party chief were sitting there drinking coffee. The rest of the crew were apparently not up yet as the inclement weather was putting a stop to the flying operations for the time.

After greetings and mutual remarks on the nasty weather I broke the news to them. After stating all the information the Constable had given me, I said, "John, is it possible to get the use of the chopper to look for Albert? I cannot pay for it, the cost will have to be born by your Company but I feel that something should be done as soon as possible as it is eight days now and I don't think he can last much longer without food."

"My permission is given right now," John replied, "but it will be up to the chopper pilot, Bob Taylor." Before I could say a word, a shout came from the tent next door, "Yes, we'll go," and in a lower voice he went on talking with the engineer.

Some minutes later the pilot and the engineer came into the tent to eat breakfast. Then we discussed the pros and cons of Albert's situation and what likelihood there was of him surviving this ordeal. "He probably has nothing but a pocket knife and his little Marble match safety case, that holds about twenty matches," I said. "He will be able to stay warm and dry at night anyway."

"As he swamped in the canyon," someone said, "he cannot follow the river shore, he will have to climb out and around and hit the river several miles below, can that be done?"

"Depending on which side of the river he is on," I answered. "If he is on the north shore there is just no way he can get out overland, but if he is on the south side, it is possible to climb out in some places only, and it is nearly four thousand feet to the top of the rim."

We all knew that he was tough and strong, but he was seventy years old and he had a crippled back that made it difficult for him to walk. Nothing much more was said. We looked at one another and murmured, "Hummm," and "Hawww," and listened to the rain beating on the tent.

The chopper engineer came in from the rain and said, "O.K. Bob, she's ready to go."

Bob turned to me, "Ready? Let's give it a try."

The head wind was probably only twenty miles an hour, but there was considerable fog mixed in with the rain and the visibility was down to a mile or less. We had the Liard to follow and could see well enough as we were flying very low. No problem, at least Bob thought not, and we continued on. The visibility improved slightly as we neared Nahanni and we settled fown in our front yard on our grassy heliport. The wind was down but it was raining the same as ever.

After lunch, Bob checked the barometer, the temperature and cast an eye on what could be seen of the weather from outside the house. "The barometer is rising, and I think I see some improvement," he said. "With any luck it should clear before sundown, and then we'll give it a whirl; there is no use in going now, we can see nothing in the rain."

"While we are waiting then," I said, "I'll scoot across river to the village, rustle up a canoe and kicker, get some gas and

grub ready and send some Indians up the river. We'll assume
he is on the left hand shore otherwise he would not get out of
the canyon at all. The boys can go ashore every mile or so and
check for tracks or any signs of him. Those lads have sharp
eyes and will miss nothing."

Mrs. Howard volunteered their ten h.p. kicker, I got
three Indians and one of their big twenty foot canoes and
brought them home. We loaded gasoline, food and camping
equipment and off they went, rain or no rain. They said a little
thing like rain would not bother them.

By three o'clock the weather was definitely starting to
improve, and we had great hopes the day would have a happy
ending. Once he got out of the canyon he would be near the
river at all times, and should be easy to spot from the chopper.

"What is the walking like, from the canyon down?" Bob
asked, over a cup of coffee.

"Hell, I wish you had not asked me that," I said. "The first
ten miles or so is good, or I should say, fair, but from Jackfish
Lake on down right to the Butte it is terrible."

"How so, the country is flat is it not?"

"Yes, it is flat, sure enough, but with myriad snyes and
swamps full of windfalls two feet high, and a tangled mess of
rose bushes and willows extending right up to the river bank.
Where the ground is dry, the timber is big, with half of it lying
on the ground, or blown half over with the wind. In a very few
places he could follow a sand bar but only for a short distance.
Once long ago when I was twenty-four years old I walked
down through the bush from Jackfish Lake and that thirty
miles took me three days. Bob, I just can't think of the old man
in those swamps, we've got to find him before he gets that
far."

By five that evening the rain had ceased. The wind was
down and the ceiling had lifted to perhaps a thousand feet. We
climbed into that beautiful little whirly-bird, fired up and spun
off up that bad old Nahanni River.

"There is one thing," I said to Bob, "he will have a fire
going for sure a day like this and we should be able to spot the
smoke easily."

All the way to the canyon there were wisps of fog rising
from the swamps, and at a distance some looked very like
smoke, but as we approached we could see it was only fog
rising from the wet ground. As we neared the canyon my
heart sank. There was no sign of smoke anywhere, and I had

been so sure he would be sitting beside a roaring fire with smoke billowing up in great gobs that could be seen for miles. Nothing. We had passed no campfire at all, I felt certain.

About five miles below the canyon we spotted the boat upside down with the stern in the water, on a sand bar. We landed and looked around. There were no footprints of any kind near it. If Albert had gone by, he must have missed it. He would have been able to turn it right-side up and float down to safety, as it was not damaged at all. But he could have passed it by without seeing it as it was out from the main shore a good ways and was hidden with alders and willows.

Now the plan was to check down stream any place his footprints would show and where the chopper could sit down. About six miles or so below the boat there was an extensive sand beach where he would surely walk, with a good chopper landing close by. Bob settled it in nicely and I hopped out the door and ran along to the sandbar.

I guess Bob heard me give a whoop from the chopper even with the engine running for he came over and we examined the tracks. "That's Albert, that's Albert," I chortled, "I'd know the old rascal's footprints anywhere, but, by God, they are not too fresh, there is rain in them. They are not many days old. He's still going strong and he can't be far."

Bob flew that chopper as if he had been born in it and never left it. We followed every bend, every twist and every crook and turn of that shore line. We circled and doubled back in any doubtful places and by God we were looking. We were not smoking or talking or gazing into the sky. We looked as closely and as carefully as two pairs of eyes can. We could see every stick, every root along the sand and rock bars. I could almost count the grains of sand, but no Albert.

"I guess we had better go back," Bob said, "we are getting low on fuel." It was getting dusk when we landed at home, tied down the chopper blade and went into the house. Vera knew from my face that there was nothing to say, and said nothing. She put supper on the table and we sat down to eat.

We were all somewhat subdued that night and there was no banter at all passing around. What was there to say? Nothing. I felt by this time Albert had had the biscuit. Perhaps tried to build a raft and been swamped in the Splits. Or exhaustion had caught up with him and he had simply fallen asleep. The possibility was entering my thick head that he might have no matches to build a fire with, or if he had some to start with he perhaps got them wet or lost them. Without a fire and in the rain the heat and strength would be sapped from his body more quickly. However there was no use in being despondent, it was yet possible he was still alive and we would find him tomorrow. And the chopper. We could not keep it much longer as we were not paying for it. J.C. Sproule and Associates or Vancouver Helicopters were paying the shot and Bob was responsible to them.

The morning dawned clear and calm. At least I think it did, for when I arose somewhat after dawn it was clear and calm.

After breakfast we fueled up the flying machine and were off again. We had a plan that Bob would drop me off where we had seen Albert's footprints, I would follow them down while Bob would follow with the chopper and check on my progress from time to time.

All the way from the mouth of Jackfish Creek on up, where there was a shoreline of sorts to follow, we flew low and stayed with every bend and turn, looking, looking. About a mile below the spot where we intended to land, Bob said, "There he is." And indeed, there he was, walking along the rock beach a hundred yards ahead. I could hardly believe my eyes. I could only mumble, "He's still going strong. Bless me, he's still going strong."

"Look," Bob spoke, "I'll land in that slough close to the river there, and you bring him down to the point half a mile below, and I'll pick you both up there. I don't think I can get out of that little slough with the two of you."

We landed on the slough grass that Bob had indicated and in thirty seconds I was through the hundred yards of bush and out to the river. I ran up the beach to meet him and grasped him by the hand. The truth is, there were tears in my eyes. His hands were cold as ice, and this is the second day of August.

"Albert," I said, "how are you?"

"Oh, I'm fine," he replied, but his voice was more squeaky than usual. "Where did you come from, Dick?"

"The chopper," I said, "didn't you hear the chopper?"

"Yeah, I thought I heard an engine but I didn't know it landed."

"We're to walk down to the point where he will pick us up, but wait, no, he's coming back to the slough, we'll go over there."

Soon we had the old rascal tucked in between us, and the chopper came out of there like a home-sick Indian headed for home. We spotted the canoe with the lads from the village and stopped beside them, gave them the news and in thirty minute more we were at the house. I noticed Vera had tears in her eyes too as she hugged Albert.

We all sat at the table talking a blue streak for over five minutes before it dawned on me. "Perhaps you should get Albert something to eat, Mother," I said, "as all he has had in nine days is nine raspberries and three puff-balls."

Vera was out of her chair, had the kettle on, and the cupboard doors open before you could say "Boo."

Then Albert said, "Don't bother, please, just a coffee for now will be fine.

I turned to Bob. "It turned out to be a fine day. I suppose your men will be chomping at the bit, what do you think?"

"Yes, we had better throw in some fuel and head back to Liard." Vera and Albert waved as we lifted off and headed south.

On the way, I said to Bob, "By jove, I forgot all about letting the constable know what our plans were before we left, but I guess the boys will tell him."

Bob put the whirly-bird down on her pad at Fort Liard, I collected my daughter, fired up the little Gray motor and resumed our journey on the river, toward Fort Nelson.

I can't remember why we were so long on this particular trip to Fort Nelson, but it was more than three weeks later when we arrived back at Nahanni.

Vera reported that Albert had stayed for two weeks, resting up and gaining back some weight. She said it was amazing he never did stuff himself with food, he ate just a moderate amount three times a day.

Someone brought his boat down from the Splits to the Butte and Albert went on to Simpson, calling it quits for that summer.

Between Vera's account from what he had told her and from talking to Albert himself later on I got the whole story of his adventure. The cause of the boat upsetting had been a terrific gusty wind in the canyon. One of the gusts caught him with increased force and threw the boat against the rocky shore. One of the twin kickers hit against the rocks and stopped. He then swung the boat out into the stream where another gust blew him sideways onto the rocks again and the other motor hit and stopped. He then grabbed a paddle to steer the boat down stream and into shore but slammed head on into a large boulder protruding from the water. The next thing he knew he was in the water and had come up under the boat which was by then upside down. He swam ashore and crawled onto the beach, and saw the upturned boat disappear around the bend. That was that. The boat was gone with no hope of retrieving it. Luckily he had gotten ashore in one of the few places where there was a shelf of heavy spruce trees and right behind them the canyon walls were broken in a narrow defile that led steeply to the rim of the canyon.

He took stock of what he had, which did not take much time. His knife was in his pocket and he had his jacket on. His hat was gone. The safety match case that he usually carried in his pocket was in the grub-box on the boat and now presumably at the bottom of the river. In his pocket was a box of matches containing twelve matches, all wet. Out of the twelve he found three that would light. One of them was used to build a fire and get dried out.

Later in the day it began to rain and it was a day and a half before the rocks were dry enough for him to attempt the steep climb out of the canyon. He did think of waiting at the camp for a boat to come by, but travellers were so few then he thought he might have to wait a month. After getting around to the foot of the canyon he would be near the river and could possibly flag down a passing boat anyway.

Getting out of the canyon was a bigger undertaking than it looked to be. Once at the top he had two more smaller canyons to navigate before he got down the the Hot Springs at the foot of the canyon. This took him three days. It was now four and a half days since he had swamped, all the matches were gone and he could build no more fires at night.

"How in the world did you keep warm?" I asked.

"I would dig a hold with a stick, as deep as I could, under a big tree and cover myself with moss, pull my jacket over my head and sleep a little."

His experience at this time was too recent to joke about, but I could not help thinking he had an easier job to break camp than Jack Mulholland had; he didn't even have to put on his cap and pick up the axe.

"Where were you Albert when Jim and Joe Donato went by? Or did you see their boat?"

"That I did," he said, "I was right on the beach on that

wide stretch about five miles below the canyon. They went by in the middle of the river. Joe was standing up steering and the other man was sitting in the bow looking at a paper. With that big kicker they were going like hell. I screamed to them, 'Help me, I'm stranded,' but they went right on by."

Going by that place with a boat later on, I tried to imagine old Albert standing on the shore shouting for help. There was a dark mud bank behind him and it is perhaps a hundred yards to the middle of the river. You wouldn't hear feeble cries above the roar of the motor. Unless you looked directly his way you could easily pass by and not see him. It must have been a keen disappointment to him to see rescue, that had been so near, vanishing up the river with the sound of the motor getting more faint each moment.

From this point he was able to stay with the shoreline until he got opposite Jackfish Lake. Here was a well worn trail going into the lake three miles away. The trail was only used in the winter time by the Indians and for some reason Albert thought there was a cabin there. If he could find some old dog chains or snare cable he might be able to tie some drift logs together and float down to the mouth. Anyway he thought it was worth a try and followed the trail into the lake. He found no cabin, and nightfall coming on, he huddled under a tree and pulled his jacket over his head. He huddled in this partial shelter until the rain eased up when he made his way back to the river again. Late in the afternoon while he was still in the bush he heard the helicopter but had no way of drawing our attention. We did not think he would be so far from the river. He realized someone was searching for him and got to the river as soon as he could where he would be seen. The next morning he heard the chopper and had a quick trip to Nahanni Butte.

What bothered Albert more than anything about this episode was the fact that when the boat swamped he lost what savings he had at that time. He apparently always carried his money with him and this time he had around four hundred dollars in bills, wrapped in tin foil, stuck in the grub box. Nothing from the boat was ever washed ashore as far as is known, and the money must be at the bottom of the river with the rest of his supplies.

I heard that robbers are supposed to take your money or your life, but that nasty old Nahanni will take both if given a chance.

Although the Nahanni River delivered what almost turned out to be a knock-out blow to Faille that summer, he spent more than thirty years in battling the river. He enjoyed every minute of it except those times when he was down for the count. All things considered, if a decision was to be awarded, I would vote it to Faille. You could say that some rounds ended in a draw, but throughout the years he survived everything the river could hand out and came bouncing back looking for more.

23

Summer of 1955

The summer of 1955 saw a continuation of the increase of the oil exploration in the north with more demand for equipment to transport the supplies necessary for the various operations.

Each summer from June to September we had geological crews camped in our front yard with aircraft coming and going and helicopters buzzing around. While Martha complained of them waking her up in the mornings I have always loved those whirly birds. The sound of the motors was music to my ears.

Don and I had two outfits operating on the rivers now, the *Go Easy* and its barge and the *Nahanni* and a barge. We had a six cylinder Gray and later a Jimmy diesel in the *Nahanni*. Late in May both these outfits left Fort Nelson with the usual fuel and geological equipment for points on the lower Mackenzie River. Don was to go to Fort McPherson on the Peel River and to work out of there for points up the Peel for Imperial Oil Limited. I had a load for Gulf Oil to deliver to the San Sault rapids; then I was to go back up to the Wells for another load for Inuvik.

At Fort Simpson we took on additional helicopter fuel in ten gallon kegs, to be left at Wrigley. We had about four hundred kegs of fuel on each barge in addition to food and camping equipment for the field crews. I picked up an Indian lad in Simpson as a deck hand and pulled out ahead of Don who was to meet me at the Wells.

We put down fuel caches at designated points along the Mackenzie River, went on to San Sault then back to the Wells for another load for Inuvik. The river is four miles wide at Norman Wells and it seems the wind if forever blowing there.

The loading dock at the Wells was a pile of rubble pushed into the river with a bull-dozer and hemmed about with old drill pipes I assume were driven into the mud with a pile-driver. This June, the dock and the banks of the river were a sea of river ice that had been forced ashore, liberally mixed with mud. The oily scum along the shore with the overflow from the refinery steamed with a nauseating stink. When we pulled into the Wells to load, the river was lapping over the so-called dock with a foot of water. There was a D-7 Cat and a couple of trucks sitting out from shore in the water and I presumed they were on the dock.

We pulled in beside the *Pelican Rapids* that was tied up, loading its tremendous barges with fuel. My little outfit looked more like a mouse alongside an elephant, and I was glad to be in the lee of the big tug, out of the wind. I went across the gang plank on to the barges to talk with Don Nailer the captain and Albert Luditt the pilot. Albert lived at Fort Providence, had spent most of his life on the Mackenzie and probably knew the river as well as anyone. He showed me over the tug. The two diesels in the engine room were each as big as a house, with the metal polished, shiny and glistening. All was absolutely spotless; you could eat off the floors. Don and Albert each had a state room with a private bath. Albert said the noise and vibration from the engine was at all times deafening and each fall when the river work was over he had to tie a kicker to the head of his bed with the motor running in order to sleep.

Don Nailer had been the Captain on the old paddle wheeler the *Distributor*, and remembered the occasion years ago when Vera and I were married at Hay River and Colonel Reed had given us a supper with a wedding cake on board the steamer. Don spent the winters trapping on the Mackenzie and later returned to Vancouver Island.

Looking with regard and awe at his beautiful tug and huge barges I said to him, "With my little outfit wind on the river is a constant worry and bother, many times it gets so rough we have to find a sheltered spot to tie up in, and it is often impossible to find a suitable place for many miles. You would not have that trouble with this huge outfit."

Don laughed and said, "Don't you ever think it. We can only stand a limited amount of wind too. Some time ago we were coming upstream from the Delta, pushing four barges ahead of us and were caught in a wind between Desolation Point and Arctic Red. As you know, there is no harbor of any kind in that thirty five miles. The wind blew up a gale and in spite of all our efforts to stay out of the river, it blew us ashore and there was absolutely nothing we could do about it. With all the power from the two big engines I could not control it. We ran cables ashore and waited for the storm to blow itself out. I thought sure we would be broken up in pieces with the pounding, but very little damage was done."

At eight o'clock that night a D-7 Cat pushed a low-boy down the bank and through the mud and water near our little barge to load from. The truck crew of course went back to their quarters and left young Bill and I to load. We had, I recall, about three hundred and fifty kegs to load, each weighing about ninety pounds, with not far to carry them. We can get loaded by midnight, I thought, and get out of this nameless place to a sheltered spot below, grab a couple of hours sleep and go on. We had over half the kegs aboard when I noticed the barge was lower in the water than it should have been. I walked back to the stern and saw water inside the barge, with some kegs already starting to float. There was plenty of water all around the barge, it would swing to one side or the other but would not budge ahead or back.

"This is a nice kettle of fish," I said to Bill, "we have likely parked the barge on a pile of iron, and ripped out the bottom planking some place. It's a new barge too, it must indeed be a very sharp chunk that we are sitting on." I was a bit unhappy at this new turn of events, and gave forth with a brief and vehement opinion of Norman Wells, the Mackenzie River, this so-called dock, and all other factors in the situation I could think of. I felt as Alf Lewis did in the glove episode.

We unloaded about one hundred kegs back on to the low-boy, left the rest floating in the barge, said "To hell with it," and went to bed. We were wet to the waist and a little cold. "Where the hell can Don be, with the *Go Easy*, I wondered out loud, "he should have been along two days ago."

I had been asleep about three hours when I awoke to a

278

gentle "thud" against the tug and the quiet throb of two little motors. Soon after, I heard someone walking along the gun'ale, and Don opened the door and put his head in.

"What is going on here?" he asked, "it looks like your barge is full of water."

"It is that," I replied, "I must have loaded it with the bow sitting on a pile of junk or something, it won't go forward or back."

"You're not the only one who can sink a barge," Don said, "we sunk our barge eight miles below Simpson."

"Well, for Christ's sake, what were you doing, to run aground?"

"I hired an Indian at Simpson for a helper, and pulled out about two in the afternoon, a day behind you. I turned the wheel over to this chap while I went to the galley to prepare dinner. Soon after, there was a crash and we had gone slam bang into the boulders on the shore, about half speed ahead. It seems he had been up all night on a drunk, and fell asleep at the wheel. He seemed all right when I hired him."

"Did you kill the bastard?"

"No," he answered, "I felt like it, but I didn't."

"Did you sink the barge?"

"Not quite, I got the pump going, got the barge unloaded, and patched from the inside, well enough to hobble back to Simpson. The tug was not damaged at all. The two lads with Gulf Oil helped me.

"How many kegs did you have besides the other stuff?" Four hundred."

Merciful heavens," I said. "You had to unload all that, go back to Simpson, haul out the barge, patch it and go back and load up again. The Gulf Oil boys will be pretty well fed up by now with us I guess."

"No, they turned in and helped and did not complain."

"God bless them." I said. "You got your load down to Wrigley all right then?"

"Yup, did O.K. from then on."

"Well, you had better get some sleep. I'll get the barge out in the morning and get it patched. I won't be far behind you."

The next day Don and his helper (a new one) loaded his barge with four hundred kegs of helicopter fuel and pulled out for McPherson.

Bill and I took the remaining kegs from our barge and

found a jagged-edged steel drilling pipe sticking up a foot through the bottom of the barge just behind the front deck. We jacked the bow up free of the pipe and backed away, stuffed some sacks in the hole and pumped out the barge.

To do a decent job of patching, the barge would have to be taken out of the water to be repaired from below. I went up to the office of the refinery and talked them into letting me have a cherry picker, to lift the barge from the water. Some distance above the dock there was an open place on the beach. Here we ran ashore, the cherry picker lifted it like an empty apple box and set it down on some timbers. With some plywood, tar, cotton and nails we soon had the barge as good as new, and by nightfall we were loaded and away.

I had never been below the San Sault rapids before and rather enjoyed the trip down, at least on the days the wind did not blow. On a calm night in June there are few more beautiful sights than looking into the setting sun over the vast expanse of river. Once the Arctic Circle is passed there are four hours when the sun is either just below or just above the horizon. In effect you have a sunset that lasts for four hours. Going North you have the reflection of the clouds in the water. On some nights with the right amount of clouds there is the most gorgeous reflections of color. Red and purple, changing to blue, yellow and gold, the complete expanse of the view ahead is a mass of slowly changing shades of the soft mingling colors of the rainbow.

Sometimes the color fades with the rising of the sun, the air is hot and still with the river stretching away in the distance like an endless sheet of lead. Other times, perhaps at midnight, perhaps at four in the morning, dark lines appear on the water, turn into wavelets, then into choppy little waves that lift and go nowhere. Sometimes long rollers appear, the boat begins to shudder, the door of the galley slams and you know you have a storm to fight.

For three hours before reaching Arctic Red River, the wind could not decide on its plan for the day. The river got into a mild chop and stayed that way. We steamed in the harbor about six in the morning with the waves slapping the bow and some spray coming over the sides. Nothing serious, just enough motion to keep you awake.

From McPherson I came back down the Peel to the big river, crossed over and went down the East Arm to Inuvik. To me the Delta is by far the most interesting part of the lower

Mackenzie. There are many small channels with islands covered with medium sized timber, spruce, and willow mostly. Water birds are numerous, the water is clear, with many fish. There were trappers' cabins on the East Arm and we met boats and kickers frequently.

We were in Inuvik for only half a day, and that town did not impress me favorably. I did not find the people very friendly, and the mess of broken beer bottles six inches deep along the beach where we landed was a poor start.

We soon unloaded the freight we had for Inuvik and were away on the return journey of eight hundred miles back to Fort Simpson.

Albert Faille was at his little house in Simpson when I went by on the way home to Nahanni. He had been rafting down driftwood from below the Liard rapids for his winter's supply of firewood. "Albert," I said, "would you like to stay at Nahanni this winter for a month to look after the place?"

"I would like to, Dick, but I would not want to tackle the job of shopkeeper."

"Gus says he will handle the store. He lives across river though and it would be a nuisance for him to keep the fires going, and we don't want things to freeze."

"Oh, well then, in that case between the two of us we can manage quite well. Where do you figure on taking flying lessons?"

"Vancouver," I answered. "I have heard it said it is warm there all winter and that would be a change."

"Are you going to buy an airplane, Dick?"

"Yes, if I can learn to fly."

"There is no reason why you can't, others do." His eyes twinkled, he put his hands on his knees as he often does and leaned toward me. "Dick, with an airplane on floats maybe we could get into some of those places I've been wanting to get to for so long. An old Indian told me of a north fork of Johnny creek, where other Indians had picked up nuggets long ago, and I'm sure that's where the McLeod boys found their gold. But it is a long way, I never could make it there, but I think there's a lake not too far away."

"Albert, you have talked me into it. I'll get what aircraft I can and if I don't kill myself first we'll get into that lake, find the gold, and we'll both be stinking rich."

"It's not the money I want, Dick. I'd just like to find it, after all these years."

"O.K., Albert, that suits me fine, you take the glory and I'll take the money and we'll all be happy." And we chuckled at this foolishness.

In January Vera and Martha flew to Fort Nelson with Jack Norcross in his Stinson, and took the air liner from there to Vancouver. In February, after Albert was established at our place, Rolf and I flew out to join them.

The aircraft lifted off the river ice, banked and headed south. I looked down at the snow-covered spruce trees, the white, winding, ice-bound river and the Indian village. Across from the island under the mountain, smoke was curling from our cabin in the clearing. With one last look into the northwest where the Nahanni valley was lost amont the distant peaks, I thought, "Perhaps with an aircraft Albert and I can locate that fabulous placer creek that Albert has been searching for these many years. Who knows what the future holds?"

I

GLOSSARY OF TRAPPERS PARLANCE

"*A*" —   A shelter constructed of upright logs in the form of an 'A', with the ends closed in with vertical logs and the whole thing chinked tightly with moss.

Bannock —   A mixture of flour, water and baking powder usually cooked over an open fire. A cup of flour, half tsp. of baking powder, pinch of salt. Mix thoroughly and add enough water for a stiff dough. Put in hot frypan with a tablespoon of melted lard. Brown on bottom over hot coals, then support the handle of the frypan with a stick and let the heat from the fire finish cooking the bannock from the top.

B.C. Heater —   A wood burning stove thirty inches in length with short legs and a flat top, and two stove lids.

Braided —   A stream of numerous swift flowing shallow channels that weave in and out and mingle with one another.

Bush —

All land surface that is covered by trees or bushes of any size and to any density. The synonym forest is never used by trappers and other woodsmen. For some reason there is almost a taboo against using the word and anyone who does say forest is instantly marked as a greenhorn or a newcomer.

Cache —

This could be anything of value that is put away for safe keeping. But the word in the north most often designates a small building of logs set high in the air on stilts to protect the contents from animals.

Carry-all —

A wrapper made of moose-hide or canvas fastened to the complete length of a toboggan with rope or moose-skin thongs and supported by a lazy-board near the rear of the toboggan.

Catch —

Usually the total number of fur pelts caught by a trapper in one season.

Cubby —

A pen of small upright sticks set in the ground or stuck in the snow to direct an animal into a trap.

Cutting trail —

In a trappers vocabulary this indicates using an axe to clear a trail through the bush about two feet in width, to be used as a winter trapline.

Dead-Heads —

Broken off stumps or tree trunks lodged in the bottom of a river or lake.

Drum oven —

A circular oven of tin set into a stove-pipe, large enough to bake one piece or two or three loaves of bread.

Grubstake —

A sum of money sufficient to provide the necessary food items for a winter's trapping, or for any other enterprise.

Hang-em-ups — Rabbit snares of string and wood, with a trigger that activates a spring pole to jerk the rabbit into the air, when sprung.

Hard-tack — A dry, long keeping biscuit, unleavened and unflavored, manufactured by biscuit companies.

Jawbone — This was the word used by Indian hunters and other trappers to indicate the receiving of goods from a trader on the promise of delayed payment.

Kicker — Any outboard motor.

Land fur — All fur bearing animals that do not live in or near the water. Such as lynx, fox, marten, fisher, wolverine and wolf.

Long Reach — A particular stretch of the Liard River that is wide with a slow current. It starts twenty-five miles below the Nahanni and runs for twenty miles.

Moccasin Telegraph — News that travels by word of mouth. Not always accurate but amazingly swift.

Mukluks — Footwear composed all or in part of animal hide and fur, coming to just below the knee.

Overflow — This is a winter term used to describe water that has oozed out of the ground or has been forced from below ice, and that lies unfrozen for many days underneath the blanket of snow.

Riffle — A short stretch of rapids in a stream, often merely the back curling waves under a sharp drop.

Snye — Any and all secondary channels of a stream. If there is no water in it at the time it is referred to as a dry snye.

Sheer-pin — A soft iron pin by which the drive-shaft of a motor turns the propeller. It is made to 'sheer' if the propeller contacts an obstruction.

Stake — The value of a winter's fur catch over and above the cost of the operation.

Swamp — (a) An extensive patch of bog or wet ground.
(b) To upset a canoe or boat in the water.

Sandbar — Any obstruction in a stream bed composed of sand, mud or loose gravel, or a combination of any of these three.

Tailboard — A term to designate the portion of a toboggan that is behind the lazy-board.

Toggle — A loose wooden pole preferrably of green spruce that the chain of a trap is attached to. This is to avoid the animal being brought up suddenly and perhaps break the chain or pull loose from the trap.

Trip — One regular journey over a trapline to the far end and back. In the summer it could mean any journey by boat.

Trapline — A winter trail of any length of from one
or line   mile to a hundred miles in length. Traps and snares are set on or near the trail to catch fur bearing animals.

Track-line — A hard-twist, oiled fishline, usually five sixteenth of an inch in diameter and three hundred feet in length, used to pull boats and canoes upstream.

Track — (a) The footprint of an animal.
(b) The act of pulling a canoe or boat up-stream by means of a track-line.

Water fur — All fur bearing animals that live in or near the water most of the time. Beaver, otter, mink and muskrats.

286

Wheeler —	The dog in a team that is closest to the sleigh. A clever wheeler can control or 'wheel' the toboggan by swinging it to the left or to the right to keep it away from trees. The terms toboggan and sleigh are interchanged indescriminately.
Windfall —	Logs and trees with or without branches that have been blown over and lie on or near the ground. They are NOT 'deadfalls'.
Trapper —	A man or woman whose full time occupation is catching fur bearing animals for a living. Anyone who traps as a part-time occupation is not considered a trapper by professional trappers. Among the elite of the professional trappers there is an insular snobbishness similar to that found in other skilled occupations, high-riggers and aircraft pilots for instance. This behaviour manifests itself in his pride of self-assurance and independence: His exaggerated air of confidence: his careful quiet manner in mixed company: and his scorn of wage earners. He will employ the words of a woodsman at every opportunity; words such as snye, kicker, bush and grubstake. Possibly because the mechanics of his occupation is considered to be cruel by the uninitiated, he subconsciously makes an effort to appear a gentle man.